ROUTLEDGE LIBRARY EDITIONS: ETHNOSCAPES

Volume 12

THE HOME

THE HOME

Words, Interpretations, Meanings and Environments

Edited, with an Introduction and Afterword by
DAVID N. BENJAMIN

Assisted by
DAVID STEA

with a Foreword by
PROFESSOR DAVID SAILE

LONDON AND NEW YORK

First published in 1995 by Avebury (Ashgate Publishing Limited)

This edition first published in 2025
by Routledge
4 Park Square, Milton Park, Abingdon, Oxon OX14 4RN

and by Routledge
605 Third Avenue, New York, NY 10158

Routledge is an imprint of the Taylor & Francis Group, an informa business

© 1995 the contributors

All rights reserved. No part of this book may be reprinted or reproduced or utilised in any form or by any electronic, mechanical, or other means, now known or hereafter invented, including photocopying and recording, or in any information storage or retrieval system, without permission in writing from the publishers.

Trademark notice: Product or corporate names may be trademarks or registered trademarks, and are used only for identification and explanation without intent to infringe.

British Library Cataloguing in Publication Data
A catalogue record for this book is available from the British Library

ISBN: 978-1-032-86590-4 (Set)
ISBN: 978-1-032-86411-2 (Volume 12) (hbk)
ISBN: 978-1-032-86423-5 (Volume 12) (pbk)
ISBN: 978-1-003-52747-3 (Volume 12) (ebk)

DOI: 10.4324/9781003527473

Publisher's Note
The publisher has gone to great lengths to ensure the quality of this reprint but points out that some imperfections in the original copies may be apparent.

Disclaimer
The publisher has made every effort to trace copyright holders and would welcome correspondence from those they have been unable to trace.

New Series Introduction to
RLE: Ethnoscapes

The neologism *Ethnoscapes*[1] was created by David Canter and David Stea in 1987 when they happened both to be in Yogjakarta at the same time. They wanted a term to cover the rapidly emerging multidisciplinary field of research into many aspects of how individuals, groups and cultures interact and transact with their surroundings. It was derived as follows:

Ethno (combining form) indicating race, people or culture.

Scape (suffix-forming nouns) indicating a scene or view of something.

Ethnoscapes (plural noun) Scholarly and/or scientific explorations of the relationships people and their activities, have with the places they create and/or inhabit; historical, psychological, anthropological, sociological, and related disciplines that study the experiences of places, attitudes towards them, or the processes of shaping, managing, or designing them. The term was subsequently used to provide an umbrella for a series of books. These cover topics that are so multidisciplinary that they do not sit comfortably in any of the constrained silos of academic and scholarly research. As indicated on the opening page of the first book in the series, many disciplines "have developed marauding sub-groups who move freely across each others' borders, carrying ideas almost like contraband, without declaring that they have crossed any disciplinary boundaries."

They include domains labelled as Behavioural or Perceptual Geography, Environmental/Architectural Psychology, Urban History, Social Ecology, Behavioural Archaeology, Urban Planning, Behavioural Architecture, and Landscape Architecture. There are also many other areas of research and practice that, whilst not being overtly psychological, social, or cultural, do explore and act on the built and natural environment in a way that recognises the importance of the human transactions with those settings. These professions include interior and product design, comparative linguistics, and even aspects of criminology and mental health providers.

Like all such implicit and explicit transactions between different domains, a community of interest and support has emerged in which those who cross the boundaries often find they have more in common with other transgressors than with their mother disciplines. This has given rise to common means and forms of communication, with a shared understanding of the issues and approaches that are of value. Although, of course, these are not always understood in the same way by all those involved,

The *Ethnoscapes* series of books provides a forum for these multifarious, cross-disciplinary, determinedly international, studies and practices. Each of the books takes on board one or more of the environmental challenges that that individuals, societies and cultures are facing. Emphasising a social perspective, rather than the dominant 'hard' science viewpoints embedded in physical, geological and climate changes.

It may now be regarded as rather prescient that it was over three decades ago that the need and importance was recognised of bringing together the many strands of environmental social research and practice. But there is no doubt that there were academics and professionals exploring Ethnoscape topics, going back to the 1960s, often in isolation and with little recognition, that are today front-page, and podcast, news. The challenges in the environmental social sciences that Ethnoscapes explores are just as pertinent now as they were when initially identified.

The series, in essence, deals with four challenges the environmental social sciences embrace.

> 1. Addressing "the awareness of governments and public alike of the problems of environmental degradation and pollution."

This includes the challenge of providing acceptable housing and related environmental conditions that also encompassed the support for environmental and related cultural heritage. It also requires detailed consideration of the assessment and evaluation of designs and design proposals as well as background research on policy related issues.

> 2. Developing ways of conceptualising human interactions with the physical surroundings.

This may seem somewhat abstract but has practical implications. The dominant view that people are passively controlled by their surroundings supports a paternalistic, management of what it is assumed people need. That ignores the active way in which people make sense of their environment, drawing on cultural and historical influences. This recognises the importance of user participation in decisions about built and natural settings. That, in turn, requires a much richer understanding of how people interact with where they are or want to be.

3. A much wider range of ways of exploring people's transactions with the environment is needed to contribute to policy and practice as well as developing richer insights into human experiences.

The stock in trade of surveys, or the inevitably artificial laboratory-based experiments, whilst of value for some explorations, need to be augmented by methodologies that enrich an understanding of what the experiences are of being in, acting on, and developing places. They need to connect not just with the endeavours of individuals but also with how cultures and societies express these transactions.

4. Finding ways to enable practitioners and researchers to express their own encounters with the contexts they are influencing or studying.

Much of the research that is carried out in what are curiously called 'Ivory Towers', even when it is studying the big wide world, allows the pretence of distancing from the direct experiences of the issues being studied. Yet the challenges of moving across disciplinary boundaries are as much personal challenges of finding new ways of thinking, communicating, and acting, as an academic demand to develop more effective intellectual systems. The Ethnoscapes series recognises the value of exploring these challenges by hosting a variety of formats. Many of these go beyond the staid and limited formulations that academic discourse assumes to be the norms.

The Ethnoscapes series brings together a vibrant mix of cutting-edge explorations, from all over the world, of human transactions with the built and natural environments. This includes, for example, consideration of vernacular architecture that contrasts with the architecture and urbanism of the colonial enterprise, the meaning of home, aesthetics, well-being and health, and consideration of how environmental psychology has become 'green'. All of these topics, and more, provide an exciting basis for dealing with current challenges in the environmental social sciences.

Note

[1] Not to be confused by the term *Ethnoscape* later concocted by Arun Appadurai in 1990, to refer to **human migration**, the flow of people across boundaries. This includes migrants, refugees, exiles, and tourists, among other moving individuals and groups, all of whom appear to affect the politics of (and between) nations to a considerable degree. Ignorant of the lexicographical origins of the term 'scape' he rather confusingly added it to many ideas of flow, such as the flow of technology – technoscapes and the flow of ideas ideoscapes. Appadurai, A. (1990). "Disjuncture and difference in the global cultural economy." *Theory, Culture and Society* 7(2–3): 295–310.

Routledge Library Editions: Ethnoscapes

1. *Environmental Perspectives* David Canter, Martin Krampen & David Stea (Eds) (1988) ISBN 978-1-032-81616-6

2. *Environmental Policy, Assessment, and Communication* David Canter, Martin Krampen & David Stea (Eds) (1988) ISBN 978-1-032-81635-7

3. *New Directions in Environmental Participation* David Canter, Martin Krampen & David Stea (Eds) (1988) ISBN 978-1-032-81646-3

4. *Vernacular Architecture: Paradigms of Environmental Response* Mete Turan (Ed.) (1990) ISBN 978-1-032-82023-1

5. *Forms of Dominance: On the Architecture and Urbanism of the Colonial Enterprise* Nezar AlSayyad (Ed.) (1992) ISBN 978-1-032-84164-9

6. *The Meaning and Use of Housing: International Perspectives, Approaches and Their Applications* Ernesto G. Arias (Ed.) (1993) ISBN 978-1-032-84781-8

7. *Placemaking: Production of Built Environment in Two Cultures* David Stea & Mete Turan (1993) ISBN 978-1-032-86434-1

8. *Environmental Psychology in Europe: From Architectural Psychology to Green Psychology* Enric Pol (1993) ISBN 978-1-032-83324-8

9. *Housing: Design, Research, Education* Marjorie Bulos & Necdet Teymur (Eds) (1993) ISBN 978-1-032-86388-7

10. *Architecture, Ritual Practice and Co-determination in the Swedish Office* Dennis Doxtater (1994) ISBN 978-1-032-81774-3

11. *On the Aesthetics of Architecture: A Psychological Approach to the Structure and the Order of Perceived Architectural Space* Ralf Weber (1995) ISBN 978-1-032-82034-7

12. *The Home: Words, Interpretations, Meanings and Environments* by David N. Benjamin (Ed.) (1995) ISBN 978-1-032-86411-2

13. *Tradition, Location and Community: Place-making and Development* Adenrele Awotona & Necdet Teymur (Eds) (1997) ISBN 978-1-032-84608-8

14. *Aesthetics, Well-being and Health: Essays within Architecture and Environmental Aesthetics* Birgit Cold (Ed.) (2001) ISBN 978-1-032-86577-5

Other Ethnoscapes series titles also available:

Integrating Programming, Evaluation and Participation in Design: A Theory Z Approach Henry Sanoff (1992) HBK 978-1-138-20338-9; EBK 978-1-315-47173-0; PBK 978-1-138-20339-6

Directions in Person-Environment Research and Practice Jack Nasar & Wolfgang F. E. Preiser (Eds) (1999) HBK 978-1-138-68674-8; EBK 978-1-315-54255-3; PBK 978-1-138-68677-9

Psychological Theories for Environmental Issues Mirilia Bonnes, Terence Lee & Marino Bonaiuto (Eds) (2003) HBK 978-0-75461-888-1; EBK 978-1-315-24572-0; PBK 978-1-138-27742-7

Housing Space and Quality of Life David L. Uzzell, Ricardo Garcia Mira, J. Eulogio Real & Joe Romay (Eds) (2005) HBK 978-0-81538-952-1; EBK 978-1-351-15636-3; PBK 978-1-138-35596-5

Doing Things with Things: The Design and Use of Everyday Objects Alan Costall & Ole Dreier (Eds) (2006) HBK 978-0-75464-656-3; EBK 978-1-315-57792-0; PBK 978-1-138-25314-8

Rethinking the Meaning of Place: Conceiving Place in Architecture-Urbanism Lineu Castello (2010) HBK 978-0-75467-814-4; EBK 978-1-315-60616-3; PBK 978-1-138-25745-0

ETHNOSCAPES
Current Challenges in the Environmental Social Sciences

Series Editors: *David Canter and David Stea*

Environmental Perspectives
David Canter, David Stea and Martin Krampen

Environmental Policy, Assessment and Communication
David Canter, David Stea and Martin Krampen

New Directions in Environmental Participation
David Canter, David Stea and Martin Krampen

Vernacular Architecture
Edited by Mete Turan

Forms of Dominance
Nezar AlSayyad

Integrating Programming, Evaluation and Participation in Design
Henry Sanoff

The Meaning and Use of Housing
Edited by Ernesto G. Arias

Placemaking
David Stea and Mete Turan

Environmental Psychology in Europe
Enric Pol

Environmental Evaluation and Planning in the Third World
Boyowa Anthony Chokor

Housing: Design, Research, Education
Edited by Marjorie Bulos and Necdet Teymur

Architecture, Ritual Practice and Co-determination in the Swedish Office
Dennis Doxtater

On the Aesthetics of Architecture
Ralf Weber

THE HOME:
WORDS, INTERPRETATIONS, MEANINGS, AND ENVIRONMENTS

Edited, with an Introduction and Afterword by
David N. Benjamin, PhD

assisted by
David Stea, PhD

with a Foreword by
Professor David Saile, PhD

Contributors:
Eje Arén, David N. Benjamin, Stefan Brink,
Marjorie Bulos & Waheed Chaker, Frands Herschend,
Susan Kent, Roderick J. Lawrence, Juhani Pallasmaa,
J. Douglas Porteous, Neil Price, Amos Rapoport,
David Saile, David Stea, Ruth Tringham,
Bror Westman, and Jørn Ørum-Nielsen

Avebury

Aldershot • Brookfield USA • Hong Kong • Singapore • Sidney

© The contributors 1995

All rights reserved.
No part of this publication may be reproduced,
stored in a retrieval system, or transmitted in any form or by any means,
electronic, mechanical, photocopying, recording or otherwise
without the prior permission of the publisher.

Published by
Avebury
Avebury Publishing Limited
Gower House
Croft Road
Aldershot
Hants GU11 3HR
England

Ashgate Publishing Company
Old Post Road
Brookfield
Vermont 05036
USA

British Library Cataloguing in Publication Data
Home: Words, Interpretations, Meanings, and Environments
I. Benjamin, David N. II. Stea, David
307.336

ISBN 1 85628 888 9

Library of Congress Catalog Card Number:
94-75560

Typeset in Berthold Baskerville Book by
Marusa Design, Denmark

This book is printed on recycled paper, SAVATREE.

Printed and bound in Great Britain by Ipswich Book Co. Ltd., Ipswich, Suffolk

Contents

Foreword
David Saile *ix*

Acknowledgements *xiii*

Introduction
David N. Benjamin *1*

Part One
Home: Toward a Definition of the Concept

1. **Home: The Term and the Concept from a Linguistic and Settlement-Historical Viewpoint.**
   Stefan Brink *17*

2. **A Critical Look at the Concept "Home"**
   Amos Rapoport *25*

3. **Deciphering Home: An Integrative Historical Perspective**
   Roderick J. Lawrence *53*

4. **The Home and Homes**
   Bror Westman *69*

Part Two
Home as a Cultural Interpretation Tool

5. Archaeological Houses, Households, Housework, and the Home
   Ruth Tringham — *79*

6. House and Home in Viking Age Iceland: Cultural Expression in Scandinavian Colonial Architecture
   Neil S. Price — *109*

7. Identity, Intimacy and Domicile – Notes on the Phenomenology of Home
   Juhani Pallasmaa — *131*

Part Three
Home as Reflection of Societal Contention and Change

8. Domicide: The Destruction of Home
   J. Douglas Porteous — *151*

9. Ethnoarchaeology and the Concept of Home: A Cross-Cultural Analysis
   Susan Kent — *163*

10. House and Home: Identity, Dichotomy, or Dialectic?
    David Stea — *181*

11. The Origin of the Hall in Southern Scandinavia
    Frands Herschend — *203*

12. Sustaining a Sense of Home and Personal Identity
    Marjorie Bulos and Waheed Chaker — *227*

Part Four
Home and House: Lessons from the Past for the Present

13. Denmark's Living Housing Tradition
    Jørn Ørum-Nielsen — *243*

14. The Home and Housing Modernization
    Tomas Wikström   *267*

15. What Can We Learn from the Reconstruction
    of Pre-Historic Buildings?
    Eje Arén   *283*

Part Five

**Afterword, or Further Research Issues
in Confronting the Home Concept**
David N. Benjamin   *293*

List of contributors   *309*

Foreword

This collection of writings is a reflection of the tensions, arguments and excitements building for the past two decades around the topic of *home*. It is an exciting topic because it appears to touch so many people in many places and times. It also has contradictory meanings and has interested scholar, corporate executive, politician, news editor, and layperson alike.

The topic's importance is shown by the breadth of cross-disciplinary scholarship and the continued call for further investigation. The concept of *home* is associated with multiple areas of experience and, although extremely rich, has been very difficult to clearly define and communicate. The writings here are the product of serious work over the past ten years by participants in a symposium titled, *The Ancient Home and the Modern Industrialized Home* in Trondheim, Norway, in August, 1992. This meet-ing was not the only meeting about *home* in recent years but it certainly was one of the broadest and richest in scope. Other meetings include *The Meaning and Use of Home and Neighborhood* in Gävle, Sweden in August, 1989, and *Home: A Place in the World* at the New School of Social Research, New York in October, 1990.

It is not surprising that *home* is considered important by so many people but it is difficult to come to terms with the complexity of the topic. Homes are places of important household rituals, tasks, negotiations, and so on. Individuals develop important components of their identities in, and in resistance to, their family homes. Homes are constructed of patterns of cultural processes and indicate important distinctions in individual and household privacy and their connections with the broader society. The meaning of *home* may also be considered as commodities which are negotiated between the dweller and the corporate and political power systems. As a product too, the economy of production is important to both producer and consumer.

DAVID SAILE

I am very excited by this collection firstly because it embraces the connections and oppositions inherent in crossing disciplinary boundaries. I see great value in these areas of hybrid scholarship and research. The work builds well upon earlier interdisciplinary investigations (Altman and Werner 1985; Seamon and Mugerauer 1985; Oliver 1987; Low and Chambers 1989; Kent 1990) but draws together even more strands of research. Illuminating and evocative insights are derived from connections among archaeology, social anthropology, geography, environment and behavior studies, architecture, urban policy, and philosophy.

This collection excites me secondly because it more than hints that multi-cultural and diverse groups are involved. Different groups have different ideals and visions of *home* and different degrees of voice, power, and control over their spaces and production. This continues the increasingly valuable discussion of gender and multi-cultural aspects of housing in other recent volumes (Wekerle, Peterson, and Morley 1980; Hayden 1981 and 1984; Ahrentzen 1992).

Thirdly, concern for the value of different community and household organizations is reiterated here. Many of the chapters eloquently show rich human strategies for living in complex societies and do not simply reinforce the stereotypical Western ideal of nuclear (young) family with children. They show the pleasures and struggles of what actually exists in all its variety. In this respect, they also build upon the growing literature and series of community experiments in recent years (Cooper-Marcus and Sarkissian 1986; McCammant and Durrett 1988; Franck and Ahrentzen 1989). Finally, and no less importantly, the topic has received major media and public attention. Arguments over the meanings and production of homes has both resulted in, and focused attention upon, children in poverty and varieties of homelessness including those associated with political gamesmanship and migration caused by coercive, military, and economic forces. These issues were discussed in the *Home: A Place in the World* symposium (*Social Research* 1991) and it is good to see them addressed in some essays here. I hope you are as excited as I was in reading this sparkling collection.

DAVID SAILE
Professor of Architecture
University of Cincinnati

References

Ahrentzen, Sherry 1992. Home as a Workplace in the Lives of Women. In *Place Attachment*. Vol. 12 of *Human Behavior and Environment. Advances in Theory and Research*, ed. Irwin Altman and Setha Low. N.Y.: Plenum Press.

Altman, Irwin and Carol Werner, eds. 1985. *Home Environments*. Vol. 8 of *Human Behavior and Environment. Advances in Theory and Research*, ed. Irwin Altman and Carol Werner. N.Y.: Plenum Press.

Cooper-Marcus, Clare and Wendy Sarkissian, 1986. *Housing as if People Mattered*. Berkeley: University of California.

Franck, Karen and Sherry Ahrentzen, eds. 1989. *New Households New Housing*. N.Y.: Van Nostrand Reinhold.

Hayden, Delores 1981. *The Grand Domestic Revolution*. Cambridge: MIT.

———. 1984. *Redesigning the American Dream. The Future of Housing, Work, and Family Life*. N.Y.: W. W. Norton.

Kent, Susan, ed. 1980. *Domestic Architecture and the Use of Space, An Interdisciplinary Cross-Cultural Study*. Cambridge: Cambridge University Press.

Low, Setha and Erve Chambers, eds. 1989. *Housing, Culture, and Design. A Comparative Perspective*. Philadelphia: University of Pennsylvania.

McCammant, Kathryn and Charles Durrett, 1988. *Cohousing. A Contemporary Approach to Housing Ourselves*. Berkeley: Habitat/Ten Speed.

Oliver, Paul, ed. 1987. *Dwellings. The House Across the World*. Austin: University of Texas.

Seamon, David and Robert Mugerauer, eds. 1985. *Dwelling, Place and Environment. Towards a Phenomenology of Person and World*. Dordrecht: Martinus Nijhoff.

Social Research. 1991 Home: A Place in the World. 58(1).

Wekerle, Gerda, Rebecca Peterson, and David Morley, eds. 1980. *New Space for Women*. Boulder: Westview.

Acknowledgements

From the University of Trondheim, I would first like to extend my warmest thanks to doctoral candidate Eli Støa for her work as my partner in putting together the original symposium *The Ancient Home and the Modern Internationalized Home: Dwelling in Scandinavia*. Thanks go also to the faculty members that oversaw our activities: Professor Tore Brantenberg and assoc. professor Liv Arvesen from the Faculty of Architecture, professor Michael Jones and assoc. professor Vidar Hepsø from the Department of Social Sciences, and Axel Christophersen of the Royal Norwegian Department of Monuments Conservation. Grete Vintervoll and Vesla Huseby at the Institute for Building Design were absolutely invaluable components of the symposium.

I would like to thank architect Inger Anne Lahnstein for her dedicated work with the working seminar to plan the symposium, and assoc. professor Houchang Fathi and professor Terje Moe for their help in putting together the graphic design for the symposium's marketing material.

Lisa J. O'Bryant and Mike Myers from Kinko's Copies in Cleveland, Ohio provided invaluable help with the final text production, as did the Teknologi- og Informatikcenteret (TIC) in Copenhagen; while thanks must also go to the designer Martin Savery for making a book that is worth looking at.

I would like to thank Gerry and Valerie Mars for taking on the task of mediating the three days of symposia. Their job was often times thankless, but they did it anyway.

I extend thanks to those who opened their home to me while editing and writing: My parents Jeanne and Stanley Benjamin, Niels-Ole Sørensen and Lucia Stacey, and Hoshiar Nooraddin and Tahany Mohamed.

I extend the warmest and heartiest thanks for their financial assistance to Nordisk Kulturfond (The Nordic Cultural Foundation), NAVF (The Norwegian Humanities Research Council), The Faculty of Architecture at the Norwegian Institute of Technology, and the University of Trondheim. The Institute for Building Design in the Faculty of Architecture provided partial compensation for salaries so that Eli Støa could work on the symposium project. This book was made possible by a generous monetary gift from private persons and the humanitarian foundation Third Planet of Copenhagen, Denmark.

Thanks also to architect Leo de Klerk, Holland.

Finally, I extend my humblest thanks to those who helped along the way that I have neglected to mention.

DAVID N. BENJAMIN

The editor may be contacted at the following address:

Naturfolkenes Verden
Dronningensgade 14
1420 Copenhagen K
Denmark
Attn. David N. Benjamin

Raphael is charged to heal the earth, and through him, the earth furnishes a home for human beings, whom he also heals of their maladies.

— Rabbi Abba
from the *Zohar*

This book is dedicated
to all those made homeless by ignorance, hate, and war.

Introduction

David N. Benjamin

This book calls into question several conventional notions about the *home,* its definition, method for its study, where homes can be found, and even whether it is a useful concept for research at all.

Thus, the popular identification of the home with the house is only one small part of the story. Lawrence has elsewhere claimed that the home for many cultural groups is in addition a locus for abstract and often subjective concepts and associations concerning the structuring of domestic processes, and the human attatchment to such loci (Lawrence 1987, 3-6). Further, scholars need to start investigating each built environment in relation to its own specific cultural situation. Homes must therefore be viewed relative to the, "ways in which they have been used and regarded by people in specific social, cultural, geographical, and historical contexts" (ibid., 31). Several cases are here presented to posit the existence of homes across spatial and temporal barriers. Thus, the northwestern European culture area may not be the only exclusive location for the home, indeed, other cultural groups may have had the home concept prior to contact with modern European civilization. Finally, the issue of whether the *home* can be seen to define anything at all unique is taken up; maybe the scholarly use of the term should be avoided in favor of a word combination that allows strict and explicit agreement about a meaning content.

Fourteen of the articles in this book stem from a 3 day symposium, held at the University of Trondheim from the 20th to the 23rd of July, 1992, entitled *The Ancient Home and the Modern Internationalized Home: Dwelling in Scandinavia.* The article by Stefan Brink was commissioned later by the editor.

The present book is the result of a 2 year process of dialogue among the contributors and the editor (in Stefan Brink's case, this was a written dialogue). This dialogue involved a two stage process, first starting with formal presentations, group discussion, and informal conversation, centered around a specific theme for each day. Second, a final plenary forum on the last day brought together researchers and practitioners from diverse fields and research attitudes to contemplate out-loud the subject of the *home*. Thus, in addition to the articles, an afterword by the editor presents the contentious and difficult issues taken up in the plenary discussion, along with his own comments on what the articles do not say, and promising or compelling avenues for future research.

During 1993 and 1994, the authors revised their articles, the face to face discussions having provided inspiration for strengthening complementary or opposing viewpoints. Final discussions between the authors and the editor led to yet further revisions, and changes in the eventual structure of the sections of the book.

From the start, the original symposium and the present volume have taken an inclusivist and relativistic attitude on how to approach and present the subject of the home. Thus, the term and the concept are examined in each article with disciplinary, cultural, and chronological relativity compared to the other articles. A sense of the richness and depth of the subject is thus given, showing that the home is a phenomenon from the ancient past to the present, it is found in several different cultures, atleast within the Euro-American geographical area, and likely beyond, and has been studied by scholars in several fields: animal behavior, psychiarty, etymology, philology, theology, political science, sociology, art history, literature studies, social and cultural anthropology, geography, archaeology, and architecture, along with important cross-disciplinary specialties such as ethno-archaeology and environment-behavior studies.

Because of this relativistic attitude, I have used subscripts in the text of the Introduction and the Afterword to indicate homes as seen from different cultural groups, from different time periods, or by different viewpoints (i.e., $home_x$).

In spite of the wealth of scholarship and multi-disciplinary debate, and the fact that the first scholarly article concerning the home was published already in 1678 (referred to by McCann 1941), *home* is still an ambigious term. This is likely due to five major reasons:

1. The home is essentially dialectic in nature (understood as a relationship of complementary phenomena that are dependent on one another's existence), as it is a name for a category of phenomena that are at once both concrete and abstract.

2. As part of this abstract nature, the home is a symbol, so that even though we recognize it, and "know" it, it will always defy a rational deconstruction and complete explication of its meaning content.
3. Most researchers have been willing to take for granted ethno-centric, often Euro-American, definitions of the term.
4. Specific cultural groups who may not have had the term or the concept prior to their discovery of the Euro-American meaning have *apparently* begun to use this Euro-American *home* to communicate through modern mass media. This confuses the issue for conventional positivistic research in two ways:

    a) Because of this influence from the mass media, it will be difficult to untangle the effects of the Euro-American $home_1$ on any $home_2$ that these other cultures may have had, or still have.

    b) There is no practical way for conventional research to ascertain how informants not native to the Euro-American culture actually understand the concept of home. It would require a long and involved psycho-historical and etymological study of all those culture groups using *home* to actually find out what they understand by the term. On the other hand, one may claim that the Euro-American etymology of the *home* is no more valid as the starting point for a comparative study of the term than any other *home*.

5. The term *home* has a long history, going back atleast to the time of the birth of Christ in Germanic and Proto-Germanic or Greek languages, and thus the term has had a great deal of time to evolve and transform (see Brink in this volume).

Because of this controversy, the importance of the concept to scholarly research is still an issue in itself. However, this editor proposes that the home as a subject for serious study is important because contemplation of its meaning and role in society can assist in the following:

1. the study of an informant delimited category in the built environment, an environment-behavior relationship (EBR) from empirical research, and thus generally relevant to environment-behavior studies (EBS)
2. the study of cultural history where written records are few or non-existant, such as in the ancient past, or in contemporary non-literate societies
3. to view the environmental debate in a new way, since the home is an expression of the values and attitudes with which societies and individuals relate to their surroundings

4. to look at therapeutic or healing environments in a new light, since the home is reported to represent the initial place of birth and growth, and the memory of this place in later life, serving as a reference for the origin of pathologies or wellness.

5. to see the socio-political significance of the home, especially topical today when masses of people both escape from economic hardship and warfare, and fight to remain at home.

In addition to the term's prevalence the world over, this ambiguity, scholarly controversy and confusion, and lacunœ in our knowledge of its meaning, make it a generally interesting topic for research.

Because of this multi-faceted nature of the home, the contemplation of the concept and the term's use from many viewpoints seems to be necessary if we want to encompass its breadth along the aforementioned dimensions of comparison of discipline, time, and culture. The spectrum of viewpoints represented here is thus a review of the testing and evaluation of a variety of methods and theories concerning the subject, showing how the home can be used as a tool in cultural interpretation, and how research can help to define or destroy the concept.

Further, the authors ask the following research questions, vitally important for environment-behavior studies: Does a scientifically describable concept of the home exist; how can the home concept be useful for diachronic and synchronic research, and finally, can the use of the concept assist in the design and rehabilitation of contemporary settlements?

The book is structured around the following five themes:

1. methods for explicating the meaning of the term

2. the home as an arena for change and contention

3. the home as symbolic expression

4. the improvement of environmental design through contemplation of the home

5. the production of knowledge on the home through empirical research.

These themes correspond closely with the sectional titles of the book. However, theme 4 is mainly contained in Part 4, Home and House: Lessons from the Past for the Present, while theme 5 can be found covered in both Parts 2 and 3, respectively Home as a Cultural Interpretation Tool and Home as Reflective of Societal Contention and Change.

INTRODUCTION

The parts of the book

Part One: Home: Toward a definition of the concept.

The authors in this section seek to explicate the meaning content of the concept itself, and how the term is understood by different groups of people, from scholars to informants. The attitudes here run the gamut from rejecting the existance of a scientifically verifiable unique definition to, on the other hand, finding a definition that is useable cross-culturally and over long time periods.

Stefan Brink. This author analyses the history of the term from its ancient origins in Greece and Germany and up to later pre-history in Scandinavia, tracing the development and transformation of the meaning of the term along the way. He draws on several different areas of evidence about the essential aspects of its meaning to come to a final definition, relating the *home* to its cognates in other languages, analyzing place names, and even looking at a Scandinavian god with *home* in his name.

Amos Rapoport. Rapoport subjects the term to a critical and skeptical examination, inspired by the worrying trend in popular and scholarly contexts for using terms to stand for ever broader sets of phenomena, i.e., *vernacular.* Through this analysis, he proposes answers to some simple but important research questions: Can the term be improved? Are there alternative terms? Should the term be discarded altogether? And so on.

The analysis is broken down into the popular and research contexts of usage, to see what if anything in either context may be helpful to construct a uniquely identifiable meaning that can be related to other variables. In doing so, Rapoport proposes for discussion a set of criteria to test for useful concepts in environment-behavior studies. Such systematization would seem to be necessary in the theoretical and empirical development of the field, in that it should lead to standardization and agreement about the essential elements of discussion.

The author uses a literature analysis to explicate how these tests can be applied. Finally, he proposes an alternative set of words that more precisely stand for that which he claims is poorly described by *home* in the scientific context.

Roderick Lawrence. Lawrence directly confronts the term as a fact in scholarly research, admitting that its complexity and ambiguity challenge any attempt to define it, yet at the same time noting its almost worldwide popularity. However, he does not merely accept the superficial meanings attributed to the term by popular culture as the last word in an empirical analysis of the concept, but digs deeper to find its historical roles in society. He proposes that this can be done by use of an historical-integrative method, and the use of a specific list of research questions.

He claims that the home can be approached by considering the sets of relationships that all human groups organize for themselves, these relationships being not merely functional, but also meaningful. One such relationship is the home itself.

Bror Westman. Westman studies the subjective behavior of human cultures. He claims that the home is an important part of this behavior, as it is both a physical and mental phenomenon. He proposes that the concept can be understood if analyzed cross-culturally, and does this by the comparative study of people's movement patterns, especially those that go back and forth between essential locations of human daily life.

By contemplating and observing movement in various cultures, Westman seems to have come upon a way to empirically study the relative definition of the home. Thus, different cultures apparently conceive of the home differently according to how they organize and think of their movement in the domestic sphere. He illustrates this way of looking at the home with a graphic model to place the home in space and time, between 'being' and movement.

Part Two: Home as a cultural interpretation tool

This section basically accepts the existence of the term in its scholarly guise, and goes further to show examples of specific areas of usefulness to humanistic research and architectural practice. All these authors see the built environment as meaningful, and this meaning as vital to research as well as to those experiencing the situation under study. Here again, both diachronic and synchronic perspectives are presented.

Ruth Tringham. Tringham asks very simply whether, in what way, and with what methodology the concept of home can be useful to prehistoric studies. She answers these questions by studying the rich domestic archaeological record from southeastern Europe between 7 to 5,000 B.C., with the viewpoint that material culture is both a passive reflection of behavior and an active symbolic expression for culture.

In this test of the home concept, she works with several innovative ideas from processualist research, such as the *use-life* of material objects, the relativity of the archaeological record, the construction of multiple prehistories, the notion of individual actors in the past, and going beyond a focus on the house as the delimitation of the entire domestic arena to consider the entire settlement area. She has illustrated this construction of the past with both an extensive set of excavation diagrams and a "fictional" narrative of domestic life.

Niel Price. By using the home as a concept to study ancient domestic life, Price shows how the following pressing issue in Viking Age archaeology can be dealt with: The recognition of personal, cultural, and ethnic identity in the archaeological record.

Previously, it was traditional to isolate artifacts traceable to Scandinavian culture, yet Price claims the problem is more involved, and provides other opportunities for interpretation. The built environment and portable material culture together have meaning for specific groups in the past, and by comparatively studying this meaning, the author claims that a culturally identifiable Scandinvian dwelling tradition can be described.

Price uses the colonial architecture of Viking era Iceland to look beyond style, size, material, etc., and finds specific forms of spatial patterning in buildings to be a determinant for cultural tradition. Finally, because of this analysis, he questions the earlier typing of Viking Age buildings, showing that there was *variation* built into the design of structures *within* the conventionally known types. This study is thus important, because it documents how such abstract concepts as the home are relative, and undergo transformation over time.

Juhani Pallasmaa. Pallasmaa looks at the home as *definitively* a human phenomenon. He uses novels, peotry, film, and critical commentary as a way of showing the importance of the concept to humanity and the tragedy of its loss to both individuals and society. The author analyzes the major aspects of the home that need to be promoted if we want to retain a sense of its quality: Imagery, emotion, identity, the return (of the prodigal son), childhood, family, intimacy, and finally causality. He thus broadens the study of the home to include these abstract, subjective factors that are very human but hard to grasp and work with in conventional positivistic research.

Through this search, Pallasmaa finally comes to a central question in contemporary environmental design: Is it still possible to attain the state of van Eyck's "homecoming" in today's architecture, the *reconciliation* between public and private life, between the place of origin and the present location of the individual?

DAVID N. BENJAMIN

Part Three: Home as reflective of societal contention and change

The authors in this section study the transformations in present or past societies with the help of ambigious concepts such as the home. They see the home as a category important to specific groups of people that assists in the categorization of experienced space and time, either in our present, or in the ancient past.

The present contention over the control and habitation of living environments all over the world certainly makes this view of the home highly topical. People's attitudes about who should live where, and for what reason, are some of the central socio-political issues of the last quarter of the twentieth century.

J. Douglas Porteous. Porteous takes up the phenomenon of the willful or natural *destruction* of home within the more general place-destruction. He implicates the system of corporate capitalism, the planning professions, and the civil bureaucracy for their decisive role in the willful annihilation of all kinds of environments meaningful to human groups. He then goes on to make a typology of destruction, and a framework for its futher study. For physical planners, this has up until now been an all too ignored aspect of the settlement process itself, that of erasing one form of settlement in order to make way for "improvements" and "development."

Porteous seeks to identify in this research who is doing this, why, and to what effect. He shows how this information can be studied by looking at three examples, in Chile, Canada, and England. He analyzes in depth the company town phenomenon which naturally leads to a pathological relationship of one-way dependence. Porteous thus deals with such topical issues as power(lessness) and control in settlements, important just now when groups in several different locations experience the destruction of places physically and psychically.

Susan Kent. Kent compares information from several different cultures undergoing specific processes of transformation for data concerning how people think about and delineate space. She structures this information according to specific measurable dimensions of social behavior and looks for generalizable correlations. This makes her investigation relatively transparent, so that criticism and repetition are made easier for future researchers.

From this careful method, Kent posits that home, even for westerners, is basically an individually constituted concept, although it is understood culture-wide. This is another thoughtful warning to researchers that they must make explicit the comparisons and analogies used in order to derive conclusions, lest we inadvertanltly transfer concepts from one culture to another, or mistake individually formed ideas for prevalent traditions.

David Stea. Stea proposes that research on the evaluations made by users of environments and the relationship of these evaluations to behavior is of utmost importance now, and is well within the conventionally accepted research program of EBS. As such, home can be an interesting concept since it is not only associated with emotionally charged and contentious evaluations, but it may be a guide to research into just those cultures that do *not* have similiar environmental concepts to the home.

The author notes that the field of community psychology is of cardinal use in this case, since systems of values are related to behavior at the societal level, going beyond the individual's solitary relationship to space. He thus deals with family, social heirarchy, and the mode of activity to study the structure of the community's use of domestic space.

Stea analyzes the use of the dwelling, and the relationship of its major constituent actors. By doing so, he finds that the time scale of change for traditional homes in Third World countries has been compressed relative to First World homes, with the impact on people and the physical environment being concomitantly greater. This make the study of meaningful environments, such as a concept of home, all the more important, since it has to do with evaluations of right/wrong, good/bad, and thus it affects our further behavior within the environment.

Frands Herschend. Herschend examines the development of the hall building type over a little known period in Scandinavian prehistory, the Roman Iron Age up to the Viking Age. The hall seems to have been a particular kind of meeting house, which served to qualify the gender, socio-economic, and political status of its users, and especially its owner.

The author takes a definitively self-critical view of the possibility of such reconstructions of the past, yet claims that it is ultimately necessary that we do so, although for reasons that have more to do with our own life, rather than an interest in some exotic past.

Herschend cogently develops this thesis around the relationship between the individual and the collective, showing how the spatiality of society in the past was very much a common concern of the entire culture. He systematically reviews examples of settlements from Norway, Sweden, and Denmark, covering a 500 year time span, and illustrates the discussion with explanatory drawings.

Through this study, it is possible to see that certain building types in prehistoric society may have even presaged the socio-economic status and role of later important actors on the historical scene: The stage was set, only the actors need be born, so to speak. Finally, Herschend relates his conclusions on space to two of the few written records that are known to illustrate the period in question, lending credence to the reconstruction task.

Marjorie Bulos – Waheed Chaker. Bulos and Chaker examine the phenomenon of working at home in Britain through both a summary literature review, and case studies illustrated by interview excerpts and photographs. These case studies make evident the diversity of homeworking situations, and the conflict and opportunities that arise from this situation.

Homeworking is still at the stage of being seen as abnormal, and by association, thus the homeworker is also seen as somehow abnormal. This is a disruption to homefulness, yet this type of work is growing more and more popular, especially in England and the U.S. It is thus a vital area of research, not least because of the impact of homeworking on areas of daily life as diverse as politics, architecture, geography, demography, behavior, public health, and architecture.

Part Four: Home and house: Lessons from the past for the present

The authors in this section seek not only to make proposals for improving the built environment, but to go beyond this: to provide inspiration and knowledge to help designers and researchers manifest and study *future* settlements that will have to deal with difficult or unimagineable problems. Thus, the scope of present challenges, such as the environmental crisis, mass emigration, forced deportation, and wilfull place-destruction on a large scale, may not even come close to encompassing the severity of the necessary environmental design and research tasks of the future.

Present trends, such as worldwide population growth and increasing migration to cities in many countries are mere indicators of the real world designers and researchers will have to deal with. Thus, we need to intensify our examination of traditional architecture and interpretation, and listen more closely to what dwellers tell us today, so that we can begin to make a healthy and meaningful future.

Jørn Ørum-Nielsen. Ørum-Nielsen claims that bureaurcratic standards and the training and conventional practice for professionals in the built environment has produced a gulf between the planner/architect and the dweller, the unavoidable dilemma of housing design: Architects are in the end left to find solutions for others based on their own personal experience. He shows that this situation may be atleast partially rectified through an examination of traditional dwelling design, here illustrated by the

Danish tradition. To do this, we must be willing to take into account intangible and non-rational ideas and modes of thought, including concepts of community/privacy, security, belonging, and a sense of home. Regulations concerning structures, life safety, and aesthetics simply do not exhaust the necessary factors that have an affect on a satisfactory life in a dwelling environment.

The author studies houses and settlements from before the advent of the professionalization and bureaucratization of the building industry, and compares these to some of the best housing designs from the twentieth century. This is not a nostalgic project, the goal is not to replicate the past, but instead to study the design principles used to help in planning a resilient and adaptable future that can mediate between the individual and the community. He goes on to identify, with photographs and diagrams, the key principles that make traditional European settlement seem so successful today. He shows how these ideas were applied in several important housing estates from after the Renaissance and up to today. Ørum-Nielsen claims that these concepts are applicable beyond Scandinavia since they deal with very general planning problems in a simple manner.

Thomas Wikström. From his empirical research into Swedish housing modernization, Wikström contemplates the spatial dimension of home. Inspired by thinkers such as Böllnow and Heidegger, he sees the home as a cultural expression in the creation of space.

For Wikström, the notion of home came not only from the literature, but was an informant-defined category in his interviews with the dwellers, showing that also the terminology used by informants should not necessarily be thrown out because of its "irrational" character. Rather, people are emotional about their surroundings, and this is an important path to learning how designers and researchers can study the settlement-dweller relationship. Indeed, the author posits that we must go beyond the prevalent reductionism inherent in the distinction between object and subject to understand the home, at once a mental and physical phenomenon. In so doing, he makes life more complex and ambiguous for designers and researchers, yet at the same time all the more exciting.

Eje Arén. Arén examines what can be learned about the environment-behavior relationship through the study of ancient house reconstructions. He presents a detailed example of a house he himself has built, exemplifying the two learning methods he uses to interpret ancient houses: Learning by doing as a craftsman, and the study of still extant construction methods from traditional cultures worldwide.

Arén goes beyond conventional reconstructions that focused solely on the house itself, and reconstructs the natural premises for architecture in the surrounding landscape. Thus, he extends the view of society to include an integration with the natural resources and landscape forms. Finally, he proposes that the real value of reconstruction for the present is not entertainment, but rather the provocation it offers to action and contemplation about issues within the realm of environment-behavior studies because of its very immediacy: standing before a building, whether "wrongly" or "correctly" built, will usually without fail produce a reaction. Such reactions can be the impetus to reinterpret our own present, and transform it to the better.

The home in environment-behavior studies

Why study the home?

The term *home* encompasses a vast subject, with a two-thousand year history. During this time, the home has been built, destroyed, transformed, defiled, scorned, revered, and continued to be what it is, while the home has in turn imprisoned or sheltered inhabitants, sanctioned and demarcated the boundaries of legally defined space, provoked people to action, and soothed the weary traveller or the returning child. All this, and more than can be mentioned here.

Beyond the prevalence of the home in daily life, EBS provides reasons to study this phenomenon within the scholarly context. This has to do with the goal and method of EBS, along with the importance of meaning and interpretation as mechanisms in EBS.

Goal. One definition of the goal of EBS is the "generation of knowledge and the discovery of processes and systems to understanding design-behavior interactions, and to develop a theory of the environment in relation to human activity," (Moore 1984, 97). More specifically, the home is one of the archtypical places in place research to study empirically, "from the perspective of the user" (ibid., 107).

Method. The conventionally accepted methods of EBS seem to allow the investigation of the concept since the investigation should be empirically based, using information provided by people who design and dwell in homes. Indeed, this information should then be checked against any available diachronic and synchronic studies to provide the basis for comparative studies, which can lead to pattern recognition and hypothesis testing or theory building (Rapoport 1990, 24, 49). The *home* is highly amenable to such investigation since it is a term that has existed since ancient times, and has been reported by several cultural groups, both within the original Germanic language groups and among diverse other cultures.

Inter-disciplinarity. According to Rapoport (ibid., 102), "an essential requirement in EBS is to establish relationships among many disciplines with similiar concerns." For many years, possibly since Hofer's article in 1678, the concept of the home has served to bring researchers from fields as diverse as psychiatry and architecture together (the 1992 symposium in Trondheim is only the latest example). It is thus a prime *inspiration* for interdisciplinary learning and knowledge creation.

Spatio-temporal extent. Further, the extent of any setting needs to be discovered, and not decided a priori (ibid., 4). Thus, the at once abstract and concrete concept of home requires investigation to also determine its extent in different cultures (both spatially and temporally), and the conventional identification of the home with the house needs to be seen as merely a particular case in the Euro-American context.

Meaning. According to Rapoport , "People seem to shape and interact with built environments/material culture through meaning, and this seems to hold over time, cross-culturally, and in all kinds of environments, contexts, and situations." Thus, "meaning is a central mechanism in EBR" (ibid., 42). Since the home is a meaning applied to specific environmental or psychic structures, we should be willing to continue to confront the concept at face value, exhausting all that the term has to say.

Interpretation. Hastrup (1985, 16–19), has written that cultural groups tend to see an order in the activities of production and reproduction, and thereby they interpret these activities, a sort of meaning production, or culture. All three, production, reproduction, and culture, guarantee the psychic and physical continuation of the particular society. More to the point, Guidoni (1978, 10, 16), claims that the notional, *interpreted,* and rationalized environment is a real component of any architectural fact, along with the habitation, settlement, and territory.

Finally, there are in use other contentious and possibly misunderstood terms in the humanities and social sciences besides *home*. The Polynesian *tapu,* or *kapu,* has thus become *taboo,* widely used in the literature (Mead 1968, 1934; Parry 1985), even though the several Polynesian subtleties of meaning were used interchangeably for the meaning of a single term by early ethnologists. Thus, Mead (1934) defines the term, and used it again in the definition of *incest* (1968). Home should be treated similarly, as a term requiring study, discussion, and concerted attempts at definition for specific cultural groups. The synthetic alternatives invented by some researchers may be more internally coherent, but have a dubious and unproven connection to informant conceptions of space and time (especially if one is studying the emotional and spiritual aspects of places and occasions), and are more unwieldly and verbose in their construction.

The above makes it seem reasonable that the home concept not only deserves further serious study, but can be an inspiration to developing new, or the testing of conventional, methods, hypotheses, theories, and environments. It should inspire researchers to view the present chaotic process of settlement from a particular user-developed concept, compare it to other user-developed concepts, and ask critical questions about design, and the effects of present interpretations of environments.

References

Guidoni, Enrico. 1978. *Primitive Architecture.* History of World Architecture Series. N.Y.: Harry N. Abrams, Inc.

Hastrup, Kirsten. 1985. *Etnografisk Grundbog.* Copenhagen: Gyldendal.

Lawrence, Roderick. 1987. *Housing, Dwellings and Homes. Design Theory, Research and Practice.* N.Y.: John Wiley & Sons.

McCann, Willis H. 1941. Nostalgia. A Review of the Literature. *Psychological Bulletin* 38.

Mead, Margaret. 1968. Incest. In *International Encyclopedia of the Social Sciences,* ed. David Sills. N.Y.: The Macmillan Co. and the Free Press.

———. 1934. Tabu. In *Encyclopedia of the Social Sciences,* ed. E.R.A. Seligman and A. Johnson. N.Y.: Macmillan and Co.

Moore, Gary T. 1984. New Directions for Environment-Behavior Research in Architecture. In *Architectural Research,* ed. James Snyder. N.Y.: Van Nostrand Reinhold.

Parry, J.P. 1985. Taboo. In *The Social Science Encyclopedia,* ed. Adam Kuper and Jessica Kuper. London: Routledge & Kegan Paul

Rapoport, Amos. 1990. *History and Precedent in Environmental Design.* N.Y.: Plenum Press.

Part One

Home: Toward a Definition of the Concept

1
Home: The Term and the Concept from a Linguistic and Settlement-Historical Viewpoint

Stefan Brink

Everyone knows and understands the word *home*, although if we were able to X-ray or dissect people's minds to see the connotations that represent that particular person's meaning of *home*, we would probably see a wide range of concepts. The modern word *home*, *hjem*, *heim*, *hem* etc. must *per definitionem* be ambiguous, due to the fact that firstly, it denotes not a concrete object but something more abstract, an observation which in fact seems to go far back in history, 1,000, maybe 2,000 years; Secondly, the word has thus lived for thousands of years with the possibility of becoming semantically wider or narrower in different languages. One can only go to oneself and ask for the meaning of *home*. The semantic core is probably shared with most other people in the same cultural context, however the semantic picture will probably fade out at the edges. What probably comes to mind, is one's living-house with various "necessities" in the vicinity. A more collective valid meaning we can look up in lexica. If we however for some reason want to use *home* as an unambiguous term in research, we of course have to give it a precise definition.

This is the synchronic life of the word *home*, its use today. What about the use of the term and the concept *home* in earlier days, hence what about the diachronic aspect?

The word *home* has equivalent cognates in most Germanic languages (here the English form *home* is used for all Germanic related words). The forms and lexical meanings in older Germanic languages are e.g. OEng. *hām* n. (collection of dwellings, village, estate, house etc.), OHGerman *heima* m. (home, world), OSaxon *hēm* (home) and OScandinavian *heimr* m. (dwelling, home, world). The meaning home, or one's farm, goes far back in history for the Scandinavian word *heimr*, *hēm*. One early example is from the mediaeval provincial law for Östergötland, the *Östgötalagen* (ms. ca. 1350), where in section two, concerning homicide, it is stated (Collin & Schlyter 1830, 46 f.):

> Nu dræpær mabær man ....
> Nu fa þe draparan ok dræpa egh ginsta.
> þa aghu þer han til þingxs föra ....
> Nu ma egh taka draparan i sialfs sins heme.
> ælla i annars manz heme
> utan þe takin han gensta uiþ drapit....

> Now someone kills another man
> Now they catch the killer and do not kill him immediately
> they shall bring him to the thing.
> You may not take a killer at his home
> or in another man's home
> if they don't catch him at once at the manslaughter

Another is from the ancient *Gutalag*, the Law Codex for the island of Gotland (ms. ca. 1350), where in the section *af haim friþi* (peace in the home) it is stated (Pipping 1905–07, 15):

> Þa ir enn huerium manni haima friþr siþan
> Drepr þu mann haima i garþi sinum eþa af hagg veitr

> Now it is about peace in home for every man
> Do you kill a man at home on his farm or mutilate him

In this last stanza, it is also interesting to notice the use of home (*haim*) corresponding to farm *garþ*. In this way the word *hem* (home) is used in Old Swedish in the Middle Ages.

When talking about *heimr* (home), it is of course impossible to leave out the name of one of the central figures in the old Scandinavian pagan religion, the divine *Heimdal(l)r*. He is mentioned by Snorri and in the *Edda*. In *Gylfaginning* Snorri writes:

> One [God] is named *Heimdal*. He is called the white asa-god. He is big and holy. He was born as the son of nine virgins, that all were sisters.... He lives in *Himinbjörg* ["Heaven-mountain"] at *Bifrost*. He is the guardian of the gods and sits there at the end of the heaven to guard the bridge against mountain-giants... He also hears the grass grow on the ground and the wool grow on sheep and everything that

sounds more than that. He has a horn, called *Gjallarhorn*, and when he blows it, it is heard in all worlds. Heimdal's sword is called *Huvud* [Head].

Heimdal is not possible to trace in place-names. Hence it is dubious if he ever has been worshiped. Maybe he is just a code-name for another god, a hypostasis. The evidence in the sagas and the silence amongst the place-names makes it difficult to label *Heimdal* as an actual god among the *asar*. The name *Heimdal* is very interesting, however difficult to interpret. The latter element *-dal(l)r* is yet not fully understood; maybe it goes back to **dal-þu*, found in other gods names as *Óðr* and *Ullr*. The first element is probably our *heimr*, most surely in the meaning world. This is also a hint that *Heimdal* has not belonged to the *asar*, but to the real world. With the word *heimr* (world) in his name, it is interesting to note that in *Rígsþula*, *Heimdal* is known by the name *Rígr* and he begets with *Edda*, *Amma*, and *Móðir* the three sons *Pæll*, *Karl*, and *Jarl*, representing the three ranks in the society: the slaves, the farmers, and the nobility. (de Vries 1962, 219; Ström 1961, 298 f.; Holtsmark 1970, 158 ff.)

The word is also found in the lost Gothic language in the form *haims*. Gothic is handed down to us with the Bible as a filtering-medium, which must be kept in mind. Here, Wulfila the translator in the 4th century A.D., used *haims* for the Greek word κωμη (village, hamlet), but even more interestingly he has used the plur. *haimos* for Greek αγροι (country, country-side) to oppose πολιξ (town). Of course, this early observation will be of importance in the following discussion. It is also worth noticing the two adjectives Gothic **af-haim(ei)s* (absent, away from home) and **ana-haim(ei)s* (present, at home) (Feist 1939, 233 f.; Lehmann 1986, 170).

The Proto-Germanic form is *$*\chi aima$*- ($-i$-), which was most probably borrowed into the Lithuanian *kiēmas* (village, farm) etc., and *káima(s)* (village, land or country as opposed to town) (Fraenkel 1962, 251). The ultimate relations of this Proto-Germanic base *$*\chi aim$*- are somewhat disputed, however most probable, and in agreement with most etymologians, it is to be understood as an abstract formation with an *m*-suffix to an IE. root **kei*- (to lie), as in Greek κειμαι (lies), κοιμαο (brings to rest), cf. κοιτε (lair, camp). It is interesting to note that the same formation is found in e.g., Latvian *saime* (family, household servants) and OSlavic *sĕmija* (household servants; slaves). (Pokorny 1959, 539 f.; Kluge 1989, 301; Hellquist 1948, 346.)

In Old Celtic languages we find a related formation that demonstrates another interesting theme, namely the meaning 'love', as e.g., in OIrish *cōim* (dear, beloved) (Pokorny 1959, 540). Also related to this formation

Proto-Germanic *χaim- are e.g., MHGerman *heimen* (take home; marry) and OEnglish *hǣman* (< *haimian*) (to have sexual intercourse; to marry), originally (bring home [a bride]), cf. (above) Greek κοιμαο (bring to the bed) etc., which certainly also puts in perspective this word *home* (Bosworth & Toller 1921, 497; Grein 1974, 294; Holthausen 1963, 145; Torp 1919, 206).

Consequently the words — now and in ancient times — that are direct cognates with, or that relate to *home*, deal with dwelling and affection, perhaps the affection for one's dwelling-place, one's *home*. There is obviously not any absolute demand for habitations in this semantic evidence. Already early on we have meanings such as country (as opposed to town), and thus, as expected also world, the home of all of us. This evidence can probably be underlined furthermore when we turn to the place-name evidence below.

A valid question in this connection is of course if there are languages that have other concepts for home than this massive demonstration of one and the same lexical formation found in most Indo-European languages. We find some scattered examples, however in the light of the popular *m*-formation of the root *kei-, they are very few. The words for hearth, fireplace normally are from notions like fire, burn, shine, heat etc., and in some few cases it has come to be used symbolically for the family dwelling house, thus (the home), as in Greek εστια, cf. ομεστιοξ (of the same household), Rumainian *cămin* and OHGerman *herd*. Another instance is Irish *baile* (town, village), which also can be used with the meaning home. (Buck 1949, 459, 474).

If we turn to the toponymical evidence, several interesting observations of great value in the discussion of the word *home* are to be found. The equivalants to *home* are found in many old place-names on centrally located settlements all over the North Germanic language area. In Germany the place-name element in question is *-heim*, whereas in England it is *-ham*. This latter element is rather problematic, since place-names in *-ham* have different origins. Besides the old OEnglish *-hām* with assumed meanings as (village, estate, farm), we have some other words that are found amongst the *-ham* names, namely OEnglish *hamm* (enclosure), *hamm* (river-meadow), *hemm* (edge, border) etc. (Sandred 1976).

In England the *-ham* names show an uneven distribution, e.g., East Anglia have many names, whereas the western Midlands have few. Normally the first element in *-ham* names are a man's name, *Amersham* (Ealhmund's village), however in some cases the first element is a topographical word, *Burnham* (village by the stream). Of special interest are the *-ingaham* names (village of X's followers), thus containing an inhabitant-name in -*inga* and the name of some leading man of this people, e.g. *Gillingham* (the homestead of the followers of Gylla), *Wokeingham* (the homestead of the followers of Wocca). These names are related to the -*ingas* names, where the element -*ingas* (the followers of X) also contains a man's name as the first element, e.g. *Reading* (the followers of Read) and *Hasting* (the followers of Hasta). Of course, these latter names do not have to denote an habitation etc., it is possible to interpret these with a more areal meaning, i.e. settlement-district (Dodgson 1973; Cox 1973; Gelling 1978, 112 ff.).

If we turn to the -*hem*, -*heim* names in the Nordic countries, we find an interesting difference compared to the British and Continental names in -*ham* and -*heim*. The first obvious thing is that the Scandinavian names never seem to contain a person's name as the first element. Instead we find topographical appellatives. (The same opposition we find regarding the Scandinavian -*inga* names!) A valid starting-point for the discussion of the Scandinavian -*hem* names, may be to contrast e.g. the names *Trondheim*, in Norway, with *Sähem*, one of several Swedish names. The former means (the settlement-district of the *trønder* [in *Trøndelag*]), while the latter means (the farm by the lake). This opposition in meaning, an area contra an habitation, has led to a vivid discussion amongst scholars what is the original meaning of -*he(i)m*. Most scholars have come to the conclusion that the latter meaning, (a farm, a settlement), represents the original meaning for this element, and one has especially used the meaning of the Greec κειμαι (lie) as a tool to come up with an older meaning (place where one has settled; settlement).

If we look at the actual material, we find that among Norway's ca. 1,000 *heim*-names, Sweden's ca. 300 *hem*-names and Denmark's ca. 200 *hem*-names, a large part are somewhat stereotypical names, e.g. *Solhem* (sun–), *Nyhem* (new–), *Opphem* (upper–), *Sähem* (lake–), *Askhem* (ashwood–), *Grythem* (stone–), etc. Many of these names must be considered to be fairly young, from the Late Iron Age. However there are some really old -*he(i)m* names as well, spread nearly all over the Iron Age settlement districts in Scandinavia. These names have probably been coined already in the centuries around the birth of Christ. With a combined onomastical, archaeological, and palaeo-ecological dating, I have been able to give the *hem*-name *Vattjom* in the province of Medelpad, northern Sweden, a precise dating to as early as ca 200 A.D., probably the most "secure" dating such an old place-name has in the whole of Scandinavia (Brink 1984, 45 ff.).

Regarding the intrinsic semantical problem with the element -*he(i)m*, it is interesting to study a -*hem* name on the island of Gotland in the Baltic Sea.

Here we find a parish-name *Elinghem* (< **Airlingiahaim*). In this parish we find the farm *Ire* (ære 1523), which contains a Proto-Scandinavian river-name **Airōn* (the copper colored stream). The farm situated beside the stream has thus metonymically taken over the name of this water, whereas the parish-name contains an inhabitant-name **AirlingiaR* (the people who lives by the **Airōn* stream) and the element *-hem*, which hence must be interpreted as (the residence, the settlement-district of the **AirlingiaR*). In this case it is obvious that the name-formation *Ire* is punctual, it denotes a specific farm by the stream. When coining another name, one has used the element *-hem* and an inhabitant-name, which obviously demonstrates that *-hem* is not the name of the farm, but bears a more areal semantic content, denoting something like (the area of resource) for the **AirlingiaR*.

In the discussions so far, one has concentrated too much on the question whether *-he(i)m* denoted (a habitation) or (a settlement-district). This has led to an academical hair-splitting. Obviously there is nothing etymologically that forces us to presuppose some kind of habitation (hence actual buildings) for the meaning of *home, haim, hem, heim, hjem* etc. Therefore, it is tempting to assume that a vital semantical component for the *-he(i)m* names has been (settlement[s] with area of resources). With this explanation, there is nothing problematic to have on the one hand names like *Trondheim* (the province of the trønder) or *Böhmen* (the district occupied by the Boii), and on the other *Sähem* (the farm by the lake) or *Stenhem* (the farm by the stone); and actually this interpretation also finds support when we look at the appellatives, such as the Gothic plural *haimos* (country) and OWScandinavian *heimr* (dwelling, home; world) (Brink 1991).

To sum up, regarding the place-name element *-ham, -hem, -heim*, what must have been of interest for the name-givers have been the area – small or large – where some people have lived. This explains names such as German *Böhmen* (Bohemia, Latin *Boioh(a)emum*) (the land of the Boii), English *Gillingham* (the district of the followers of Gylla), Norwegian *Trondheim* (the district of the trønder), Swedish *Grythem* (the farm on the stony terrain [and its possessions]). And if we turn back to the etymological considerations of the appellatives, this areal component seems to be vital. Thus one could end this discussion by stating that some kind of semantical core, regarding the word *home* and its cognates, is the area and place where you live, a place with its surroundings that you normally take an affection to and have a very special relationship to, throughout your lifetime.

Hence, after more than 20 years in Uppsala and several other places around our world, I still say *home* when refering to the place (and

Holthausen, F. 1963. *Altenglisches Etymologisches Wörterbuch.* 2nd ed. Heidelberg: Carl Winter. Universitätsverlag.

Holtsmark, A. 1970. *Norrøn Mytologi. Tro og Myter i Vikingetiden.* Oslo: Det Norske Samlaget.

Kluge, F. 1989. *Etymologisches Wörterbuch der Deutschen Sprache.* 22nd ed. Berlin & New York: Walter de Gruyter.

Lehman, W. P. 1986. *A Gothic Etymological Dictionary.* Leiden: E. J. Brill.

Pipping, H. 1905-07. *Guta lag och Guta saga. Jämte Ordbok.* Samfund til udgivelse af gammel nordisk litteratur 33. Copenhagen.

Pokorny, J. 1959. *Indogermanisches Etymologisches Wörterbuch 1.* Bern & München: Franke Verlag.

Sandred, K. I. 1976. The Element *hamm* in English Place-Names. A Linguistic Investigation. *Namn och Bygd* 64 : 69-87.

Ström. F. 1961. Heimdal(l). In *Kulturhistoriskt Lexikon för Nordisk Medeltid från Vikingatid till Reformationstid.* Vol. 6. Malmö: Allhems förlag.

Torp, A. 1919. *Norsk Etymologisk Ordbok.* Kristiania: H. Aschehoug & Co.

de Vries, J. 1962. *Altnordisches Etymologisches Wörterbuch.* 2 ed. Leiden: E. J. Brill.

province!) where I was born and spent my first 18 years, that is in the northwestern part of the province of Hälsingland in northern Sweden. I will always be an Hälsingian, and my *real home* is there, although my *present home* has for many years been situated in Uppsala.

References

Bosworth, J., and T. N. Toller, 1921. *An Anglo-Saxon Dictionary.* Supplement. Oxford: Oxford University Press.

Brink, S. 1984. Absolut Datering av Bebeyggelsenamn. In *Bebyggelsers og bebyggelsesnavnes alder.* NORNA-rapporter no. 26. Uppsala: NORNA-förlaget.

———. 1991. Iakttagelser Rörande Namnen på *-hem* i Sverige. In *Heidersskrift til Nils Hallan på 65-årsdagen 13. desember 1991,* ed. G. Alhaug, K. Kruken, and H. Salvesen. Oslo: Novus.

Buck, C. D. 1949. *A Dictionary of Selected Synonyms in the Principal Indo-European Languages. A Contribution to the History of Ideas.* 3rd impression 1971. Chicago & London: The University of Chicago Press.

Collin, H. S., and C. J. Schlyter, 1830. Östgöta-Lagen. In *Corpus Iuris Sueo-Gotorum Antiqui.* Vol. 2. Stockholm: P. A. Norstedt & Söner.

Cox, B. 1973. The Significance of the Distribution of English Place-Names in *-ham* in the Midlands and East Anglia. *English Place-Name Society Journal* 5.

Dodgson, J. M. 1973. Place-Names from *ham,* Distinguished from *hamm* Names, in Relation to the Settlement of Kent, Surrey and Sussex. *Anglo-Saxon England* 2.

Feist, S. 1939. *Vergleichendes Wörterbuch der Gotischen Sprache.* 3rd ed. Leiden: E. J. Brill.

Fraenkel, E. 1962. *Litauisches Etymologisches Wörterbuch.* Indogermanische Bibliothek 2. reihe. Wörterbücher. Heidelberg: Carl Winter Universitätsverlag.

Gelling, M. 1978. *Signposts to the Past. Place-Names and the History of England.* London, Melbourne & Toronto: J. M. Dent & Sons Ltd.

Grein, C. W. M. 1974. *Sprachschatz der Angelsächsischen Dichter.* 2nd ed. Heidelberg: Carl Winter Universitätsverlag.

Hellquist, E. 1948. *Svensk Etymologisk Ordbok.* 3rd ed. Lund: C. W. K. Gleerups förlag.

2

A Critical Look at the Concept "Home"[1]

Amos Rapoport

Introduction

From the perspective of Environment-Behavior Studies (EBS) as a scientific discipline concerned with understanding and explaining Environment-Behavior Relations (EBR), it is important that terms and concepts be precise. It is essential that definitions and concepts be clear and as unambiguous as possible: They must be clear enough to be made operational (usable) and hence capable of being related explicitly to other variables. Conceptual clarity is essential in any field.

A term or concept is useful only if it is clear, well-defined, and only changes slowly and systematically as a function of the empirical and theoretical development of a field. Without standardization and agreement such terms cannot help discriminate among entities.

When theoretical terms and concepts do not possess such attributes progress in a field is impossible, since there must be consensibility before there can be consensuality (Ziman 1978).

From that point of view, certain current developments are worrying. One is the increasing use of terms which are used too loosely for broader and broader sets of things, for example *vernacular*. I pointed out recently that if that term can be used for so many types of environments, it is not useful. It is only useful if it can distinguish or discriminate A from not A, i.e., from B, C, D... N, if it helps decide if something is A and also says what is not A (Rapoport 1990a). Another such development is the use of vague, subjective, and emotive terms in ways that can mean whatever users want them to mean at any given moment. One major example is *place* which I have recently examined critically (Rapoport 1985a, 1994).

There I argue that although *place* and related terms such as *placelessness*, *placemaking*, and *attachment to place* are ever more prevalent and widely used, not only are they not needed and not useful, but are actually harmful. This is because they are vague, they mean whatever a given author wants them to mean, and are normative on subjective grounds. *Placeless*, like *chaotic* cultural landscapes, merely refers to settings that a given observer does not like, does not understand, or does not find appropriate. Since cultural landscapes are related to the culture, they cannot be chaotic: There is no disorder, merely different orders. Similarly, there is no *placelessness*, only different kinds of places (Rapoport 1984, 1992). It also seems clear that one person's place is another's non-place. This also applies to *home* which has also seen ever increasing use and seems to have very similar and comparable characteristics, seemingly violating all of the desiderata described above. One can therefore ask a series of questions about its attributes or characteristics to see whether it meets the general attributes that any scientific or theoretical term needs to possess before it becomes useful in research or practice. This may be a model for the more general issues of how EBS concepts can be made explicit, more carefully defined, articulated and dismantled, related to other concepts, and also how this process may lead to conceptual frameworks and theory building.

I will therefore subject the term *home* and its utility to skeptical and critical examination, analyzing its usage, examining its conceptual and theoretical underpinnings (if any), and thereby clarify my objections to it by drawing attention to problems connected with its use. In this way, one might discover whether the term might be improved and it (or a new version) made more useful, or whether it should be given up, and also whether there already exist alternative concepts which might do the job better and avoid the problems its use presents. In doing this, I will also try to identify what (if anything) introducing the term was intended to accomplish, i.e., why there is interest and increasing preoccupation with it. This question then is what, if anything, is missing from other concepts that *home* introduces and what are the potential advantages, if any?

To begin to answer these questions, I will do an informal and non-systematic content analysis of some examples of both popular (folk) and research uses of the term.[2]

Use of the term *home*

Popular.

The term certainly exists in popular usage or the folk vocabulary, where it is often used in lieu of *house*. For example, in Australia people typically buy and sell homes rather than houses, they are *homeowners* rather than owning houses, and will commonly pay a compliment by saying "oh, what a lovely home." This is also the case in the U.S., so that in advertisements, for example, one finds references to "refinancing your home" or installing an air conditioning system "designed for your home" (e.g., *Milwaukee Journal,* 1992). In a business report *(New York Times,* 1992) the headline refers to the resale of homes, and references are made to sales of existing homes, single-family homes, home prices, the median price of homes, and home ownership. Clearly in all cases reference is to *houses* (or *units* which are used once), which can be substituted without any loss. This usage alone would seem to be a major problem with the use of the term *home* because it confounds the actual artifact with certain other aspects of people's reactions to them which, I suspect, the use of *home* is intended to emphasize.

In ordinary usage there is also a series of sayings, proverbs, and quips which might provide a clue as to what these reactions are. It might also suggest what the folk theory behind them might be – a topic which I will not explore in any detail.

One common usage is, I feel at home (with people, places, ideas, situations, a language, etc.). This meaning of being at ease is also well illustrated by a *Heathcliff* cartoon by Gately (1991). This shows a mouse sitting in front of a mousehole with a huge portrait of the cat Heathcliff over it, saying to a fellow mouse, "It just doesn't seem like home anymore." The proverb, home is where the heart is, emphasizes the *affective core* of the concept as effectively as the others do the elements of *security, control,* and being at ease and *relaxed.*

Significant are also sayings such as you can't go home again (implying it is a *mental state),* and, home is where when you go there, they have to let you in, implying *ownership, kinship* and, again, *control.* In the tradition of analyzing advertising and other popular media (Rapoport 1977, 1985b,c, 1990b,c) consider a series of advertisements for Smirnoff Vodka. These show some very "unlikely" settings (including bars, ski slopes, etc.) with the slogan "Home is where you find it." Home is identified as a place where we *feel comfortable,* defined by *family* and *friendships,* where one finds *laughter* and *contentment.* This is about as good a definition as any in the literature and, combined with the attributes identified earlier, seems closely

27

to resemble the research usage (as we shall see). In fact, we can ask if the latter goes any further and, if not, whether it can be a useful concept in research. At the same time this usage in advertising shows how vague the term is and how applicable to an extraordinary variety of settings, so that it does not seem to distinguish or discriminate among them effectively.

Another important aspect is well illustrated by a Norwegian cartoon by Arvid Andreassen (1974). It shows two people having a picnic in the country with all the contents of a house – but no walls. Although the caption is "Isn't it just wonderful to be out in the country so close to nature," it also (and mainly) shows the importance of semi-fixed elements and owned objects in creating home. This tends to be neglected in the professional literature, although as an aspect of *personalization* and *taking possession* it is implicit. I have discussed the importance of personalization in popular usage (Rapoport 1977, 1985b, 1990c). One example, of the importance of pets, draws attention, once again, to the issue of control, whereas another example, the Milwaukee See-for-Yourself Auto Tour (slogan: "Discover Milwaukee, a great home town") draws attention to the fact that *home* can refer to *large entities* like cities, and also emphasizes the role of various physical attributes (water, trees, parks, etc.) in creating a *positive evaluation* of environments which, in some way, seems related to home. One can thus infer or suggest that, like *place, home* is used to communicate certain positive attributes, i.e., something one likes. A home is then a *positive evaluation* of something, such as a house, dwelling, or neighborhood (Fried 1963), or a whole city or country (Fried 1986), suggesting that these have certain attributes, some of which people see as *homelike,* and it then becomes possible to study these attributes (e.g., Robinson et al. 1984; Deitz 1984; Rapoport 1985c). One can also study the schema of *homelike* that is used to match or evaluate these attributes. One can also ask who does the evaluation (which groups, cultures, etc.), and whether there is any agreement, cross-culturally or over time? In this connection, the problem of "slums" is of interest, i.e., the variability in the evaluation of environmental quality, attributes, and standards which must play a role in the positive (or negative) evaluation of any environment (e.g. Fried 1963; Fried and Gleicher 1961; Rapoport 1977, 1990c; Spalding 1992). Two further points can be made. One is that in any given locale only some people have deeper bonds with it than satisfaction with the tangible environment so that, if it is lost, one "grieves for a lost home" (Fried 1963; but see later discussion of Feldman 1990; Hummon 1990, for a different view). The other is that this is often linked to identity, but for some groups this may be non-environmental (Rapoport 1981) and for others this may be neither the dwelling nor the neighborhood, but a different element altogether (The *Kgotla* among the Tswana or the *Marae* among the Maori, see later discussion of problems with the cross-cultural use of *home)*.

Popular usage of terms is typically *implicitly* linked to what have been called folk theories, which not only need to be made explicit, but are usually highly unsatisfactory. There are two views about those: One, that they must be *replaced* since they never work, and two (a weaker version), that after being made explicit they can be clarified, articulated, improved, made more rigorous, terms defined, and mechanisms specified. Although I will not deal with this issue, I would suggest and will try to show that the current use of *home* in research does not go beyond the popular usage, and hence beyond whatever folk theory exists; it has not even been realized that the term is not only vague and fuzzy (and "warm" in feeling) but that there is an implicit folk theory behind it that needs to be made explicit and examined.

The question is whether there is any hope of improving the folk theory and hence the *term,* and I will briefly consider the latter at the end. At this point one needs to ask what the usage of this term, both popular and professional, is intended to communicate. I.e., what is it people are trying to express when they use *home* as opposed to *house*. Its popular usage seems to involve its being used *in lieu* of *house* or *dwelling,* possibly because it is "warmer." This creates one of the major problems with its usage, since it is also used to describe certain mental states. There is thus confusion between its use to refer to a *product* (the thing) and a *process* (a mental state or positive evaluation). These need to be distinguished clearly, and the current confusion is another major general problem. The *mental states* seem to involve an *affective core,* feelings of *security, control, being at ease and relaxed,* are related to *ownership* and to *family, kinship, comfort, friendship, laughter,* and other *positive attributes;* it involves *personalization, owned objects,* and *taking possession.* It can apply to larger entities and involves *positive evaluations* of attributes of environments matching certain *schemata* or *ideals.* Note that evaluation is a general process: All environments are evaluated (Rapoport 1977, 1985b, 1990c, d). I will elaborate on this in the conclusion.

One other way of thinking about what the use of *home* (as opposed to *house)* is meant to communicate (and one to which I will return) is that possibly home = house + x. If that is the case, one can ask what that "x" might be that makes a home more than a house. The above list gives some suggestions and, again, popular usage has an answer. In the *Milwaukee Journal* in a feature *Zingers* by Doug Larson (1992) one finds: "It takes a *lot of loving* to make a house a home, not to mention a *substantial down payment* and *30 years* of monthly ones" (my italics). Here, x = affect, resources, owner-ship, and time.

However, now we should analyze the use of *home* in some examples of the research literature to see whether it has gone beyond the popular usage and whether it has articulated its attributes.

Research

I begin, as in the case of popular usage, with cases where *home* is used in lieu of *house* or *dwelling,* or interchangeably with it, or where it makes no difference if one substitutes one for the other (as is the case almost throughout). This is rather more common than one might expect. For example, the McGill University School of Architecture Affordable Homes Program clearly refers to affordable *houses* and the Project Paper No. 3 of 1990 on the Grow Home clearly refers to a house. Similarly Colson (1980) uses *home* strictly instead of *house:* Nothing is added. Or consider the title of this symposium: *The Ancient Home and the Modern Internationalized Home: Dwelling in Scandinavia.* Nothing is lost by rephrasing it: *The Ancient House and the Modern Internationalized House: Dwelling in Scandinavia,* or by using *dwelling* as both noun and verb, *The Ancient Dwelling and the Modern Internationalized Dwelling: Dwelling in Scandinavia.*

Sebba and Churchman (1986), in discussing the "Uniqueness of the home" are in fact, dealing with the uniqueness of the house or dwelling as a type of setting. On page 8, the response categories of social and psychological needs filled by the home (dwelling) include:

1. The home is the sole area of *control* for the individual.

2. The home is the most appropriate *physical framework for the family.*

3. The home is the place of *self-expression.*

4. The home provides a *feeling of security.*

I would suggest that nothing seems to be lost by substituting *dwelling,* and *dwelling unit* (as a socio-spatial system) is, in fact, used once (Sebba and Churchman 1986, 11). What the above says is that the dwelling unit is a setting for the family in which maximum control may be exerted allowing self-expression and leading to feelings of security. The result is that it acquires unique psychological and social meanings which, if you will, turn it into a home, i.e., which establish particular relationships between people and that setting. That this is the intended meaning is clear from their page 21, where the "uniqueness of the home" is identified as its psychological and social meaning, and the opportunity it affords occupants to exert control over space and behavior in it. Clearly there is no loss in substituting *dwelling:* In fact, by distinguishing clearly between the object and the meanings it has for people, confusion and circularity are avoided and conceptual clarity improved.

Similarly when Ahrentzen (1989) speaks of the "home as office" or "working at home," she clearly refers to *house* or *dwelling*. Nothing is lost by the substitution and some respondents insisted on using *house* in lieu of *home* (Ahrnetzen 1989, 281). The effects of working in it, on feelings about the house, were in terms of *refuge* and *privacy*, weakening the positive qualities of being a *sanctum,* or increasing the negative feelings of *isolation* or *entrapment*. One result of working in the house is that the neighborhood gains in importance (ibid., 277) so that the system of settings which is the dwelling (Rapoport 1980, 1985b, 1990e) is at issue rather than merely the house. In effect, the study is of the dwelling, with certain relationships between it and people changing. Separating these "feelings of home" and the thing itself is, in fact, helpful.

Sadalla et al. (1987) refer to subjects being able to infer homeowners' self-concepts to a significant degree from the style of their houses; clearly house-owners are meant. Horelli (1990) refers to *dwelling* and occasionally *home* (with the usual confusion) and discusses the "elements of home" but also refers to "parts of the house," such as the kitchen, dining room, living room, garden, sauna, etc.. She points out that these may evoke *associations* (e.g., about *social relationships, memories of childhood rhythms,* etc.); a whole spectrum of affective states (all of which we have already seen and will see below) are taken as aspects of home, but clearly evoked by parts of houses. Many of these affective states, such as family cohesion and the importance of the childhood dwelling, are parts of home in Hayward's (1976) taxonomy (see below), but they relate to physical aspects of the house, for example, plan type. Clearly, all these affective responses are the result of residents' interactions with certain important physical elements of the house: there are strong psycho-social and socio-cultural relationships between residents and material aspects of the dwelling. The use of *home* tends to confound these responses and relationships with the physical elements themselves. Another finding is the importance of semi-fixed features (furnishings, decorations, etc.) which, as I predicted (Rapoport 1990c), are more important for those people who were not involved in the original planning and construction of the dwellings.

A number of major studies on the feelings and evaluations, positive and negative, of dwellings in which other studies would use home use *housing, house, dwelling,* or *site* with no reference to *home* – and with no loss (c.f. Hunt Thompson Assoc. 1988; Coleman 1985; Cooper-Marcus and Sarkassian 1986). In the latter, a reference to the inability to find one's way home clearly means house. In the case of some recent studies of a number of other cultures, *home* is not used, yet all the relevant relationships of people with their cultural landscapes and dwellings as systems of settings, such as affect and attachment, privacy, control, meaning, and preference are studied; *home* is clearly not needed (e.g., Ross 1987; Heppell 1979; Memmott 1991; Kamau, 1978/79; Kent 1990).

The confusion in usage, and the circularity which is found repeatedly in this survey, can be seen in Stanton (1986). A distinction is proposed (Stanton 1986, 299) between *home ground* and *neighborhood* – although *micro-neighborhood* or *core area* have been used for some time. This is described (p. 300) as those places that evoke a feeling of being near home, the use of two vague terms which are far from clear. A more formal definition (ibid., 305) of a home ground as a mental form and geographical extent of those places that evoke a feeling of being near home, is not much more helpful. Moreover, the last word *home* can easily be replaced by *house* or *dwelling* with no apparent loss.

There exist in the literature a series of attempts to identify more formally the attributes or dimensions of home. While these are to be applauded, given the need to dismantle concepts and to use polythetic sets (e.g., Rapoport 1990a), these often suffer from the fact that *house* and *home* often mean the same thing, confusing the object and the feelings evoked. The attributes also often do not hang together, being sets of unlike elements, resulting in conceptual confusion. Tognoli (1987, 655) for example, points out that *residential environment* is a neutral term which includes both *home* and *housing, neighborhood* and *community* (which I would identify with a system of settings). He then concentrates on the difference between home and housing as a major theme in the literature, emphasizing that the literature on home is concerned with private and personal space, although clearly both private and personal space in the house or dwelling can easily be studied; *home* is not needed. He also argues (ibid., 656) that *housing* is in the public rather than private sphere, being the knowable physical and spatial aspects rather than the behavior of only one individual in one house, which he seems to identify with *home*. If that is the case, it is not useful in research (or design), particularly since Tognoli adds that this is highly idiosyncratic and ephemeral.

Tognoli then argues that although home is both a *physical place* and a *cognitive concept* (although others emphasize the *affective*), generally the literature on home underemphasizes the former in favor of social, cognitive, cultural, and behavioral aspects. I would add that a concept that is both the physical object and the ways people use it, feel about it, relate it, and so on is potentially confusing, and its use potentially dangerous. Furthermore, these non-physical aspects which supposedly characterize home, e.g.

feelings of *security* and *comfort*, being a symbol of *continuity* and *return* (implying going forth), can equally well be aspects of dwellings. In Tognoli (ibid., 657), six categories of aspects of home are given more formally which seem to present many problems, only a few of which I can discuss.

1) *Centrality, Rootedness, and Place Attachment.* Comment: *Centrality* can be related to "primary setting" (Stokols' term), or seen as the anchor/base in the system of settings or house-settlement system. *Rootedness* may be problematic given mobility (c.f., Hummon 1990; Feldman 1990; J.B. Jackson's discussion of the United States experience generally, nomadic cultures, etc.). This also applies to *place attachment* (apart from the fact that this has its own set of problems, Rapoport 1994).

2) *Continuity, Unity, and Order.* Comment: *Continuity* is, once again, problematic in terms of mobility (see above); *unity* is quite unclear. *Order* raises the issue that all built environments and cultural landscapes have order. There are many different orders so that order cannot be an attribute of home (Rapoport 1984, 1992). Moreover, the order of houses, dwellings, settlements, and so on can be studied.

3) *Privacy, Refuge, Security, and Ownership.* Comment: Not only are these all very different concepts (e.g., regarding security c.f., Rainwater 1966) but they apply to houses, dwellings, and other settings. Also, in Switzerland, ownership of dwellings is particularly low, yet does not seem to affect people's relationships to their dwellings; it thus seems a highly ethnocentric attribute suspect for cross-cultural research.

4) *Self Identity and Gender Differences.* Comment: These seem to be totally different concepts and do not seem to belong in one category. There can be self-identity which is *not* related to environments (c.f., Rapoport 1981) and when it is, houses, neighborhoods, furnishings, landscaping, and the like, and their attributes, can (and do) provide them. Gender differences can be studied in houses, urban spaces, and many other settings; how they help define *home* is quite unclear.

5) *Social and Family Relationships.* Comment: These occur in houses, open spaces, and many other culture-specific settings (Rapoport 1977, 1990c,e); since they can be studied in houses, urban neighborhoods, regions, etc., they cannot characterize home.

6) *Socio-cultural Context.* Comment: All environments and settings occur in a socio-cultural context and this applies to houses and dwellings, neighborhoods, settlements, regions, cultural landscapes, etc.

This list of attributes, even given this rather minimal critique, hardly seems to define or characterize home, nor give one much faith in the utility of the concept. This is also the conclusion I reach from my analysis of many other statements Tognoli makes about home – all of them can be applied to houses, dwellings, or other settings and systems of settings: The notion of ideals and schemata, or of evaluation, preference, and satisfaction (see later). Moreover, there is the usual circularity of reference of attachment to home, whereas it is attachment to a dwelling, neighborhood, or cultural landscape that engenders those feelings that some call *home*.

I myself (Rapoport 1985b) have tried to give an attribute of home by saying that "if it isn't chosen, it isn't home." But in fact it is a house or dwelling, in a particular location, that is chosen, but this does add *choice* as a potential attribute of whatever home might be.

One of the earliest explicit lists of attributes of home is that of Hayward (1976). He identifies nine dimensions of home in order of importance:

1. as a set of relationships with others

2. as a relationship with the wider social group and community

3. as a statement about one's self-image and self-identity

4. as a place of privacy and refuge (c.f., Roberts 1977)

5. as a continuous and stable relationship with other sources of meaning about the home

6. as a personalized place

7. as a base of activity

8. as a relationship with one's parents and place of upbringing

9. as a relationship with a physical structure, setting, or shelter

Again, eschewing a detailed analysis, several things are clear. First, that at issue is a set of relationships with fixed, semi-fixed, and non-fixed features of the environment. Second, that there is some confusion and difficulty in using some of these categories (e.g., 5). Third, that in all cases *dwelling, system of settings, primary setting, social networks,* and a number of other EBS concepts already in use, would work equally well, if not better and that *home* is not needed. Fourth, that cross-cultural (and historical), considerations make this particular, highly influential formulation too ethnocentric (particularly since the study is based on a small sample of young residents of Manhattan, possibly atypical even of the U.S. in the 1970's).

Hayward's list appears in other studies and is partly incorporated and partly modified in a recent Ph.D. dissertation (Després 1991). The categories of meaning of *home* are derived from six previous studies as well as her research. There are ten categories of home as:

1. security and control

2. a reflection of one's ideas and values

3. acting upon and modifying one's dwelling

4. permanence and continuity

5. relationship with family and friends (center of love and togetherness)

6. a center of activities

7. a refuge from the outside world

8. an indicator of personal status

9. as a material structure (in a particular location)

10. a place to own.

Després (1991, 45) tries to account for these in terms of both micro and macro variables and proposes a model in which individual thoughts, actions, and socio-demographic characteristics, housing as a built environment and ideologies, cultural norms and housing policies, interact to generate a particular meaning for that setting. *It is that meaning which is home,* in other words it is an EBR. Thus while she speaks of the "meaning of home" she looks at dwellings (as she must). There is the usual lack of a clear distinction between the human relationships with dwellings or primary settings in terms of meaning, behavior, affect, experience, etc., and that setting or dwelling, the process, and the product. The overlap with Haywood's (1975) list, other studies, and my analysis of popular usage suggests that some consensus exists about the attributes of the relationships between people and dwellings or other culturally primary settings. This will be supported by the remaining examples.

It is necessary, however, to reiterate reservations about some of the categories of meaning of *home*. I have already referred, in commenting on Tognoli (1987), to the work of Hummon (1990), and Feldman (1990). These two are related to each other through their finding that many people in the U.S. identify with *types* of environments rather than specific places, and that it is the former that are linked to identity. Thus mobility is common, rootedness and the like are absent, and continuity is of a new kind which seems at odds with the intuitive sense of home that the literature communicates. Hummon (1990) argues that identity results from a symbolic placement of the self providing symbolic structure for affiliation and disaffiliation such as a city person, suburban person, or small town person. On page 141, Hummon points out that "place identity is communicated by the home, along with its interior objects and exterior decoration, which often serves as a significant locus of self and sign of biographical social and temporal identities." *House* or *dwelling* is clearly meant; moreover he points out that neighborhoods also play that role. I would add that this neglects religious, ethnic, occupational, ideological, etc., identity, and the fact that the environment may play no role in identity in some cases, whereas in others, urban locations, or culture-specific settings such as the *Kgotla* (among the Tswana), the *Marae* (among the Maori), or *country* (the land among Australian Aborigines), may play that role (Rapoport 1981, 1990c).

Feldman (1990) discusses how people maintain continuity although highly mobile by establishing psychological links to *types* of settlements. Unlike Hummon, she only discusses two (city and suburb), omitting small towns. Settlement identity is achieved by maintaining psychological bonds with places while mobile by substituting residence in similar types of settlements for residence in one specific home place (ibid., 186). This is an extremely broad use of *home* with problems like those I discussed earlier concerning *vernacular* (Rapoport 1990a). There is some confusion, and contradiction, when she (Feldman 1990) discusses the common threads in *the development of psychological bonds with home places,* which are said to occur through long-term focused involvement in a residential setting. It seems that the major new insight suffers as a result of trying to force a relationship onto the concept of *home place* which is unnecessary.[3]

Fried (1986, 333) defines home as the "core of place experience," confirming the link between these two concepts. "It is the realm in which we live, *from* which we move out into the wider world and to which we return." This can be captured by the house as anchor of what I would call the house-settlement system. He points out that the conditions that generate a "sense of home" and its diverse meanings vary with social structure, culture, and psychological characteristics and, further, that for work-oriented people, *the workplace may become home* and that the conception of home may expand to a whole country. These two latter points are typical of excessively broad and vague terms. It would seem preferable to say that certain feelings may attach to a variety of settings at various scales.

In a sociological analysis of *home* as it applies to the city, Lenz-Romeiss (1973) defines it as the "feeling of belonging to a place and the ability to identify with it" and interprets it in terms of a symbolic attachment to "place" (once again demonstrating the link between these two terms). This is clearly a relationship that is more a property of people than of settings, although among the attributes identified, in addition to belonging, contentment, haven, freedom, public spirit, feelings of being protected, fitting in, emotional security, and familiarity, are added "an area (or defined space)" and "place of abode" – the usual confusion between the setting and the feelings and relations it elicits.

In analyzing Altman and Werner (1985), one finds things already encountered. First, typically there is no loss in using terms like *house, dwelling,* and the like in lieu of *home,* and in fact, these are often used. Second, one finds the typically varied, contradictory, and ambiguous usage and circular reasoning. Consider a few examples. On p. xvi the point is made that "homes in different cultures have different forms and functions and...a thorough understanding of homes requires a cross-cultural perspective." Clearly houses or dwellings are meant, particularly since, on the same page, *home* is defined as the psychological response to dwelling or the feeling of being at home. It is difficult to see how psychological responses or feelings can have forms and functions in the sense intended. There is the usual confusion between the object and the relationships with it. Home is also defined as a residence invested with psychological meaning; in the case of Australian Aborigines it is *not* the residence but the landscape and kin group that are invested with such meaning.

On p. 1 it is suggested that homes can be studied in terms of their physical qualities, use patterns, and satisfaction and experience with them. Again, it is obviously houses or dwellings that are meant, and human responses to them – which need to be distinguished one from the other. The whole chapter by Werner, Altman, and Oxley can be transcribed using *house* or *dwelling*.[4] On p. 22, they discuss the utilitarian aspects of home when house or dwelling is clearly meant, and are more appropriate in dealing with what I would call the instrumental aspects, because both the popular and professional usage largely emphasizes what I would call latent aspects. In several other chapters there is the usual confusion and circularity, confounding the house or dwelling, as part of the environment with home as a kind of relationship between it and people – a subjective, affective, meaningful relationship with or experience of the dwelling: *Home,* if it is anything, is the meaning one attaches to the dwelling, which makes usages such as "meaning of home" very confusing. Although Dovey does make the distinction between a house as part of the environment and home as a kind of relationship between people and the environment, one which is emotionally based and meaningful, I think that *home* is an unfortunate term for those relationships, given the confusion of usage. It *would be preferable to specify the range of relationships* which, as we have seen, the literature (both popular and professional), begins to provide. The importance of keeping the basic distinction unmistakable becomes even clearer when the discussion concerns, on the one hand, visible behaviors such as personalization and marking, and on the other hand, human conceptions of ideal social orders (which enter into the evaluation of dwellings and other settings). Weidemann and Anderson in their chapter refer (see Altman and Werner 1985, 154) to the "evaluation of home" when they mean "of dwelling;" a positive evaluation is then part of the particular relationship with it which the term *home* is meant to describe. Satisfaction is with dwellings, and it is part of a particular relationship between those and people, particularly if dwellings are defined as systems of settings (which is what Taylor and Brower discuss). In other chapters, e.g., by Saile and Duncan, the authors move back and forth among the different uses of these terms. The major problem here, as elsewhere, is that it is dwellings as settings or environments that are being discussed and analyzed, whereas it is the experience of those, and relationships with them, whether symbolic, economic, affective, or whatever which the authors try to identify. The term *home* confuses the issue and makes both tasks more difficult.

Consider three special issues of journals dealing with the topic: The first is a special issue on *Home and Housing* of the journal *People and Physical Environment Research Paper,* (Australia) no. 36, April 1991. The material on housing makes it clear that one can deal with all the most important issues by using that concept. With regard to home, there is a report on a Polish conference which refers to *home* as a term rather than a concept. The suggestion is made that three main aspects or factors are involved:

1. the material aspect – house or apartment, the fitment and furnishings (what I call semi-fixed feature elements) and its immediate environment (the relevant system of settings)

2. the inhabitants

3. the symbolic meaning of home [*sic*] (what I would call the latent aspects of the dwellings) and its value in satisfying human life

Other than confusing the issue in (3) above, the term *home* is not needed: The topic as formulated can be studied as I have always done and propose below, and in terms of the three basic EBS questions.[5] Concerning institutions, we find the attributes of home as: comfort, involvement, intimacy, caring atmosphere, bonds among inhabitants, and domestic service. This neglects the physical attributes of the building which may communicate domesticity or institutionality (c.f., Robinson et al. 1984). Other attributes of home include the already familiar security and control (both of which are culturally variable) and meaning at different hierarchical levels: Cultural, intermediate, and personal (see below cultural, group, and individual filters in the evaluation model; c.f., my notion of levels of meaning Rapoport 1988, 1990c). Thorne makes it clear that the "meaning of home," (*sic*) in Australia, is intimately related to ownership (in spite of the counter example of Switzerland), and to the type of unit: Apartments are not considered home even by people who live in them. There is clearly a cultural model present. Also important are the various visual attributes of the house. Home, then, is a particular kind and style of house which one can own, and which gives security, pride of ownership, and freedom of behavior to modify. It is clear, once again, that all these issues can be discussed in terms of house and dwelling, and of how people evaluate, prefer, relate to, and interpret those, i.e., how people relate to their dwellings.

The second is a special issue of *Environment and Behavior*, vol. 19, no. 2, March 1987, on *Home Interiors: A European Perspective*. Again, one finds that everything that needs to be said could be said by referring to *house interiors* or *interiors of dwellings*. Lawrence, who uses Hayward's (1976) attributes, argues that a house with psychological resonance and social meaning becomes a home, which is a complex entity defined by cultural, sociodemographic, psychological, political, and economic factors. However, I use a similar range of factors in *House Form and Culture* (1969) referring to the house. Again, *home* just draws attention to certain relationships between people and dwellings. The discussion (by Giuliani) of naming rooms can be done equally well by using *house* (and in terms of domain definition, this is exactly what I and others have done). In fact, the objectives of all the remaining papers (by Werner, Bonnes, and Amaturo, et al.) can be achieved by using *house*, settings, semi-fixed objects (furnishings, decoration, etc.), as communicating status and identity in culturally specific ways (c.f., Rapoport 1990c).

Third is a special issue of the *Journal of Architectural and Planning Research*, vol. 8, no. 2, Summer 1991, dealing with *The Meaning and Use of Home*. Apart from the fact that one uses houses, not homes, one finds that *home* is defined, once again, largely in terms of Hayward's (1976) criteria. The point is made that it is a variable concept varying with culture, social groups, and individuals (and, I would add, over time). I would interpret this to mean that the evaluations, meanings, and other relationships between people and dwellings vary. The meaning of home (*sic*), (the meaning attached to dwelling which some call *home)* involves: (1) materials structure, (2) refuge, (3) security and control, (4) reflection of personal ideas and values (although, I would add, this is achieved through the material attributes of the dwelling and its furnishings (Rapoport 1990c; Suchar and

Rotenberg 1988); this also neglects *group* values, (5) locus of activities, (6) locus of social relations with kin, (7) something one can act upon and modify, (8) a locus for appropriation, (9) private property and, (10) an indicator of personal status (and, I would add, *group* status and identity). The list is already familiar.

Giuliani argues that *home* involves the development of affective bonds and attachment. The latter is multi-dimensional and involves a range of psychological and sociological dimensions, and includes cultural context, social history, and an individual's residential history. Home defines and is mutually defined by overt human behavior, including residential mobility and stability, health consequences of relocation, social interaction, residential satisfaction, and affective and cognitive processes. Home attachment involves mental representations and has three main constituents: Objects, people, and object/people relations. This again points out the problem with *home* which tends to be used to refer both to the object and the object/people relationship. Also, as already mentioned and as I will discuss later, it is a concept difficult to study cross-culturally and historically, particularly since Guiliani (like several others) emphasizes the individual and personal nature of home, whereas I argue that only groups and the patterns they exhibit can be the subject of research and most design (other than the individual detached house for a single person).

Finally, as part of a study of place attachment, there is a recent unpublished but widely circulated list of meanings of home (by Rivlin, Valmont, and Foster of the Environment Psychology Program at CUNY). This lists over 50 meanings in nine major categories: Individual meanings, social, physical, political, economic, developmental, safety, emotional, and symbolic/metaphorical. These are also based on a content analysis of previous work, with little overlap with the work to which I refer. This, in effect, greatly extends the range of work analyzed. There are some overlaps with the attributes that I have already discussed, i.e., some closure, but there are also a number of new attributes. In fact, it is a list with a very large variety of meanings, usages which I find very confusing. Many of them can attach to *dwelling* or *house,* others involve circular reasoning, others yet are Environment-Behavior Relationships.

Thus, having reviewed some of the research literature, there appear to be a number of patterns in it, some of which are also found in popular usage. These will be considered in the next section.

Critical discussion

Although the research literature expands somewhat the attributes present in popular usage, adding to them, it does not really go much beyond that (nor analyze the folk theory underlying that usage). In fact, in some ways popular usage seems to be highly effective in drawing attention to some of the most important attributes of people's relationships to certain settings that the research literature emphasizes. It also seems clearly to make the point that there is something missing when houses are being discussed, that home is house (or dwelling) + x, and I will shortly discuss the question of what that "x" might be.

At the same time however, the research literature does articulate and dismantle the notion of home to some extent, with many attributes discussed. About some of these there seems to be widespread agreement – they constitute a core, as it were; others are more idiosyncratic and form a scattered field about the core. The use of these attributes is not generally systematic and the results seem to be confused and confusing. The term, like *place,* remains extremely vague and ambiguous, unclear and inconsistently used. As a result, it can mean whatever one wishes it to mean, although there is less of this than I expected: There seems to be some implicit, albeit unclear consensus of what is intended. A problem with that consensus, however, is that (like *place)* it is often normative on emotive, subjective grounds: What one likes is *place* or *home,* what one does not, is not. As a result of all this however, the term is not very useful. It does not seem to be able to identify a clear, consensual concept or theoretical construct, even one defined polythetically (as it would have to be, Rapoport 1990a). Moreover, as we have seen, many of the sets of attributes are disparate and diverse, belong to different analytic categories, are inconsistent, and do not "hang together."

There is more consistency relative to the major problems found in the literature. First is the fact that both in popular and research usage, the term *home* is often used as a synonym for *house*. This usage introduces a major element of confusion which cannot be eliminated and fatally "contaminates" the use of the term to draw attention to other aspects of the dwelling – people's affective, psychological, social, cultural, and behavioral relationships with the relevant systems of settings. This then, is closely related to the second major problem. Both in popular and professional usage the term *home* often refers both to an object, artefact, or physical thing in the environment as well as people's reactions to it, their links and relationships with it. This confusion between the objects and the relations that various people have with them at various times makes the term highly questionable and creates an impossible situation. One cannot confound an affective reaction with the object. Doing so leads to confusion between *product* and *process,* with *home* referring to both. Yet, as we shall see below, the concept of home seems to have been introduced in order to draw attention to these processes, and current usage thus interferes with this goal.

A third major problem is that there is a frequent and prevalent circularity, with *home* being defined as "the meaning of home." This is worse than confusing, it seems meaningless. The intended meaning seems to be that a component of the concept of home is a particular meaning attached to dwelling (or house). Such circularity is also found in another form where the meaning of home is said to be attachment to home. Clearly, what is intended is that the meaning of home is attachment to something (an object or artefact in the environment) which cannot itself be home.

A fourth problem is the neglect of the physical aspects. Physical features seem to play a minor role in the research literature on home (smaller than in the popular), although a few exceptions are found in my analysis. Spatial and physical (including semi-fixed) attributes are de-emphasized in favor of social, psychological, cognitive, affective, and behavioral issues (even cultural issues are *relatively* neglected). Yet it seems that these spatial and physical elements and their attributes are a critical component in people's relationships to settings (e.g., Robinson et al. 1984; Thorne in *Paper* no. 36, etc.). As Wohlwill reminded us, "The environment is not [all] in the head." Often, the physical elements and their physical attributes are all that one finds for historical and cross-cultural studies; they are also what is designed, built, and manipulated. Moreover, in EBS generally much more is known about people than about environments. Thus the emphasis on *home,* rather than helping rectify that problem, exacerbates it.

Of course, as already suggested, the concept *home* seems to have originated precisely to draw attention to certain psychological, temporal, economic, affective, behavioral, and other links of people to certain settings. In other words, *it was intended to refer to particular EBRs.* As already pointed out, current usage obscures and interferes with this goal, which was certainly worthwhile and hence useful – although nothing new. If I am correct in my assertion that all the commotion about home is to show that it is more than house, then it hardly seems worth the excitement. After all, in *House Form and Culture* (Rapoport 1969, 46) I made the point that a "house is an institution not just a structure, created for a complex set of purposes. [It is] more than shelter...and from the beginning 'function' was much more than a physical or utilitarian concept...its positive purpose is the creation of an environment best suited to the way of life of a people – in other words a social unit of space." Yet I was using *house,* not even dwelling (as redefined in Rapoport 1980, 1990e; see below), and in more recent work I was able to deal with the ideal schemata which underlie this creation, with the role of modification, personalization, and semi-fixed elements, with communication of status and identity, with evaluation, satisfaction, preference and choice, with social and family relationships and networks, activity systems and so on. It seems to be the case that everything necessary can be achieved without introducing the term *home,* which only confuses things (and I will present an alternative below). The use of the term can be interpreted as merely restating my long-standing argument about the associational aspects of the environment being more important than the perceptual, about the latent aspects being more important than the manifest or instrumental, so that meaning is the most important function, and about affective links being primary.

I have already suggested briefly that the use of *home* may present particular problems with regard to cross-cultural and historical research and analysis. I have shown that even *house* is inadequate for such analysis and one needs to use a more neutral concept such as *dwelling,* redefined in a more neutral fashion as a system of settings within which a system of activities takes place (including their latent aspects, Rapoport 1980, 1990e). *Home* is even less neutral than *house* cross-culturally, particularly due to its affective, emotive, subjective, and normative aspects (quite apart from its general unsuitability due to vagueness and lack of clarity). An additional problem is that data about *home* are not available; typically all one has is the house (or traces of it). It is difficult to reconstruct the system of settings which is the dwelling. About relationships, one can only make inferences and these become easier if defined as specific types of relationships. One studies houses to identify dwellings (or other relevant settings) and make inferences about people's relationships with these (Rapoport 1990f). Also, one cannot study individuals' psychological links, one can make inferences about patterns of *groups* (or *aggregates*), using poetry, myth, literature, songs, pictorial materials, etc. (Rapoport 1990b). In the case of the many non-literate cultures and those in the remote past (where only archaeological traces remain), one can, at best, starting with these physical traces, study environment-behavior interaction in terms of activity systems, and make inferences about cognitive schemata and the affective and other relationships that a particular group had to particular systems of settings and features on the cultural landscape.

Note also that from a cross-cultural perspective the type of relationships described by, say, *attachment to home* may involve very different "things." For example, among the Tswana, attachment is to three locales, and the *Kgotla* may be more important than the house. Among the Maori, attachment to the *Marae* may be equally or more significant. Among Australian Aborigines it may be locale and land, certain features on it, and the people living in it. In Nigeria, attachment may be to one's native village even when living elsewhere. We have already seen that in the U.S., for many (but not all) people, (group- and culture-specific) attachment is not to a specific dwelling or locale, but to a type of milieu. In Switzerland, ownership and type of unit seem to be relatively unimportant compared to, say, Australia. In other cases yet, the physical environment may not play any role, there may be no attachment, it may not be psychological. In connection with this particular question, one needs to do research to identify to what attributes of which settings which groups of people are attached at which period.

Conclusion – and an alternative

The serious problems with the term *home,* which I have discussed, make its use so problematical that there does not seem to be enough potential in the term to persevere with attempts to improve it. Moreover, the term is not needed: By relying on already existing more useful concepts and frameworks, one can do all the necessary research (contemporary, historical, and cross-cultural), including research on the set of environment-behavior relationships emphasized by the proponents of *home*. These can be seen as a repertoire of possible relationships from which different groups will draw at different periods. In that sense, as already pointed out, some of the work on *home* has been useful in asking what some of these relationships might be, without making the use of *home* either necessary or desirable.

This alternative, a more useful already existing conceptual framework, is one that I have developed over the years. It involves:

1. Using the concept of dwelling (defined as a system of settings) as the physical object, embedded in the larger system of settings, with the primary setting as anchor.

2. Linking the settings in that system through systems of activities, including their latent aspects.

3. Defining the group in which one is interested in terms of lifestyle, social structure, and the like ("dismantling" culture).

4. Identifying the desired relationships between the group in question and the system of settings. The evaluation of that system in terms of values, ideal schemata, norms, etc., results in its environmental quality

being judged as positive, neutral, or negative. As a result certain decisions, choices, modifications, etc., are made and relationships established with these systems of settings which may be those subsumed by *home*.

In other words, having defined the system of settings and the group (at a given time), one can then study the interaction processes and relationships such as evaluation, preference and choice, attachment and other psychological links, relation to status and identity, furnishings, decoration, landscaping and other personalization, and so on. The question is what kinds of relationships link which people to what attributes of which settings, why and through which mechanisms, which becomes a specific case of the three basic questions of EBS – as it should and must.

This suggestion also answers the question of what is the x that is added to *house* to turn it into *home*. There is no x added to house; x refers to a set of relationships between people and important systems of settings of which the house may be the primary setting or anchoring point. But it may be sacred sites in a landscape, a neighborhood, a city or country, a work setting, or not an environment at all.

I have suggested several times a link between the concepts home and place. If these are used, then home becomes a special kind of place. Place can be studied in the same way, by identifying particular settings with certain attributes, characteristics and ambience, and defined by systems of activities (including their latent aspects). These are evaluated and various relationships established with the settings by members of the group in question. This has, in fact, been proposed recently (Bonnes 1991, 152). There, place is defined as the psychological or perceived unity of the geographical environment involving a system with three principal components: The physical properties of the environment, the activities performed within it (behavioral aspects), and the cognitive and evaluative psychological representations of both the physical properties and activities of the environment in question. Bonnes comments that little empirical research has tried to establish how a particular urban surrounding becomes a place for its users in terms of physical, behavioral, cognitive, evaluative, etc., components. The same can be said about home, and the type of research needed is the same and eliminates the need for place, since one can also use system of settings or cultural landscape (but that is another story, c.f. Rapoport 1994).

In the case of both *place* and *home,* the nonverbal communication approach to meaning is useful (Rapoport 1990c). One can ask which cues communicate those meanings, for example identifying a setting or system of settings as homelike. This is equivalent to identifying the ideal schema, so that attributes of settings can be matched against it. Research can identify those attributes that communicate particular meanings (in this case those currently subsumed under *home*) and thereby identify the schema homelike (e.g., Robinson et al., 1984). We have already seen that in Australia apartments are never *home*, in the U.S. hotels and mobile homes (!) are never *home* – they fail to match the relevant schemata. Regarding the latter, a student (Mark Proffitt in a term paper, Fall, 1991) identified changes to mobile homes that make them homelike by making them more like the appropriate houses and their arrangement more suburban. Note that as I suggested earlier, homelike involves a positive evaluation of an environment.

These schemata play a role in evaluation which, in turn, is general, since *all* environments are evaluated (Rapoport 1977, 1985b, 1990d, 1992)(Fig. 2.1).

The evaluation of some setting systems, if positive, is then what some call *home,* but it is preferable to study the different relationships between the thing being evaluated (houses, dwellings, sites, landscapes, etc.), the different groups at specific times, and what actions or behaviors make such evaluations more positive. One can study change over time – culture change, changes in lifestyle, values, ideals or images, etc., so that historical study (dynamics) becomes possible as well as cross-cultural studies.

As I have long argued, the things evaluated, the evaluations, and hence also the relationships established will vary. For example, three groups at the same time, in the same gentrifying neighborhood of one city, have very different evaluations of the same houses, using three modes of judging: As a stage for social performance, as a setting for expressing one's unique individuality, as providing the atmosphere for private family life and domesticity (Suchar and Rotenberg 1988). In each case the arrangements, transformations, and furnishings vary, as do openness or closedness between inside and outside (c.f., Borchert 1979; Hanson and Hillier 1982/83).

Note an important point: The three modes of judgement (and some of the responses), are among the attributes of home which I discussed, i.e., part of the repertoire. Yet only one is actually used by members of each group. Thus, assuming that all of these attributes, and many others, somehow act together to describe a single concept, *home* is a serious mistake. By using a series of more constant, well-defined, and relatively well-developed and cross-culturally neutral concepts, it is possible to study the specific relationships between particular groups and particular systems of settings. Since there is an extraordinary variety of settings (even though activities in them are much more constant), and many groups, all changing over long periods of time, the types of relationships will also be highly variable. To try and subsume them under the single term *home,* with all its problems I have identified, hardly seems prudent.

A Critical Look at the Concept "Home"

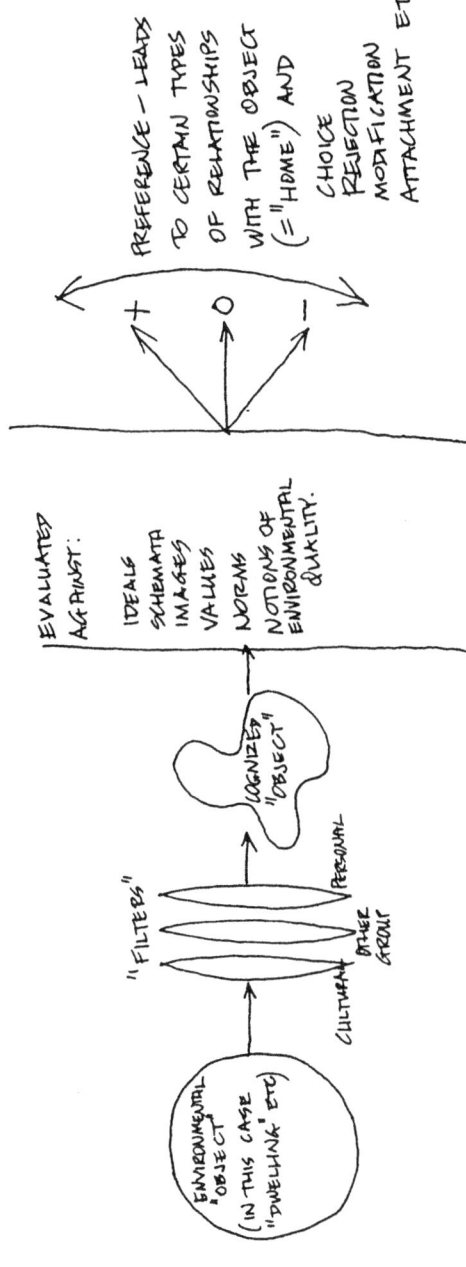

Fig 2.1. (Based in part on Rapoport 1977, Fig. 2.1, p47; Rapoport 1992, Fig. 1, p37).

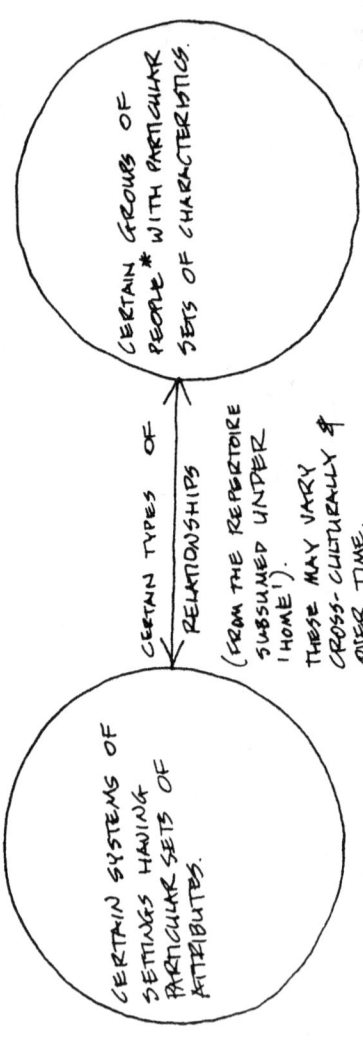

Fig. 2.2. * Both research and design are only regarding groups.
Open-endedness of designs is the means of providing for individual variability which may be small (in traditional societies) or large (today). This also allows for personalization etc.

Endnotes

1. Invited paper presented at the Symposium on Dwelling in Scandinavia, Trondheim, Norway, August 1992.

2. In this review I ignore many other aspects of the work which may be interesting or even *indirectly* relevant. Nor am I concerned with substantive – empirical, theoretical, or methodological issues about which nothing is said and nothing implied.

3. Note that R. Swanson, in a geography Ph.D. at the University of Wisconsin-Milwaukee, showed that attachment can also exist to agricultural land and the farming way of life, i.e., be work related.

4. Of course, there is also a problem with *dwelling* vis-a-vis *house,* because they also are often used interchangeably (e.g. Zgusta 1991 uses *dwelling* meaning *house*). Therefore, an important general point is to reach consensibility on terminology and its consistent use.

5. These, as I have often suggested, are:

   (i) What are the bio-social, psychological, and cultural characteristics of people, as individuals and as members of various groups, that influence (and in design should influence) how environments are organized and shaped.

   (ii) What effects do what attributes of which environments have on members of which groups of people, under what conditions, in what circumstances, and why.

   (iii) Given this two-way interaction between people and environments, they must be linked through some mechanisms; this question concerns the nature of these mechanisms.

References

Andreassen, Arvid. 1974. *Milwaukee Journal* (May 21).

Ahrentzen, S. 1989 A Place of Peace, Prospect and ... a P.C.: The Home as Office. *Journal of Architectural and Planning Research* 6(4) (Winter).

Altman, I. and C.M. Werner, eds. 1985. *Home Environments*. Vol.8 of *Human Behavior and Environment. Advances in Theory and Research.* N. Y.: Plenum Press.

Bonnes, M., ed. 1991. *MAB11 – Urban Ecology Applied to the City of Rome.* UNESCO.

Borchert, J. 1979. Alley Landscapes of Washington. *Landscape* 23(3).

Coleman, A. 1985. *Utopia on Trial (Vision and Reality in Planned Housing).* London: Hilary Shipman.

Colson, N. 1980. Space around the Home. *Architect's Journal* (Dec. 24–31).

Cooper-Marcus, C., and W. Sarkassian. 1986. *Housing as if People Mattered.* Berkeley: University of California Press.

Deitz, P. 1984. A Gentle Redesign for a 1949 Project. *New York Times* (Jan. 21).

Després, C. 1991. Form, Experience and Meaning of Home in Shared Housing. Ph.D. Diss., Dept. of Architecture, University of Wisconsin, Milwaukee.

Feldman, R.M. 1990. Settlement Identity: Psychological Bonds with Home Places in a Mobile Society. *Environment and Behavior,* 22(2) (March).

Fried, M. 1963. Grieving for a Lost Home. In *The Urban Condition,* ed. L.J. Duhl. N. Y.: Basic Books.

———. 1986. The Neighborhood in Metropolitan Life: Its Psychosocial Significance. In *Urban Neighborhoods-Research and Policy,* ed. R. B. Taylor. N.Y.: Praeger.

Fried, M., and P. Gleicher. 1961. Some Sources of Residential Satisfaction in an Urban Slum. *AIP Journal,* 27(4) (November).

Gately, George. 1991. Heathcliff. *Milwaukee Journal* (Nov. 12).

Hanson, J., and B. Hiller 1982/83. Domestic Space Organization. *Architecture and Behavior* 2(1).

Hayward, D.G. 1976. Dimensions of Home. In *Priorities for Environmental Design Research.* EDRA 8, ed. S. Weidemann and J. R. Anderson. Washington, D.C.: EDRA.

Heppell, M., ed. 1979. *A Black Reality (Aboriginal Camps and Housing in Remote Australia).* Canberra: Australian Institute of Aboriginal Studies.

Horelli, L. 1990. Psychosocial and Socio-Cultural Meanings of Dwelling (in the Context of a Self-Planned Community). Paper read at EDRA 22 Conference, March 1991, Mexico.

Hummon, D. M. 1990. *Commonplaces – Community Ideology and Identity in American Culture.* Albany: SUNY Press.

Hunt Thompson Associates 1988. *Maiden Lane Feasibility Study.* London.

Kamau, L.J. 1978/79. Semi-Public, Private and Hidden Rooms: Symbolic Aspects of Domestic Space in Urban Kenya. *African Urban Studies* 3 (Winter).

Kent, S., ed. 1990. *Domestic Architecture and Use of Space. An Interdisciplinary Cross-Cultural Study*. Cambridge: Cambridge University Press.
Larson, Doug. 1992. Zingers. *Milwaukee Journal* (April 22).
Lenz-Romeiss, F. 1973. *The City–New Town or Home Town*. N.Y.: Praeger.
Memmott, P. 1991. *Humpy, House and Tin Shed (Aboriginal Settlement History on the Darling River)*. Faculty of Architecture, University of Sydney, Ian Buchan Fell Research Centre, Sydney.
Milwaukee Journal. 1992. Green Sheet. (April 12).
New York Times. 1992. Resales of homes rose 12.5% last month. (April 28).
Rainwater, L. 1966. Fear and House-as-Haven in the Lower Class. *AIP Journal* 32(1).
Rapoport, A. 1969. *House Form and Culture*. Englewood Cliffs, N.J.: Prentice-Hall.
———. 1977. *Human Aspects of Urban Form*. Oxford: Pergamon Press.
———. 1980. Towards a Cross-Culturally Valid Definition of Housing. In *Optimizing Environments Research, Practice, and Theory*. EDRA 11, ed. R. R. Stough and A. Wandersman. Washington, D.C.: EDRA.
———. 1981. Identity and Environment: A Cross-Cultural Perspective. In *Housing and Identity: Cross-Cultural Perspectives*, ed. J. Duncan. London: Croom Helm
———. 1984. Culture and the Urban Order. In *The City in Cultural Context*, ed. J. Agnew, J. Mercer, and D. Sopher. London: Allen and Unwin.
———. 1985a. Place, Image and Placemaking. Keynote paper read at conference, Place and Placemaking, June 1985, Melbourne, Australia.
———. 1985b. Thinking about Home Environments: A Conceptual Framework. In *Home Environments*. Vol.8 of *Human Behavior and Environment. Advances in Theory and Research*, ed. I. Altman and C. Werner. N.Y: Plenum Press.
———. 1985c. On Diversity and Designing for Diversity. In *Housing Issues 1: Design for Diversification*, ed. B. Judd, J. Dean, and D. Brown. Canberra: RAIA.
———. 1988. Levels of Meaning in the Built Environment. In *Cross-Cultural Perspectives in Nonverbal Communication*, ed. F. Poyatas. Toronto: C.J. Hogrefe.
———. 1989. On the Attributes of Tradition. In *Dwellings, Settlements and Tradition. Cross-Cultural Perspectives*, ed. J.-P. Bourdier and N. Al-Sayyad. Lanham, MD.: University Press of America.
———. 1990a. Defining Vernacular Design. In *Vernacular Architecture*, ed. M. Turan. Aldershot: Avebury.
———. 1990b. Indirect Approaches to Environment-Behavior Research. *National Geographical Journal of India* 36, Pts. 1-2 (March-June). Reprinted in *Literature and Humanistic Geography*, ed. R. L. Singh and R. P. B. Singh.

National Geographic Society of India Research Publications 37, Banaras Hindu University, Varanasi.

———. 1990c. *The Meaning of the Built Environment.* Rev. ed. Tucson: University of Arizona Press.

———. 1990d. Environmental Quality and Environmental Quality Profiles. In *Quality in the Built Environment,* ed. N. Wilkinson. Newcastle, U.K.: Urban International Press.

———. 1990e. Systems of Activities and Systems of Settings. In *Domestic Architecture and Use of Space. An Interdisciplinary Cross-cultural Study,* ed. S. Kent. Cambridge: Cambridge University Press.

———. 1990f. *History and Precedent in Environmental Design.* N.Y.: Plenum Press.

———. 1992. On Cultural Landscapes. *Traditional Dwellings and Settlements Review* 3(2) (Spring).

———. 1994. A critical look at the concept 'place.' *National Georgraphical Journal of India* 40(1-2). Also in *The Spirit and Power of Place,* ed. R. P. B. Singh. Varanasi: Banaras Hindu University.

Roberts, C. 1977. Stressful Experiences in Urban Places: Some Implications for Design. Paper read at EDRA 8 Conference, April 1977, Washington, D.C.

Robinson, J.W., et al. 1984. *Towards an Architectural Definition of Normalization.* Minneapolis: University of Minnesota,

Ross, H. 1987. *Just for Living (Aboriginal Perceptions of Housing in Northwest Australia).* Canberra: Aboriginal Studies Press.

Sadalla, E. K., B. Verschure, and J. Burroughs. 1987. Identity Symbolism in Housing. *Environment and Behavior* 19(5) (September).

Sebba, R., and A. Churchman. 1986. The Uniqueness of the Home. *Architecture and Behavior* 3(1).

Spalding, S. 1992. The Myth of the Classic Slum: Contradictory Perceptions of Boyle Heights Flats, 1900-1991. *Journal of Architectural Education* 45(2) (Febuary).

Stanton, B. H. 1986. The Incidence of Home Grounds and Experiential Networks (Some Implications). *Environment and Behavior* 18(3) (May).

Suchar, C. S., and R. Rotenberg. 1988. Judging the Adequacy of Shelter: A Case from Lincoln Park. Paper presented at the Society of Applied Anthropology meeting in April, Tampa, Florida.

Tognoli, J. 1987. Residential Environments. In *Handbook of Environmental Psychology,* ed. D. Stokols and I. Altman. N.Y.: Wiley Interscience.

Zgusta, R. 1991. *Dwelling Space in Eastern Asia.* University of Foreign Studies Publication no. 4/1991. Osaka.

Ziman, J. 1978. *Reliable Knowledge.* N. Y.: Cambridge University Press.

3

Deciphering Home: An Integrative Historical Perspective

Roderick J. Lawrence

Introduction

Several years ago, Claude Lévi-Strauss, the well known French anthropologist, argued that food is a good subject for contemplation. This chapter argues and illustrates that home is also good to think about. There are several reasons for this. First, home is a complex subject which cannot be studied adequately by applying traditional academic theories or methods that rarely transcend disciplinary boundaries or sectorial approaches. Second, there are a growing number of conflicting accounts and images of home: On the one hand, the mass media presents painful reports of increasing numbers of people sleeping on the streets of many cities around the world. There are also accounts of domestic violence including child abuse. Then there are those reports of the plight of migrants and refugees fleeing or exiled from their homelands owing to ethnic rivalry, religious discrimination, political supression or natural disasters, such as drought or flood that lead to famine. On the other hand, these negative accounts and illustrations coexist with persistent ideals of home as a cherished place of comfort, security, and refuge which may refer to a country, a town, or a housing unit. Consequently, today we live at a time in the history of human civilization when the concept of home requires a reappraisal.

The aim of this chapter is to show that the concept of home is ambiguous, and therefore, it cannot be taken for granted. In particular, the common association between domestic space and home is contentious, and therefore, it is an interesting subject of study. Indeed, there have been a number of ironical reversals of the meaning and uses of terms in recent centuries; for example, the common use of *home* as an euphemism for house such as the real estate industries use of *homes for sale*. In principle, however, a person can purchase a house but one cannot buy a home! Similarly, architects can design houses but not homes. A house may be uninhabited temporarily, or abandoned, but a home has an experiential dimension at one or more geographical scales – generally, from a dwelling unit to a country – as well as over time.

This chapter begins by examining the concepts of home and homelessness, which transcend geographical areas, cultural norms, linguistic connotations, religious doctrines, and temporal boundaries: *They are fundamental human conceptions which are grounded in sets of relationships that order and define the status of individuals in relation to society at large.* Then a multi-dimensional interpretation is applied in the first section of this chapter to distinguish between terms including *house, dwelling, and home*. The second section provides a brief historical overview of interpretations of home in relation to the definition and development of independent housing units for households. It shows that home, family, and place of domicile gradually became coterminous in several fields, including literature, painting and law, during the eighteenth and nineteenth centuries. It also discusses how these developments have been largely overtaken by other societal trends and transformations in many countries during this century and especially since the 1960s. In this respect, demographic trends and technological innovations are mentioned. These sets of longstanding and recent developments indicate that the multi-dimensional nature of the concept of home ought to be examined in precise contexts using integrative, and historical research methods. This means that critical and innovative approaches need to be applied. In order to achieve this goal five questions are tabled for researchers in the concluding section.

The multi-dimensional nature of home

Unfortunately, despite the rapid growth of studies about home during the last two decades, academics and professionals have rarely developed and applied either critical or innovative theories and methods. In order to reorientate contemporary interpretations of home it is fruitful to ask and answer the following questions:

1. What are the meanings of home and homelessness in a precise locality at specific points in time ?

2. What philosophical and ideological frameworks commonly underly these meanings and other interpretations?

3. How can current knowledge of these frameworks and of the meanings of home and homelessness be developed and applied?

These are not simple questions that can be easily answered. Moreover, there is a lack of consensus about uses of terminology including *housing, dwelling* and *home* (Lawrence 1987). The distinction between these terms concerns the definition of house, dwelling and home, which have already been discussed by some authors including Altman and Werner (1985), Bachelard (1964), Dovey (1985), Heidegger (1971), and Porteous (1976). For example, according to Bachelard (1964), "home is our corner of the world...our first universe, a real cosmos in every sense of the word" whereas, for Porteous (1976), home is "the territorial core," a preferred space and a "fixed point of reference" for daily activities. From a similar perspective, Dovey (1985) suggests that home is "an ordering principle in space" and that the notion of place underlines the opposition between home and journey. Yet, as Dovey states, this emphasis on spatial characteristics yields an interpretation of homes which is too restrictive. It implies that home is predominantly spatial and has no meaning unless there is a journey.

From the perspectives of economics and politics, the tenure status of housing, with its implications for personal control, is considered to be the critical variable that defines "what makes a house a home" (Johnson 1971). Yet, like the emphasis on spatial dimensions, the tenure status of housing is also too restrictive; it cannot account for the large portion of the population, in many countries, including Switzerland, that chooses to rent housing units.

In recognition of these restrictive interpretations, it is interesting to examine those common dimensions of home identified by Hayward (1975): "Home as physical structure," "as territory," "as locus in space," "as self and self-identity" and "as a social and cultural unit." This review suggests that affective qualities and human relations are equally important, if not more important, than physical dimensions. In this respect it is noteworthy that the terms *house* and *home* have different meanings in diverse languages, as Sopher (1979, 130) discusses with respect to home:

> The distinguished characteristic of the English word, which it shares to a certain extent with its equivalent in other Germanic languages, is the enormous extension of scale that it incorporates and has done throughout its history. It can refer with equal ease to house, land, village, city, district, country, or indeed, the world. It transmits the sentimental associations of one scale to all the others in a way that the Romance languages, for example, cannot. To speak of 'hometown' or

'homeland,' in which the scale is made specific as a matter of convenience, is to transfer the same warm feelings of security and familiarity that we experience at the scale of the family dwelling to a city or a country, in a way that speakers of French and Spanish do not. In those languages, and many others, house and home are one and the same: to be at home is literally to be 'inside one's house.' The Romance word for 'house' then takes on some of the warmth associated with 'home' in English, but it remains a symbol for firmly bounded and enclosed space, which 'home' is not.

Beyond these fundamental semantic qualifications, there are other reasons for distinguishing between *house, dwelling,* and *home*. The notion of dwelling does not assume that the physical unit of a house defines the experience of home. Houses are commodities produced and marketed in many contemporary societies for financial profit within particular economic and technological constraints. Hence, beyond semantic variations, differences occur within and between cultures and societies with respect to the construction and ownership of houses, and also with respect to the experience and image of home (Duncan 1981; Pratt 1981; Seamon 1979). According to Sopher (1979, 136):

> It is necesary to emphasize the elasticity of the scale of home, both semantically and experientially, as well as the mythic quality of 'attachment to place.'

Furthermore, as Saegert (1985) notes, home is a more elusive notion than house: "Not only is it a place, but it has psychological resonance and social meaning. It is part of the experience of dwelling – something we do, a way of weaving up a life in particular geographical spaces." Moreover, Saegert (1985, 287–8) states:

> The notion of dwelling highlights the contrast between house and home. First it does not assume that the physical housing unit defines the experience of home. It connotes a more active and mobile relationship of individuals to the physical, social, and psychological spaces around them. It points to a spiritual and symbolic connection between the self and the physical world...(and) emphasizes the necessity for continuing active making of a place for ourselves in time and place. Simultaneously, it points to the way in which our personal and social identities are shaped through the process of dwelling.

In essence, the concepts of home and homelessness can be interpreted with respect to sets of human relationships between individuals and society which are contextually located in time and place. These relationships are meaningful and not simply functional. They are created and maintained over time by the experience of daily life. These relationships are mediated by at least seven sets of affiliations including the family, community, government, education, employment, religion, and recreation. Collectively these affiliations define and are mutually defined by the duties and claims, the rights and obligations, and the social status and role of persons. They also underlie self, social, and place identities which are inextricably associated with how the concept of home is interpreted in precise situations by individuals and groups.

This interpretation means that although the term *home* commonly evokes images of a place of domicile, it does not necessarily encompass a family, a household, or a fixed abode. Consequently, living outside a nuclear or extended family, without a permanent address, does not mean that a sailor, a soldier, or a priest are homeless; on the contrary, a person who occupies the same lodging in a welfare hostel for several weeks, months, or years is commonly considered to be homeless. These kinds of interpretations have a long-standing history.

Although homelessness is scorned in many contemporary societies, it was widely interpreted as an admirable way of life in past times. The exaltation of homelessness as an ideal is a recurrent theme of Christian doctrine, recorded in the Scriptures and upheld by principles of monasticism: Poverty, detachment from the past, the abandonment of materialism, and vagrancy were preached by St. Francis of Assisi and the Franciscan order. A parallel ethos is found in Muslim history, in which Mulai Abd al-Qadir al-Jilani (1078-1166) is the patron of the needy and suffering. In addition to friars, hermits, and vagrants, Christianity and Islam recognize and honour the pilgrim who is a homeless wanderer. The ethos of vagrancy is also present in Buddhism: Buddha and his disciples were members of an ancient order of wandering almsmen.

These traditional types of homelessness are still observable today but they have become secondary to other types that can be related to processes of colonization, industrialization, urbanization, and de-colonization. Contemporary types of homelessness include refugees and migratory workers. Although involuntary migration has occurred throughout human history – it is recorded in the Old Testament, for example – population flows have been unprecedented in scale, scope, and duration during this century. The involuntary migration of refugees can be contrasted with voluntary migration in search for personal and family betterment. Refugees are persons who migrate owing to reasons for which they cannot be held responsible, including actual or threatened persecution related to race, religion, political conviction, or warfare. In contrast, voluntary migration includes seasonal labour which is required especially for agricultural production. In such cases the population flow may be internal, transnational, or international. The migrant work force may comprise only single men, or families, or both. In either case, migrants can be denied the possibility of forming or retaining their known sets of affiliations in their host country, and this can lead to the experience of homelessness.

These examples show that house and home may or may not overlap, just as family and household may or may not be synonymous. In principle, home is attributed meanings and values by each individual according to a number of implicit and explicit societal, cultural, and human dimensions that may vary over time. Hence there are different layers of meaning that can be interpreted in relation to:

1. *spatial and temporal dimensions* including formal structural properties across diverse geographical scales and time periods

2. *societal dimensions* including ideological, political and socio-economic factors (that are frequently ignored in studies of home)

3. *experiential dimensions* including emotions and values related to the residential biography of each individual and household

The diverse content of, and the range interrelations between these three sets of dimensions confirm that the meaning of home may vary from person to person, between households and social groups in the same society, across cultures, and over geographical scales and periods of time (Lawrence 1987). Consequently, home is a relative concept, not an absolute one that can be defined in a dictionary by a linguist, or by a researcher. Given that it transcends quantitative, measurable dimensions and includes qualitative subjective ones, it is a complex, ambiguous concept that generates contention as shown by a comparison of several contributions to this book. Therefore, it is interesting and useful to study the multi-dimensional nature of home using an integrative, historical perspective.

Societal developments, trends, and transformations

The relativity of the meaning of home in specific countries is ably illustrated by historical and cultural studies. For example, conceptions of the family, households, and domestic space have varied over time (Aries 1962; Flandrin 1979; Shorter 1976; Tilly 1976). These studies collectively show that the close association between the family and a place of domicile is relatively recent. From the late eighteenth century an important shift occurred in the layout, meaning, and use of domestic space intended for the middle and upper classes of many European countries. These shifts reflected changes in ideology, economics, and social organization, that have been studied by numerous authors, and been reflected in paintings and novels. What many of these contributions fail to note is that these transformations in the composition and structure of households were not only concurrent with changes to the layout of residential buildings but also with the morphology of the urban quarters of cities. Fortunately, however, Daunton (1983, 37) has noted:

> The change in the physical structure of the city relates closely to changes in (the definition of) the family. Essentially the connection was through the notion of domesticity.... The assertion of a physical threshold and the encapsulated house style implied a redefinition of the boundary line between the family and surrounding community.... The emergence of the private, encapsulated dwelling was a physical demonstration of the social value attached to the conjugal family and domestic life.

These developments meant that from the nineteenth century the terms *home, family,* and *place* of domicile became more coterminous in literature, painting, and law, while concurrently there was an increase in the architectural, functional, social, and spatial segmentation of daily affairs.

During this century, and especially since the 1960s, many industrialized and undeveloped societies around the World have undergone important developments that have had direct consequences on the meaning and use of housing and home. For example, there have been significant demographic trends in many industrialized countries. Much attention has focused on the consequences of an ageing population, of the effects of a steady decline in household size, as well as changes to household composition and structure. It is noteworthy that these demographic trends have been more significant than changes to the provision of kinds of housing units in most industrialized countries. Hence, the disparity between the housing stock and households has increased during the last three decades in many countries (Haumont and Segaud 1989).

Concurrently, there have been increasing levels of housing poverty, people sleeping on streets, and unemployment in many industrialized countries. These developments have been prominent in Britain and North America irrespective of the fact that governments in these countries have offered fiscal policies to incite citizens to live in owner-occupied dwelling units. While the private ownership of housing has generally increased it is noteworthy that levels of public expenditure on housing and social services have decreased. There is an ideological framework underpinning these policies and trends which explicitly ties the tenure status of housing to the meaning of home. From this perspective, Saunders (1990) maintains that the marginalization of rented housing in Britain during the 1980s is the result of a natural law founded on innate biological and psychological principles that are reflected in the quest for 'ontological security' which is achieved by the owner occupation of housing and other personal possessions. This restrictive interpretation, which focuses solely on tenure, fails to account for an increasing portion of owner-occupiers in Britain, North America, and other industrialized countries who are unable to meet their mortgage repayments and eventually become depossessed. Furthermore, this emphasis on tenure ignores that portion of the population – including affluent countries like Switzerland – that choose to rent. Hence this interpretation, like any one-dimensional approach, is too restrictive as Lawrence (1987) has shown. In contrast, this article argues that the meaning of home and housing is contextually defined according to a range of cultural, societal, and individual human factors as well as the interrelations between them over time.

Intended and unintended consequences

Today most societies around the World have reached a level of complexity previously unknown, and often unpredicted. With respect to demographic trends, for example, the complete reversal of the baby boom after the Second World War was not forecast. Today it is difficult to predict whether the current decline in the birthrate, or the ageing of the population in many European countries, will continue beyond the year 2000. This complex subject is not only related to fertility and mortality but also migration and immigration.

Given the complexity of contemporary societies, and the increasing unpredictability of future developments, it is noteworthy, at a general level, that:

1. Traditions are no longer a core influence in all sectors of daily life like they were during the lives of our forefathers. Today, marriage and the family have not only been challenged but also discarded by a large portion of the population of industrialized countries. Consequently, although administrative norms still refer to a married couple with two children, such households are a minority in many countries. From

this perspective, it is necessary to identify what home means to an elderly person who is confined to live in an institution; likewise to the hostage, or the prisoner; or the itinerant entrepreneur who sleeps in numerous hotels; and the person who is obliged to sleep on the pavement. Clearly, the meaning of home will be different for each of these citizens.

2. Societal values reflect and express an increasing level of pluralism in contrast to consensus. It is precisely for this reason that there is no shared definition of home. From this perspective it is necessary to identify what home means for the immigrant, the foreign worker, the refugee, or the local citizen who has been obliged to move from his or her place of residence owing to a projected motorway and redevelopment project. Again, the meaning of home will be different for each of these citizens.

3. Technological innovations are transforming the use of space and time at a faster rate than at any other period since Antiquity. Following the agricultural and industrial revolutions, and more recently the impact of mass transportation, the radio, telegraph, television, and microtechnology are effacing some of the traditional spatial and temporal demarcations in the World.

It is necessary to identify the consequences of all these transformations on the concept of home. Firstly, face to face contacts associated with many traditional forms of exchange – banking and shopping for example – have declined or become redundant, owing to innovations in communication technology, economic exchange, and transportation. This means that social exchanges (indeed society itself) are maintained by less tangible ties between people, whereas in the past people were obliged to meet face to face to enact exchanges. This trend reflects and expresses the growing autonomization of societies. Second, the corollary of the decline of face to face contact is that social relationships have been stretched over space and time. Consequently, peoples' daily lives may no longer be directly related to their place of domicile, or their place of birth. Hence, there may be direct implications on the use of domestic space, such as when one's place of domicile serves only the function of a dormitory, as shown by a recent unpublished study in Geneva. Last, but not least, the effects of all these trends may be compounded so that individuals have difficulty in locating a place of belonging (Dovey 1985). When such consequences are reality the human costs and benefits can be grave, resulting in anxiety, stress, and anomie. Such consequences have been found amongst those populations who were forcibly displaced to enable urban renewal programmes to be enacted (Andrews 1979; Fried 1963; Teymur, Markus, and Woolley 1988). People were submitted to rapid changes in the organization of their physical surroundings and their social networks; whole new residential areas with unknown spatial and temporal envelopes were imposed: Usually, there were no consultations between administrators, architects, and the local population. The legacy for current and future generations in many industrialized countries has still to be calculated (Prak and Priemus 1985).

The question of theory and method

The preceding sections of this paper have briefly illustrated that there are significant developments, trends, and transformations in the World that have either direct or indirect influences on the daily lives of people in general, and the meaning of home, in particular. This section argues that, owing to this state of affairs, it is necessary to reconsider theories and methods in architectural and the social sciences in general, and with respect to housing and home, in particular. The remainder of this chapter will focus on those principles that can enable us to improve our understanding of home as that concept is construed and interpreted by people. This section will not develop a linguistic study of the meaning of home, which has already been done by several authors including Benveniste (1973) and Klein (1971). Yet, it is noteworthy that the concept of home has linguistic roots in many languages from at least since Antiquity.

The ambiguity and the contention about the association between domestic space and home stem, at least in part, from the ideal and imagery of the hearth of the ancestral fire, which is not necessarily represented by the primal hut. According to many archaeological and anthropoligical studies, human-made fire is a unique characteristic of culture that partly distinguishes homo sapiens from all other biological organisms. Fire leaves a trace of human activities. Hearths and middens are some of the earliest remnants of human habitations. In many ancient societies the hearth or fireplace served as a metonym for *household* and *family*. In litera-ture dating from the era of Greek mythology, the hearth is the centre of domestic space. Modern fables in most European countries closely relate hearth and home, and these literary associations are supported by legal interpretations stemming from mediaeval Scandinavian law, written records of Anglo-Norman law, and contemporary legal definitions. Black's Law Dictionary (1979, 660) for example, states that home is "one's own dwelling place; the house in which one lives, especially the house in which one lives with his family." Yet, home is also "that place in which one in fact resides with the intention of residence, or in which one has so resided, and with regard to which one retains residence or to which one intends to return." Last, but not least, home is also defined legally as the "place where a person dwells and which is the center of his domestic, social and civic life." These citations indicate that the rights of households to a dwelling have been institutionalized by law and that although house and home may be coterminous, a direct association between them cannot be taken for granted. These terms have and still are attributed meanings which depend on contextual conditions, which ought to be culturally, geographically, and historically specified.

In principle, 'the natural world' does not provide domestic space for humans. Dwellings must be construed. The domestification of landscapes implies that geographical space, resources, and time are cultivated by people. Cultivation is a multi-dimensional process in which implicit cognitive structures, individual and group practices, social rules and conventions, institutional structures, and human consciousness are purposely interrelated. Hence, the intentional use of space, time, and resources at any geographical scale implies that a part of the World is appropriated psychologically and physically. The term appropriation has etymological roots in the latin word *appropriare* (to make one's own). Cultivation is therefore related to attachment to place, people, objects, and actions.

Since the dawn of human civilization, conceptual, behavioural, material, symbolic, and temporal boundaries have been constituents of the cultivation of landscapes. These diverse kinds of boundaries provide a framework for the appropriation of domestic places. Boundaries define and are mutually defined by principles of social classification. Consequently, it is necessary to understand the 'world' as it is constituted by and for people according to their categories. Durkheim and Mauss (1963) are generally credited as being the first to underline the practise of social classification. They maintained that the human mind does not have the innate capacity to construct sets of categories commonly discernable in human societies. Rather, social classification is a cultural construct and a collective project not found in nature. In principle, when people, settings, objects, and events are classified, human boundaries are construed in otherwise non-bounded space, matter, and time in order to distinguish between 'here and there,' 'this and that,' and 'now and then.' Hence home may be 'here' or 'there' and it may include 'this and that' in relation to past and present (Sopher, 1979). From this perspective, home may be situated in a precise locality but it is not necessarily fixed in space and time, as the former case of the soldier, sailor, and priest, or the gypsy caravan, the Bedouin tent, and the homeless in many societies illustrate.

When house and home are synonymous, in order to cultivate a home one must define and delimit space. This is the first, generic act of creating domestic space. This space occupies a bounded territory which has geographical, material, and (perhaps) symbolic dimensions that may vary over time. It is attributed meaning and values at a precise point in time in relation to other profane and symbolic constituents of society. From this perspective, domestic space is 'the ethnic domain' (Langer 1957) defined in relation to cultural, societal, and individual human factors, both at one point in time and historically.

The concept of cultivation highlights the contrast that may exist between house and home. In essence, it does not assume that a housing unit is synonymous with home. Rather, it seeks to identify the active, perhaps mobile interrelations between individuals and their milieu; it can account for the cognitive and symbolic interrelations between individuals, groups, and their past and present. It underlines the importance of intentionality in the ongoing practices of domesticity, especially the way that self and social identities are construed, expressed, and communicated.

The preceding principles can be applied to analyze the meaning of home from the viewpoint of individuals and groups in precise localities. When this approach is adopted in architectural and social science research at least five fundamental questions ought to be posed and answered. These questions are:

1. *What are the units of analysis?*

    E.g.: Is home synonymous with a place of domicile?
    It is necessary to ascertain whether public institutions, social groups, households, and individuals distinguish between home, place of residence and domicile. In this respect, many northern Europeans have more than one residence; in such circumstances it is important to ascertain whether either of them are considered to be home. Traditionally, sociologists have not clarified possible distinctions of this kind. Rather, they have assumed that the place of domicile is home. In contrast, a recent, unpublished study in the Swiss Canton of Geneva not only found that 35 per cent of all respondents had access to what sociologists assumed to be a secondary residence, but also that this dwelling unit was home for many.

2. *How does one delimit the subject of study?*

E.g.: What conceptual, material, and behavioural boundaries relate to the definition of home?

The constituents of home depend on the point-of-view of each individual. The fundamental definition of domicile of origin, that associated with place of birth, means that residential biographies should be examined. In many contemporary societies, the ways in which a place of residence ceases to be co-extensive with domicile of origin should be accounted for. In this respect, the domicile of choice is a useful analytical concept. This concept accounts for the goals and intentions of all those people including migrants who chose to move residence for personal or family betterment. In contrast, this concept also distinguishes all other persons who are forced to move residence, including households displaced by urban renewal projects and refugees. Whereas the former commonly evoke a sense of belonging, the latter mention a sense of alienation.

3. *What characteristics are common to the homes and daily lives of people in a specific locality ?*

E.g.: How does one interpret differences across diverse geographical scales?

Home can be a room inside a residential building, a house in an urban residential area or the countryside, a neighbourhood, a village, a city, or a whole country. Given that the concept of home transcends the material culture of housing units, larger built environments and domestic activities, it is necessary to identify and study both the tangible and intangible constituents of interpersonal relationships. As these sets of relationships may involve the family, community, government, education, employment, religion, and recreation, it is necessary to examine all of these in terms of the daily lives of individuals and groups.

4. *How does one account for consensual meanings and uses as well as individual differences?*

It is necessary to consider the point-of-view of each individual in terms of age, gender. nationality, profession or occupation, length of domicile, tenure, access to a secondary residence, and presence of kith and kin. In a recent. unpublished study in Geneva, it was found that the sense of attachment to a place of domicile increased with the age of the respondents and their length of tenancy. At the same time, however, recollections of past residential activities (especially family gatherings and memorable occasions) also increased. Consequently, it cannot be assumed that the material culture of housing units is more significant to people than the activities and interpersonal relations they accommodate.

5. *How can a temporal perspective be applied?*

The interrelations between people and their residential environment acquires form and meaning from numerous sources related to social history and the residential biography of each individual and household. Therefore, in order to apply an integrative, historical perspective it is necessary to complete an historical analysis of extant residential environments by field work and the study of documents, as well as the study of domestic and daily life, human ideals and values. This dual approach, and the thesis of this chapter, contradict a current trend in architectural history and practice which has been applied to study house and home. It upholds that the form of a building has inherent, objective meaning that communicates itself to the public. This misunderstanding of the meaning of the built environment has been refuted (Lawrence 1987) and this chapter has outlined an alternative.

Conclusion

This chapter has meant to show that home is a good subject for contemplation, largely because it is complex, multi-dimensional, and sometimes it is ambiguous. For these reasons the concept of home, like that of homelessness, cannot be taken for granted. Consequently, this chapter has indirectly challenged those interpretations of home which assume it is synonymous with house or place of domicile. Indeed, this chapter has argued that in a rapidly changing world it is necessary to develop a contextual understanding of the concept of home which transcends the material characteristics of domestic space to include qualitative dimensions of daily life, and especially interpersonal relationships. These relationships define self, social, and place identities which underlie the meaning of home in precise localities.

References

Altman, I. and Werner, C., eds. 1985. *Home Environments*. Vol. 8 of *Human Behavior and Environment. Advances in Theory and Research*. N.Y.: Plenum Press.

Aries, P. 1962. *Centuries of Childhood: A Social History of Family Life*. N.Y.: Random House.

Andrews, C. 1979. *Tenants and Town Hall*. London: HMSO.

Bachelard, G. 1964. *The Poetics of Space*. N.Y.: Orion Press.

Benveniste, E. 1973. *Indo-European Language and Society*. London: Faber and Faber.

Black, H. 1979. *Black's Law Dictionary*. 5th ed. St. Paul, Minn.: West Publishing Company.

Daunton, M. 1983. *House and Home in the Victorian City: Working-Class Housing 1850-1914*. London: Edward Arnold.

Dovey, K. 1985. Home and Homelessness. In *Home Environments*. Vol. 8 of *Human Behavior and Environment. Advances in Theory and Research*, eds. I. Altman and C. Werner. N.Y.: Plenum Press.

Duncan, J. 1981. *Housing and Identity: Cross-Cultural Perspectives*. London: Croom Helm.

Durkheim, E., and M. Mauss, 1963. *Primitive Classification*. London: Cohen and West.

Flandrin, J.-L. 1979. *Families in Former Times: Kinship, Household and Sexuality*. Cambridge: Cambridge University Press.

Fried, M. 1963. Grieving for a Lost Home. In *The Urban Condition*, ed. L. J. Duhl. N.Y.: Basic Books.

Haumont, N. and M. Segaud. 1989. *Familles, modes de vie et habitat*. Paris: Editions de L'Harmattan.

Hayward, G. 1975. Home as an Environmental and Psychological Concept. *Landscape* 20(1).

Heiddegger, M. 1971. *Poetry, Language, Thought*. London: Harper and Row.

Johnson, M. 1971. *Household Behaviour: Consumption, Income and Wealth*. Hammondsworth, U.K.: Penguin.

Klein, E. 1971. *Comprehensive Etymological Dictionary of the English Language*. Amsterdam: Elsevier.

Langer, S. 1957. *Philosophy in a New Key*. 3rd ed. Cambridge, Mass.: Harvard University Press.

Lawrence, R. 1987. *Housing, Dwellings and Homes: Design Theory, Research and Practice*. Chichester, UK: John Wiley.

Porteous, D. 1976. Home: the Territorial Core. *Geographical Review* 66(4).
Prak, N., and H. Priemus. 1985. *Post-War Housing in Trouble*. Delft: Delft University Press.
Pratt, G. 1981. The House as Expression of Social Worlds. In *Housing and Identity: Cross-Cultural Perspectives,* ed. J. Duncan. London: Croom Helm.
Saegert, S. 1985. The Role of Housing in the Experience of Dwelling. In *Home Environments*. Vol. 8 of *Human Behavior and Environment. Advances in Theory and Research,* ed. I. Altman, and C. Werner. N.Y.: Plenum Press.
Saunders, P. 1990. *A Nation of Home-Owners*. London: Unwin Hyman.
Seamon, D. 1979. *A Geography of the Lifeworld*. London: Croom Helm.
Shorter, E. 1976. *The Making of the Modern Family*. London: Fontana Books.
Sopher, E. 1976. The Landscape of Home: Myth, Experience, Social Meaning. In *The Interpretation of Ordinary Landscapes: Geographical Essays,* ed. D. Meinig. N.Y.: Oxford University Press.
Teymur, N., T. Markus, and T. Woolley. 1988. *Rehumanizing Housing*. London: Butterworths.
Tilly, C. 1976. *Historical Studies of Changing Fertility*. Princeton: Princeton University Press.

4
The Home and Homes

Bror Westman

When I speak of *home*, I do not mean the children's home or the home of elderly people; I mean the dwelling and its surroundings.

The concept of home is different in different countries and cultures. I do not speak of the Danish *hygge* (cosiness inside by the fire or candlelight), although it might be an important aspect of the home. By the home I do not mean nation, country, or part of a country.*

I place my main weight on the viewpoint that the movements to and from such places as the dwelling, the fireplace, or the candlelight are extremely important in understanding the home cross-culturally. A key to this understanding is the comparison of movement patterns. Therefore, I look at the home as a turning point consisting of turning points for the movements of humans.

In the following I first present some general reflections on my theoretical position. Then I try to establish a series of events useful for understanding movements in relation to the dwelling place, cross-culturally drawing on a few examples. Finally I present my total model for this understanding, concluding with the help of the Australian aborigines.

Considerations and premises

Below I try to make two trains of thought crossing each other i.e., a temporal and a spatial. The temporal is a hypothetical course of events. The spatial is a description at the level of the meaning of words.

The home can be treated on two levels: Either at a general or specific level. Especially it is part of what I call *the cultural subjectivity*. My interest in this subjectivity has developed inside a frame of cross-cultural comparisons of variations in ways of living in relation to the dwelling place. My general and hypothetical ideas are in this way a sort of a reconstruction on the basis of scattered cross-cultural experiences. You may say that my interest in the reconstruction of a sequence of events concerning homes is an attempt to explain contradictionally the more phenomenological oriented understanding of reality (Heidegger 1954; Schutz 1975; Norberg-Schulz 1978, 1986). All these phenomenological thinkers have inspired my own work and I use many of their concepts. They focus on the concept of 'being,' however they are minimizing the analysis of movements in relation to the home. This possible antagonism has particularly nurtured my ideas about movements – the movements of the body – more important than some kind of 'being' in some place.

I would like to articulate myself in relation to the mentioned phenomenologists. In this way I might be approaching another understanding of the home, which is no less phenomenological. You could for example talk about the phenomenology of movement, and thus I try to enlighten by empirical and comparative analysis.

This applies as well to a description of the relation to other people, tribes, nations towards their homes, as well as to an interpretation of their expressions in an attempt to familiarize oneself with it. In this respect my research is a continuous looking back trying to understand how modes of speech relate to patterns of behavior.

My hypothesis implies that the home is a complex phenomena concerning people in all cultures. Through this train of thought it is easily understood that there are great differences in homes illustrated in a cross-cultural perspective. I establish a name, the *home*, which I keep constant. From this point, I examine the cross-cultural variations of it.

My first basic hypothesis is that we can divide the dwelling into two concepts: the *house* and the *home*. The house is the part of the dwelling which renders shelter; the shelter protecting the fireplace (Cooper 1974). The home, on the other hand, is that entity in which we invest our feeling, represented by symbols "binding" us to places and things. Now the question is how this "binding" takes place. On this point my hypotheses and comparisons step in. We are now talking of a comparison of dualisms, such as close-distant, open-closed, identity-community and inside-outside. It is possible to compare with the concept of dialectics used by Altman and Gauvain (1981), who claim that by the help of pairs of oppositions, they are able to analyze the home cross-culturally by using the above mentioned concepts. Where they place their main interest in conceptual areas, I place more importance on the movements of the bodies and the significances between the spatial areas.

Movements

Many researchers mention physical movement as an important element in the understanding of the home (Stea 1968; Bechtel 1970; Schutz 1975; Seamon 1979, 1980; Sopher 1979; Westman 1991; and many others). I do not disagree with these authors. I wish to clalrify the relation between the home and culture more precisely with the help of the following assumptions. Establishing that may "explain" what I conceive of as a possible sequence:

1. You establish a place and possibly a borderline around the place. It might be the fireplace, or it might be the "original" place in relation to a mythical-cosmological interpretation.

2. You repeat movements in relation to this place – cross the established borderlines. These repeated movements become ritual. They tend towards being performed in a fixed way, which means they begin to "bind" you. Places and things get symbolically meaningful by this process of *timebinding* (Merloo 1966, 239).

3. As time passes the "accessories" used in the movements may lose their meaning. The symbols may now depend on the repeated movements that "recharge" these "accessories."

4. The symbols are employed for handing over *place-feeling* to the next generation i.e., reproduction. This reproduction involves a consciousness about the differences of generations and the sexes.

5. The repetition implies wear and tear, and innovation, further implying cultural variation i.e., styles.

These events happen constantly, yet the sequence is a sort of unreal explanation. It may even seem commonplace, but the commonplace is exactly our subject. The above mentioned course of events is hypothetical. A way you try to make a scientific explanation – a series of causal events – that may seem like an aetiological myth.

This sequence of postulated events is not enough for me in my search for an understanding of the home and how it in some way may be considered the "speach of culture," what it says about the unique in a culture. It must be transected by a spatial model, which shows us the movements in their spatial course. Therefore, I propose a sequence which may only be considered an example.

This sequence is inspired by my field work in North Africa, which intended to understand the relations between dwellings and image production in arts and crafts. The spatial sequence is as follows:

1. inside the body, including dreams

2. the body, especially its surfaces, for example tatoos and clothes

3. the dwelling with its surfaces, rooms and openings

4. the neighborhood quarter

5. the town

6. the surrounding landscape

7. and finally, the cosmos reflected by the 'world view'

This sequence is physical as well as symbolic. The following is an example of the sequence from Morocco (Boughali 1974; Westman 1988). In Morocco, we learn that the house, which is called *dar*, from the Arabic *dara* (to turn over) has a *sdr* (breast), a *foum* (mouth), and a *rass* (head). The breast is the middle of the room. The door is the mouth of the house, and the alley where the house lies has a head where one enters. When a newborn child enters the world, it is called *sboula* (cornsheaf). The newborn must remain with its mother for seven days in the room of the house in which it was born. Thereafter it is given its first name in connection with a celebration. At about the same time it is presented to the invisible beings of the house, and a sheep is sacrificed. On the fortieth day after the birth, the child is presented to the patron saint of the village and local town. This is followed, for the boys, by circumcision, which is regarded as a new birth. Later comes marriage, and notably for men, the pilgrimage to Mecca. We can see how the body follows in the footsteps of language, or is it the other way round? As the Arabic word *dar* suggests, we can see the house as the place to which one returns.

This example shows the close connection between a child's years of growth and the spatial universe of meanings. From my point of view, it is important to accentuate the movement to and from the house.

Another example derives from the Hopi of Arizona (Saile 1985), a people that divide their year in such a way that they work in summer villages. Their proper homes are the winter villages. The movement to and from this latter place contributes in itself to establish it as a home. In Europe we have the same movements. Connected with mountain pasturing, a clear distinction is made between summer and winter houses, or up and down in the landscape. We also have our own model for using second homes (summer cottages), according to the season (Schwartz 1989). All these movements contribute to the establishment of the home.

An extreme example of the connection between movement and the home is from the Panare in South America who move house several times during the year within their home range. The Panare in Venezuela are hunters, fishermen, and gatherers of fruits. They live, according to their own interpretation, between forest and savannah. As well as the daily movement between the common house and the huts, they travel during the course of the year between four points. Two of these points comprise the main living place, where the common house is found.

In the middle of the dry season they move to a camp a small distance away. In contrast to this, they move in the rainy season to huts which are a half hour to one hour's walking distance from the main living place. Here, the group is spread out and each family lives alone. These people not only carry out to and fro movements in the course of the day's 24 hours, but also make two forward and backward movements during a year, which are related to the dry and wet season. The Panare are not nomadic, they are shifting cultivators (Dumont 1976).

All these examples tell us that the home is a complex concept dealing with movement. You may say that the home is the place that takes place. The movement makes this meaningful.

What happens in this process? It is a course of events that makes social life spatial – and makes space social. In this connection, I want to refer to a concept from Bourdieu's fieldwork among the Berber of Kabylia in Algeria and Pred's theoretical work (Bordieu 1972, note 42; Pred 1986, 198). The geographical space is connected to the social space with the help of the mythic-ritual system, where the social becomes spatial – the spatial becomes social. The home is what takes place for a time, and thus, essentially, it is to dwell in the movement.

It is interesting to note that the Danish word for dwelling or homestead is *bolig*. The ending *lig* is a suffix from the Middle Ages *lek*, or the modern *leg*, meaning play, in the sense of movement. Compare this with *vejrlig* (climate), something that takes place for a time, as with the movements of a yo-yo, and the movements to and fro inside the home between the focal points, such as the kitchen, the bed, the dining table, the fire place, and the television, etc.

My approach to an understanding of other cultures is to understand how people move and where do they find their symbols in all this? In conclusion, I want to present a model of a culture's home as its pattern of movements, and the way it can be reflected in words and images.

BROR WESTMAN

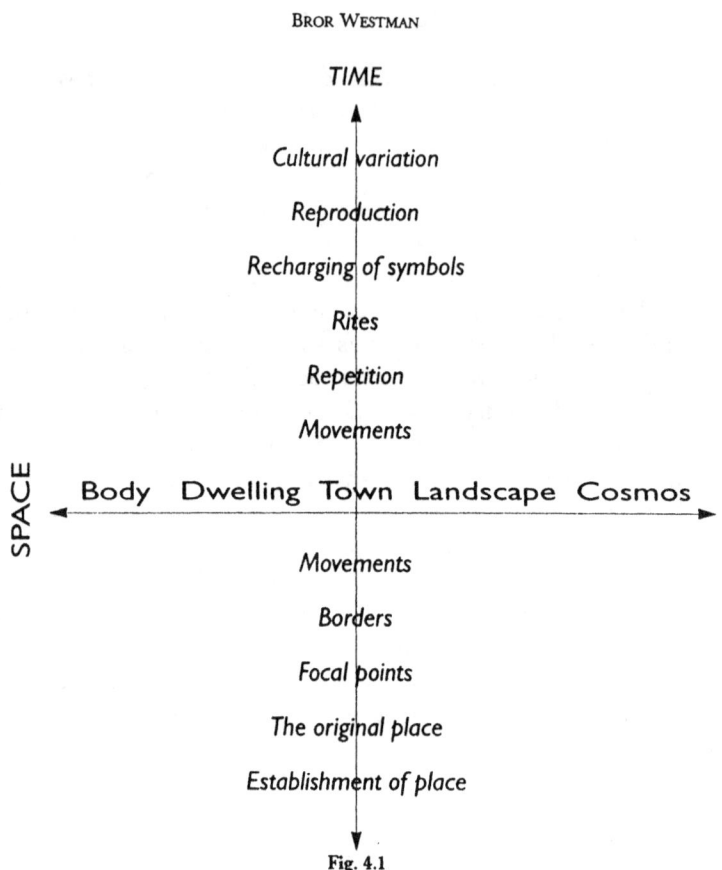

Fig. 4.1

Thus, we find that a culture's concept of home is its own way of cultivating its relation to places and the movements between them, across two sequences, the sequences of time and space as shown in Figure 4.1.

Many phenomenological elucidations often neglect the dimension of time. I think that it is in relation to time that cultural subjectivity appears, or perhaps it is in the "work up" of the relation between time and space that culture shows its face. *The ritual of home* is the "place" of action where this work finds its manifestation, the intersection of events in time and places.

Some Australian aborigines as a custom depict on wood or stone the circles and lines representing campsites and the routes of travelling among them (Munn 1973; Brandenstein 1972, 223–238; Rappoport 1975, 45). We find the same pictures on the holy stones named Tjurunga by the Aranda. They may also be seen on bull-roarers, musical instruments, which in this way yield voices to the movements in the landscape.

References

Altman, I. and M. Gauvain. 1981. A Cross-Cultural and Dialectic Analysis of Homes. In *Spatial Behavior Across the Life-Span*, ed. L. Liben, et al. London: Academic Press.
Bechtel, R.R. 1970. Human Movement and Architecture. In *Environmental Psychology. Man and His Psychic Setting*, ed. H. M. Proshansky. N.Y.: Holt, Rinehart and Winston.
Boughali, M. 1974. *La representation de l'espace chez le marocain illitre*. Paris: Edition Anthropos.
Bourdieu, P. 1972. La Maison Kabyle ou le Monde Renverse. In *Esqusse d'une theorie de la pratique*. Geneva: Droz.
von Brandenstein, C.G. 1977. The Symbolism of Zig Zag Design. *Oceania* 47(3).
Cooper, C.C. 1972. The House as a Symbol of Self. In *Designing for Human Behavior*, ed. J. Lang. Stroudsburg: Dowden
Dumont, P. 1976. *Under the Rainbow*. "The Texas Pan-American Series." Austin: University of Texas Press.
Heidegger, M. 1954. *Vortrage und Aufsatse*. Pfullingen: Gunther Neske.
Merloo, J.A.M. 1966. The Timesense in Psychiatry. In *The Voices of Time*, ed. J.T. Fraser. N.Y.: George Braziller.
Munn, N.D. 1973. *Walbiri Iconography*. Ithaca: Cornell University Press.
Porteous, J.D. 1976. Home: The Territorial Core. *The Geographical Review* 66(4).
Pred, A. 1986. *Place, Practice and Structure. Social and Spatial Life in Southern Sweden 1750–1850*. Cambridge: Polity Press.
Rapoport, A. 1975. Australian Aborigines and the Definition of Place. In *Shelter, Sign and Symbol*, ed. P. Oliver. London: Barrie and Jenkins.
Saile, D.G. 1985. The Ritual Establishment of Home. In *Home Environments;* Vol. 8 of *Human Behavior and Environment. Advances in Theory and Research*, ed. I. Altman and C. Werner. N.Y.: Plenum Press.
Schutz, A. 1975. *Hverdagslivets sociologi*. Copenhagen: Reitzels Forlag.
Schwartz, J. 1989. In Defense of Homesickness. *Kultursociologiske skrifter* 26.
Seamon, D. 1979. *A Geography of the Life World*. New York: St. Martin's Press.
———. 1980. Body-Subject, Time-Space-Ballets. In *The Human Experience of Space and Place*, eds. A. Buttimer and D. Seamon. London: Croom Helm.
Sopher, D.E. 1979. The Landscape of Home. In *The Interpretation of Ordinary Landscapes*, ed. D.W. Meinig. Oxford: Oxford University Press.

Stea, D. 1965. Space, Territory and Human Movements. *Landscape* (Autumn).

Tuan, Yi-Fu. 1975. Place, an Experiential Perspective. *The Geographical Review* LXV 2 (April).

Westman, B. 1989. Manden, kvinden, hjemmet. Fra et feltarbejde i Nordafrika. In *Kulturanalyse,* ed. K. Hastrup and R. Ramløv. Copenhagen: Akademisk Forlag.

———, ed. 1989. *Hjemfølelse.* Copenhagen: Kunstadademiets Arkitektskole.

———. 1991. What does it Mean to Feel at Home? In *Social Space,* ed. O. Grøn, E. Engelstad, and L. Lindblom. Odense, Denmark: Odense University Press.

Part Two
Home as a Cultural Interpretation Tool

5
Archaeological Houses, Households, Housework and the Home

Ruth Tringham

Archaeologists and the home

Archaeologists do not frequently write about *homes* or the *home*. We write a lot about *architecture, spatial patterns, buildings, dwellings, shelter,* and we make inferences about *houses*. Only recently have we even begun to make explicit inferences about *households*. But the home is a wildly cultural concept, evoking emotional nostalgia, whose apparent ambiguity leads it forever beyond the reach of the traditional archaeological record. And so it is rationalized as being irrelevant to investigation by archaeologists, as being a constant and not a variable in the big picture of human cultural evolution. From this point of view its demise on the part of people who study prehistory is similar to that of *gender*, the *family*, and *housework* (Tringham 1991a, in press).

In the 1970s, until the unfortunate early death of Glyn Isaac, there was a lively debate on whether early hominids were human enough to have a *home base* that would have been the focus of food-sharing and other social actions. Following on from this was the idea that the communication through speech and the social relations that went on in the home base were the source of the earliest cultural evolution of human beings (Binford 1981, 1983; Isaac 1976).

The term *home base* was only ever used to refer to hunters and gatherers. With the consideration of sedentary people, whether hunter-gatherer, pastoralist, or agriculturalist, more familiar and apparently objective terms are used, like *village* or *settlement* – at most, *house* – to express the living arrangements, the term *home* undoubtedly being considered too interpretive, individualistic, and not relevant to the grand trajectory of cultural evolution. My quest in this article is to examine whether the study of the home could ever become interesting and relevant to prehistorians.

Ruth Tringham

Ways of looking at archaeological data

As the archaeological papers in this symposium alone show, several different theoretical perspectives are currently practiced in the discipline of archaeology. My own perspective assumes that material culture is both a passive reflection of behaviour *and* – in a dialectical relationship – an "active" medium for, and symbolic expression of, the social actions, practices, negotiations, and dominance structures of the prehistoric inhabitants. Architecture – that element of material culture most relevant to this paper – thus can be seen as both a container and arena of social action. This view of architecture is in keeping with that of a number of social theorists, including anthropologists, archaeologists, human geographers, and a few architects, in whom elements of neo-Marxism, post-structuralism, and post-modernism have been merged to form structuration theory, the theory of place, and social action theory (Bourdier 1989; Bourdieu 1990; Cosgrove 1984; Donley-Reid 1990; Giddens 1979, 1984; Hodder 1986, 1987, 1991; Moore 1986; Pred 1984, 1990; Rapoport 1990; Soja 1989; Stea and Turan 1990).

This perspective is not mutually exclusive of the view that is more traditional and mainstream in archaeology – that the archaeological record reflects behavior. The latter has formed in the past the basis for much of my own research in European prehistory, and is certainly the theoretical context in which most of the archaeological record has been accumulated and interpreted (Binford 1981; Kent 1990).

My plan in this paper is to introduce the rich archaeological data base of domestic architectural remains from Europe's prehistoric past from the different theoretical perspectives of archaeological architecture. The archaeological architecture of Neolithic and Eneolithic southeast Europe, five to seven thousand years old, may seem very distant in time and space from the subject of this conference. It does not represent the origins of architecture from which the Scandinavian house stemmed. It is not particularly spectacular or monumental. But it *does* represent perhaps the richest archaeological record of domestic architecture in prehistoric Europe, and one that has been excavated and interpreted by archaeologists with many different perspectives. Fire – whether accidental or deliberate, whether individual or village-wide – has been the main contributing factor to the excellent preservation of these architectural remains.

First, my aim is to show that, even within the traditional theoretical orientation of material culture as reflection and architecture as container of human behaviour, the archaeological record is not a fixed entity. It is expandable and changeable as different questions are asked of it (Patrik

1985). Then I shall show that, just as we think we have squeezed the true prehistory out of the archaeological record, we can expand it qualitatively and quantitatively. As shown by post-processual archaeologists, this can be done by considering:

1. material culture as an active component of social action
2. architecture as an arena of that social action
3. the biographies of the individual social actors as crucial parts of constructing the narratives of prehistory.

Moreover, within this more recent orientation, it is clear that there is no one true "prehistory" to be re-constructed, but that prehistory comprises multiple interpretations of the archaeological record and multiple narratives that can be constructed.

The use-lives of prehistoric houses in southeast Europe

A focus on the *use-life* of artifacts was developed by North American processualist archaeologists as a reaction against the traditional interest in formal variation of finished artifacts that had characterized much of culture-historical archaeology (Schiffer 1987; Tringham 1978). This new interest immensely expanded the archaeological record to include the procurement of raw materials, techniques of manufacture, utilization of artifacts, and the circumstances leading up to their eventual discard or re-use, all of which contributed to the artifacts' particular manifestation in the archaeological record.

The concept of use-life was applied to archaeological architecture (McGuire and Schiffer 1983; Tringham 1991a, Fig. 5.3). The result was an exciting expansion of information over the more traditional prehistoric architectural studies that focused on variability of the form and style of buildings as finished artifacts (which by the way is still popular), (Brukner 1990; Coudart 1987). At Opovo for example, our 1983–89 excavations provided information on variability in construction, spatial arrangement of the built environment and its surroundings in general, the expected versus actual duration of the building, the attempts to prolong a structure's use-life, the re-use of materials, and the nature of a building's destruction and eventual abandonment (Tringham et al. 1992).

House construction.

The architecture of Neolithic and Eneolithic Southeast Europe may be generalized as follows. It is characterized by rectangular detached buildings – presumably houses, ca. 6 meters wide, and varying in length from 6 to 20 meters. (Figs. 5.1.a, b, and c show floor plans of houses in various building horizons at Ovcha-rovo, Bulgaria. (After Todorova 1983)). These were traditionally built on a frame-work of upright wooden posts dug into the ground with walls of horizontal planks, logs, or wattling covered on one or both surfaces by a thick layer of clay daub. Their floors comprise a thick layer of clay which was frequently spread over a substructure of horizontal logs or planks. Generally the buildings have only one story, but two-storied houses have been excavated. The roof, which has never been preserved, has been reconstructed as gabled.

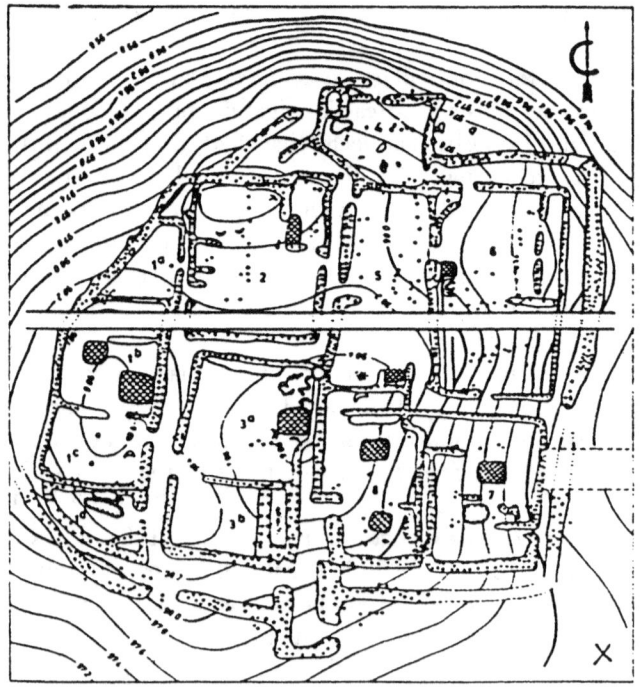

Fig. 5.1.a

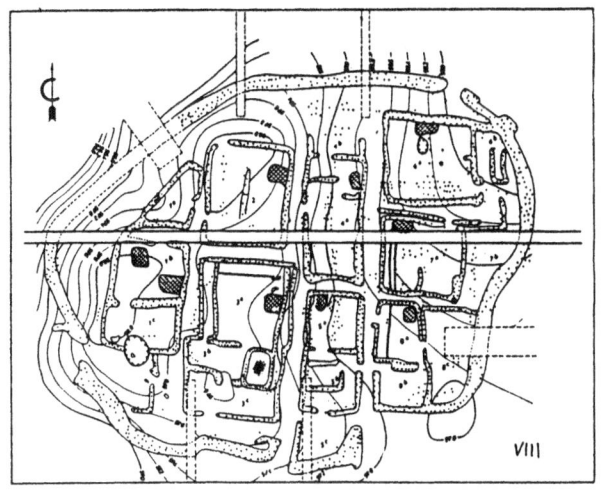

Fig. 5.1.b

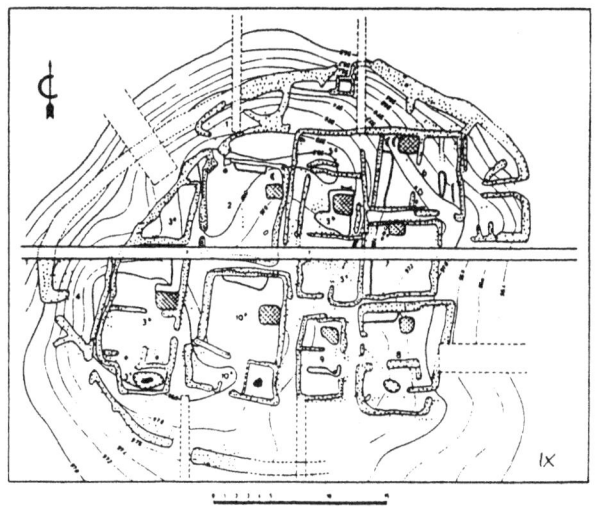

Fig. 5.1.c

On archaeological sites, the entire structures appear as bright orange or red masses of burned, collapsed clay rubble in which is impressed the shadows of the wooden framework (Fig. 5.2). Postholes, including one to three rows of internal posts, are visible beneath the collapsed superstructures and floors.

Figure 5.2 Burned and collapsed floor and superstructure of House 3 at Opovo, Serbia. (Photo: M. Trninic)

The traditional interpretation of this archaeological record of architecture has focused on how it reflects human behaviour concerning the technology of house construction, including the amount of labour (usually man-hours) involved. Many aspects of house construction can be inferred with a good deal of plausibility and consensus, since they involve the properties and manipulations of materials that are subject to principles of physics, chemistry, and biology.

House Occupation.

A focus of all prehistoric architectural studies has been on the spatial organization of partitioning and activities within houses, and the distribution of houses within a village (Kent 1991). Traditionally in European archaeology, this interest manifested itself in cleaning the house remains of all debris until the floor level was reached, at which point a map could be made of the subdivisions into rooms, and of the distribution of artifacts and furnishings (such as hearths, platforms) that were found on the floor (Fig. 5.1) (Brukner 1990; Gimbutas 1991; Kalicz and Raczky 1987; Stalio 1968; Todorova 1978; Todorovic and Cermanovic 1961). The assumption here is that, since the fires were sudden unintentional events, the situation on the floors of the house must reflect a Pompeii-type of situation — social action frozen in the midst of disaster.

The New Archaeologists of North America have fostered a growing interest in the processes by which archaeological sites are formed, as a result of which those archaeologists have become very aware of the complexities of making inferences about tasks, room functions, and the number of inhabitants on the basis of such distributions (Binford 1982, 1983; Schiffer 1987). The archaeological record of household tasks and behavior has been increased to include garbage disposal, re-use of materials, as well as off-site tasks such as gardening (Chapman 1989, 1990a). Thus the materials reflecting domestic behaviours (systems of activities) are being sought now in those areas suggested by Rapoport (Rapoport 1990) in his system of settings. That is, the areas that surround houses as well as their floors themselves, areas off-site, and in garbage pits (Coudart 1987; Hayden and Cannon 1983; McGuire and Schiffer 1983; Moore 1986; Tringham et al. 1992; Tringham, Brukner, and Voytek 1985).

The pottery and other materials excavated on the house-floors can indicate more than the distribution of tasks being carried out at the time of the fire. For example, at Gomolava we noticed that there was an uneven distribution of artifacts on the floors (Brukner 1980, 1988). This in itself has several possible interpretations. We could assume, as has so often been done in the past, that the house full of artifacts (e.g., House 80/3) was the center of domestic activity at the time of the fire, and that the emptier floor (e.g., House 80/4) represented a house that was already abandoned, or even was "poorer." Alternatively, the artifacts on the floor might be placed there deliberately, as part of the intentional act of house-burning; or floor spaces of an abandoned house might be re-used in the garbage disposal of a later neighbouring house, and the latest house might be the one with few artifacts on its floor. All of these possibilities would encourage us to seek more detailed micro-stratigraphic evidence from the floors, including details of the use-lives of the artifacts, their fragments on the floors, and in the superstructural rubble, as we did at Opovo (Tringham et al. 1992).

It has traditionally been assumed that the farmers and gardeners represented by the neolithic and eneolithic sites of southeast Europe were "egalitarian", and that we should not expect to find any evidence of social inequality in the house remains. Such a concept has been given its most eloquent expression in the Utopian scheme of peaceful co-existing matrifocal societies of Marija Gimbutas (Gimbutas 1991). In recent years however, a number of archaeologists have challenged this assumption, and have suggested that we should look for and expect short-term but very real inequalities in terms of dominance and access to human and material resources between and within households, and between genders (Bogucki 1988; Chapman 1990a, 1990b; Kaiser and Voytek 1983; Tringham 1990, 1991a).

The idea of inequality between and within the households encourages a much more detailed comparison of household units within villages. The kind of materials that are expected to reflect such behaviour include elaboration of houses, accommodation in houses of more people, evidence of access to products and the production process of, for example, minerals and clays, stone tools and ceramics, agricultural products, as well as the more obvious exotic materials (Bailey 1990; Chapman 1989, 1990a, 1990b).

The latter days of the use-life of houses

The traditional interest in the *production* (construction and maintenance) of houses has led to a focus of excavation on the house plan and any still standing architecture (wall bases) and foundations (postholes and trenches), with a relatively quick removal and undetailed record of the "messy" debris which lay above it (Todorova et al. 1983). The concept that houses have use-lives however, makes relevant several aspects of architecture that have been the object of a great deal of assumptions and superficial explanation in traditional archaeology in Europe. Nor have they been much in evidence in other archaeological practices. These aspects comprise the latter days in the life of a building; that is, the sequence of events that led to its formation as part of the archaeological record: its decay, collapse, abandonment, destruction, looting for the raw materials to build later buildings, burial and eventual replacement. How long did a house last? How did it reach the end of its use-life? When does a house die? Where is a new house to be placed? Interestingly enough, even architects themselves are shy of talking about this topic.

Destruction of houses.

The houses of the southeast European Neolithic and Eneolithic periods are characterized by evidence of house-burning which surpasses in terms of its volume and universality those settlements preceding and succeeding this period and those found anywhere else in Europe. Yet this "Burned House Horizon" has traditionally been taken for granted in European prehistory. It has been assumed that explanation was not needed beyond an intuitive common-sense reasoning that the fires were accidental, resulting from the increased use of fire within houses or the denser crowding of houses within the villages; or deliberately set fires due to inter-settlement competition, unrest, raiding, and even invasion. Once one starts to question such an assumption however, and to suggest that the coincidence of the apparently universal occurrence of house-fires with such socio-economic changes as the intensification of production, permanence of settlement, and organizational importance of autonomous households may be very significant, then all sorts of other data have to be wrested from this same "archaeological record" so that the record itself changes.

This was in fact the basis of our systematic investigation of the causes of the house fires at Opovo in the former Yugoslavia (Tringham 1990; Tringham et al. 1992, 1985). We looked for houses that did not burn and found none in the area excavated. We looked carefully in the collapsed debris – the data which is usually shoveled away as quickly as possible – for data reflecting the path and nature of the fires. The lack of burned materials in the areas between houses indicates that the houses burned in separate fires (Fig. 5.3), and burned at temperatures that in some parts of each house reached over $1000°$ C. Such temperatures are regarded as very high for accidental fires of wattle-and-daub houses and indicate that the fires are likely to have been "helped" by deliberate fueling and tending (Kirk 1969). For example, the central part of House 5 at Opovo is characterized by a massive area (ca. 3 x 3 m) of vitrified structural clay and ceramics, indicating a fire of high intensity at this point. This represents the rubble of the upper story, which collapsed along with its melted pots, which were fused to the floor in the heat of the combustion, and fell onto the lower floor along with the collapsing side walls burying, burning, crushing, and preserving the ceramics, stone, and other contents (including textile and string) of the lower floor.

Therefore, we have found data that reflect behaviour consistent with burning a single house, probably deliberately. This empirical conclusion may be interpreted in a number of ways. It may be explained, for example, as a measure to eradicate pests, insects, disease, or to signify the death of the household head as a symbolic end of the household cycle. We have shown that the fires are not something whose cause can be assumed and generalized, but must be questioned and investigated.

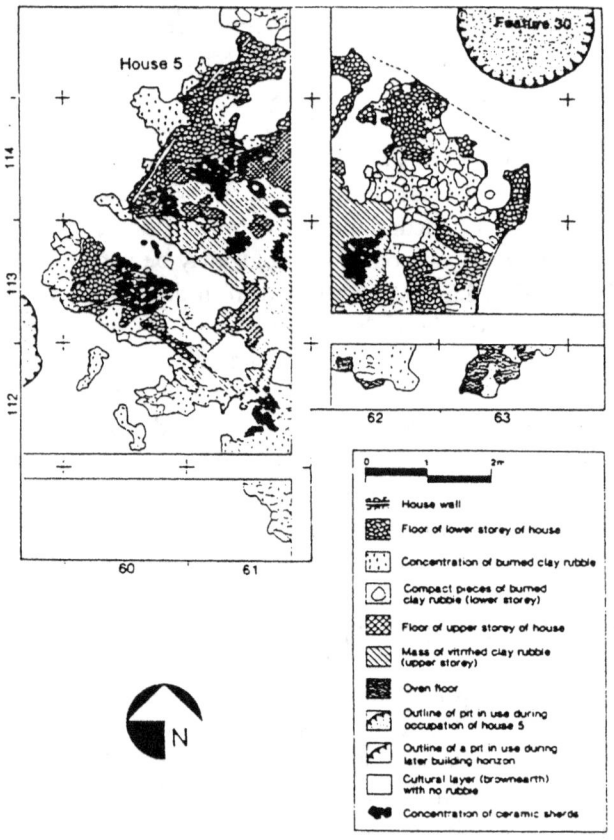

Figure 5.3: Architectural features of building horizon 3 at the Eneolithic village of Opovo.

House replacement

The Neolithic and Eneolithic villages in southeast Europe are traditionally excavated with a strategy that exposes their maximum area (hopefully the whole village) horizontally at a given time, and elucidates their chronological cultural sequence. It is a recognized practice to fuse the many years of occupation of the various houses at "a particular phase of time," and the thousands of depositional events that make up their formation as part of an archaeological site, into one generic time-frame. In such practice, individual houses and households at a particular settlement are fused into an *occupation horizon* or *building horizon* in which their individual histories (or use-lives) are concealed under an umbrella of a static time period (lasting perhaps several generations). Stratigraphy thus becomes a way of monitoring the chronological sequence of building or occupation horizons (Fig. 5.4).

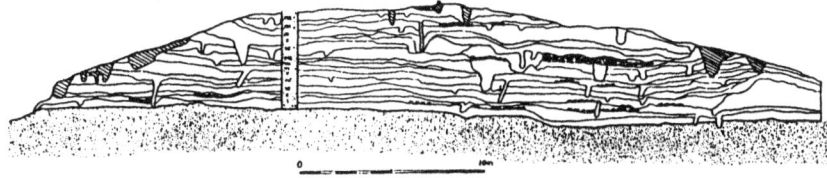

Figure 5.4: Vertical cross-section through the settlement mound (tell) of Ovcharovo, Bulgaria, showing the different building horizons (After Todorova et al. 1983).

Such a practice has also enabled the monitoring and measuring of cultural or behavioral variation through time at a particular site, as well as the establishment of cultural links and comparisons from one site to another. But it has prevented or at least discouraged the investigation of the *organic history* of a site. By this latter term I mean the processes of the destruction and abandonment of houses, and the relationship of abandoned houses to the construction of new houses (house replacement), by which the stratified occupational deposits were formed into either tells (settlement mounds) or open stratified sites. In fact, there is often an underlying assumption in the archaeology of southeast Europe that a sequence of building horizons is formed by the houses of one building horizon somehow being replaced by houses of another building horizon as a single depositional event (Bailey 1990; Chapman 1989; Todorova et al. 1983).

It is clear by now that by considering these aspects of destruction, abandonment, and replacement of houses as objects of investigation, the archaeological record is quantitatively and qualitatively increased, not only in the ways that existing excavated materials are interpreted, but also in the actual excavation methods used to retrieve the data from the ground. In directing the Opovo Archaeological Project, where we were interested in the use-lives of each house from its foundation to its burial, we developed a technology in 1983-89 to excavate and record the collapsed debris of the burned house superstructure carefully layer by layer (Fig. 5.5).

Figure 5.5: Excavation of the burned daub of the collapsed superstructure of House 2 at Opovo.

Moreover, since I was interested in the relationship of a household to a locus or loci through time, the details of the modification, destruction, and replacement history of *each* house became important. This meant that it was essential to follow an excavation strategy that would enable us to recognize the micro-stratigraphic record of the placement of one building in relation to others in time as well as in space, and of the depositional events by which a house gradually became a part of the archaeological record (Banning and Byrd 1989; Harris 1979). This was really the first time that such a scale of resolution in archaeological observation of architecture was carried out in southeast Europe.

Even at Opovo however, we did not dispense entirely with lumping the depositional events into building horizons. The settlement debris piled up over a period of about 200 years more or less continuous occupation to form a low mound over what was already a natural island in the marshes. We recognized in the area excavated (Block I), three building horizons, two of which had well preserved architectural remains (BH 1 and BH 3). The buildings of these two phases of occupation are not chronologically contiguous, being separated perhaps by one or two generations (Fig. 5.6).

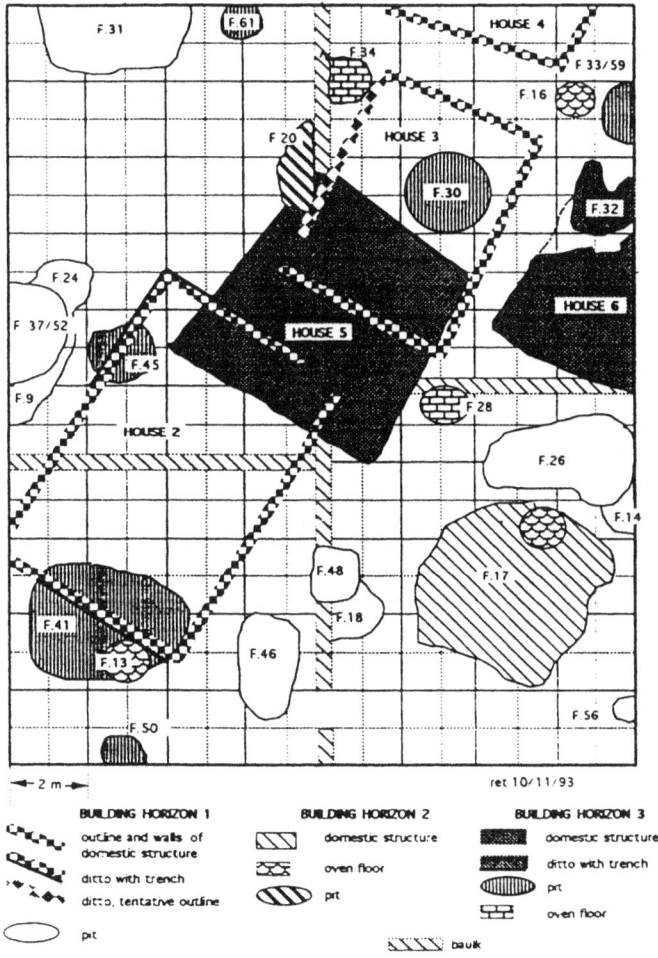

Figure 5.6: The three superimposed building horizons recognized in Block I at Opovo.

During Opovo's prehistory, efforts were made, sometimes immediately after the conflagration, to flatten the burned remains of the houses and deposit it in pits, in one case filling a probable well (Fig. 5.7). In many other cases the rubble was used, long after it had lain on the surface and had weathered, to top off garbage pits just before a new building was started. The aim of the builders of BH 1 was to use these old remains to their advantage in the construction of their dwellings, allowing old ovens and clay floors to provide a stable foundation layer and avoiding places of obvious weakness, such as filled-in pits. Thus the builders of the BH 1 structures were probably well aware of the remains of earlier building horizons, either through tradition or direct observation on or near their occupation surface. But the new houses display a certain amount of (but not complete), horizontal displacement in that their locations are not exactly above that of the old ones, I suspect because the exact location of the previous house was not known. This impression is made more plausible when we see that the corner of one of the new houses was placed directly over a previous well that had been filled in immediately after the fire of the old house (Fig. 5.7).

This pattern of house replacement at Opovo conforms to the pattern of house replacement in contexts where the area for residence was restricted by the surrounding landscape – in this case by marshland. It reminds us however, that in the southeast European Neolithic and Eneolithic periods, very contrasting patterns of house replacement have been recognized. This is the contrast between the tell or mound settlements, on the one hand, some of which were occupied for 2000 years continuously and are greater than 12 m high, and flat or open settlements, (Bailey 1990; Chapman 1989; Davidson 1976; Tringham 1990). The formation of tells are the result of a restricted settlement area in combination with intensive but not necessarily continuous occupation, and intensive accumulation of domestic debris caused, for example, by the burning of large amounts of clay daub. Some of the classic tell settlements of southeast Europe, especially those of the west Balkans such as Gomolava and Vinca, involve like Opovo a certain amount of horizontal displacement of consecutive buildings. In Bulgaria and Rumania however, the tells such as Ovcharovo and Karanovo are characterized by the vertical superimposition of buildings (Figs. 5.1 and 5.4).

As with many aspects of architectural destruction and re-location, these contrasts have traditionally not been regarded as objects of investigation, being explained by an underlying assumption that they are an adaptive response to particular topographic restrictions on settlement, such as river or marshland. But there are certainly many other reasons to restrict

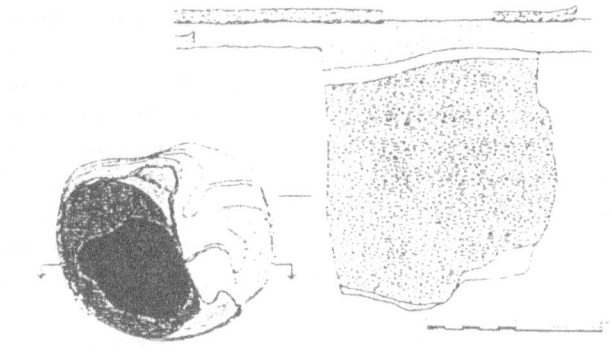

Figure 5.7: Plan, cross-section, and photographic profile of the well (Feature 30) next to House 5 at Opovo.

residence locus, such as unequal social access through inheritance and ownership of land for residence.

In his recent study of the tell question, John Chapman has suggested that the key to the contrast lies in the relationship of built to non-built land in terms of access, especially to cultivation and grazing areas (Chapman 1989). He suggests that tells reflect a situation in which cultivation land is held in common and its distribution and holding is organized at a village level. He suggests that the residence pattern of tells reflects a situation in which social stability is at a maximum and that disputes and inequalities at a minimum, in other words, a highly regulated society.

Open (non-tell) sites, on the other hand, Chapman suggests reflect a society in which the holding of land is more flexible and linked more directly to the land on which a residence is located, and where the whole is organized at a household level. In this case, it reflects a social order in which inequalities between households within a village are more marked. His ideas have encouraged him to investigate many aspects of the built environment that had been ignored (or rather whose variability had seemed irrelevant), such as the ratio of built to unbuilt space, the location and access to cultivation and grazing land, and possible patterns of cultivation.

House to home, space to place, and evolution to history

I shall argue in the rest of this paper that as the destruction and replacement of prehistoric houses become objects of investigation rather than the subject of underlying assumptions, we learn about site formation and we expand the archaeological record of architecture. Much more significantly however, these investigations enable us to progress beyond the investigation of space and house in prehistory; they enable us to consider the cultural construction of place and home in prehistory.

In this conceptual transition from space to *place* and house to home, there is another crucial factor to be considered: that is the *scale of resolution* at which archaeological observations are interpreted. I have hinted already that the traditional practice of excavating by building horizons masks the rich mosaic of individual events in the histories of houses and of the human actors, even though it allows archaeologists to compare and contrast different data sets. The history of archaeological practice has witnessed a constant struggle between the "macroscale" standpoint that considers the aim of archaeology is the recognition of evolutionary trends in prehistory, and the "microscale" standpoint that emphasizes the importance of individual histories and social actions. In the current established archaeological practice of North America and much of Europe, the former is dominant, whereas the latter is characteristic of much of the more radical standpoint of post-processual archaeology, including the feminist critique. The feminist critique of archaeological practice advocates a *multiscalar* interpretation that has not often been put into practice, but which I shall describe in more detail below.

The interpretation of archaeological architecture is a reflection of these different standpoints, many of which are represented in this volume. Amos Rapoport and Susan Kent advocate the value of cross-cultural generalizations to be made about the evolution of cultures and people-environment relations (Kent 1990, 1991; Rapoport 1976, 1990). They have emphasized the possibilities of coming up with real general principles about bounding space, spatial organization of tasks in space, and so on, that could be used for consideration in the design of modern living spaces. These are based on a comparative analysis of worldwide and timewide ethnographic and archaeological samples. Such "macroscale" questions relating to the evolution of architectural styles, social complexity, and man [sic] -environment relations are ultimately the focus of most examinations of archaeological architecture, whether by archaeologists or architects.[1]

Such "macroscale" questions comprise the main aim of the European archaeologists, whom I have been discussing, including myself at one point in my life. In this process of asking "macroscale" questions, it is understandable that individual houses from specific sites become normalized to be typical of and to "stand for" the cultural whole. In the process of discovering explanatory general principles, individual variability is understood as exceptional and of secondary relevance. In such generalizing, the "microscale" interpretation of house histories, the causes of individual house-fires, and the small inequalities between households in access to land and resources tend to be undervalued as irrelevant.

My own orientation however, has recently come to focus on "microscale" and historical questions such as these. Without denying the value of the evolutionary comparative viewpoint and questioning, I prefer to consider archaeology's contribution as a multiscalar exploration – both temporal and spatial – of variability and cultural expression in prehistory and history. In such an exploration, the lives and actions of individual families and members of those families are given equal priority to the longer, and wider-scale view in which these individual acts and perceptions are normalized and homogenized.

There are many paths to this humanistic and historical approach. The path which interests me is inspired by the structuration theory of Anthony Giddens, the theory of social practice of Pierre Bourdieu, and the theory of place of Allan Pred. Of these, Pred's concept of place that focuses on the transformation of spatial structures in a historical context, seem most relevant to my own investigation of archaeological architecture.

Pred has rewritten Marx's statement that "men [and women] make their own history, but they do not make it just as they please; they do not make it under circumstances chosen for themselves, but under circumstances directly encountered, given and transmitted from the past" to read:

Women and men make histories and produce places, not under circumstances of their own choosing but in the context of already existing, directly encountered social and spatial structures, in the context of already existing social and spatial relations that both enable and constrain the purposeful conduct of life. (Pred 1990, 9)

What occurs in the course of any local or larger-scaled transformation is not merely the making of histories but the making of historical geographies. And the unchosen circumstances under which historical geographies are constructed always subsume both existing power relations and their associated social logics, rules of behaviour, and modes of regulation (social structures), on the one hand, and the buildings, land-use patterns, and other features of humanly transformed nature already existing within a given geographical area (spatial structures), on the other. (Pred 1990, 229)

In Pred's concept, the production of place is a historically contingent process by which universally present components such as an unbroken flow of local events and "projects" (the reproduction of social and cultural forms), the formation of biographies of social actors (men and women), and the life histories of made objects such as the built environment (the transformation of nature) are interwoven differently with each local historical circumstance (Pred 1984, 284). Places are constantly changing, as is their meaning to the actors involved in their production, and as are people's relations to each other. Local places are interwoven dialectically to larger places, daily paths and practices to life paths and generational and long-term paths.

For an archaeologist, the investigation of places that are always "becoming" can serve as a viable alternative object of knowledge to testing a generally applicable theory by formal cross-cultural observation. Thus, the universal components of *place-becoming* or *place-production* are not subject to universal laws or general principles (Pred 1984, 291). In this respect, his concept of place-production contrasts with that of Stea and Turan (Stea and Turan, 1990). In Pred's opinion, it is the interweaving of the universal components in the formation and transformation of actual places in real historical situations that becomes the object of knowledge. Our aim then, as archaeologists, is the interpretive writing or construction of prehistoric narratives, rather than the analysis of the archaeological record to reconstruct prehistory.

In constructing the prehistory of different places in southeast Europe, I have relied heavily on the information of domestic architecture. Most of what we excavate is from the everyday world of housework. The theories of Pred, Giddens, Bourdieu, and even Tuan suggest that the rich variability of human relations in the domestic sphere is relevant to the course of human history; that what men and women do in relation to domestic space, their negotiations for power, their negotiations about housework and where to put the garbage, *do* affect the ways in which cultural rules are formed and transformed and the ways that societies reproduce themselves.

Archaeology of the home: The ancient home

I will now consider the interplay of the following components of place-production in prehistory, such as:

1. house biographies

2. the biographies of the actors (the dialectic between their life path and daily path, and between their individual and institutional roles)

3. the social action itself (production and distribution projects as social forms, the dominance structure of social practice)

In doing this, I know that I have to face the challenge of the ambiguity of archaeological data (Tringham 1991a). Rather than shy away from these topics because they cannot be "found" in the archaeological data, I prefer to change my strategy of archaeological investigation by celebrating the ambiguity of the archaeological record, by considering multiple interpretations of the same data, and by a more explicit use of creative imagination. In other words, I must begin to practice a more interpretive archaeology (Hodder 1991; Shanks 1991; Shanks and Tilley 1987; Tringham 1991b, Tringham Forthcoming). For it seems to me that this is the only way that space can be linked to place, that house can be linked to housework and to household and, that all, ultimately, can be linked to the cultural construction of home. In the end, much about the definition of place overlaps with that of home.

My starting point in this interpretive study of what is essentially the prehistoric home in southeast Europe has comprised the material constraints on our interpretations, built up by all the generations of archaeologists and their research that I have outlined above. At this point, I can begin to interpret the archaeological record in terms of the interplay of architecture and its surrounding landscape as arena and construct of social action.

The (pre)history of the cultural construction of place and home can be told through the archaeological investigation of the *life-history* of each house.

In such a study, the house has to be considered as an individual, as a dynamic entity whose every month of life is significant for the men and women who act in and around it. It seems to me that the concept of life-history of the house has a more historical and humanistic significance than the term *use-life*. It concerns the time aspect – the duration of the house, the continuity of its next generation (its replacement), its ancestors and descendants, the memories of it that are held by its actors, the ghosts that are held within its walls and under its foundations. In other words, I become interested in its biography. In this respect, I am interested not only in its appearance of external wall and bounded interior space, but its appearance on the broader landscape through time. In archaeological terms this is the study of "space as a vertical construct" (Bailey 1990).

Douglass Bailey is one of the few archaeologists who has attempted this kind of biography in his re-interpretation of the excavations of the tell settlement of Ovcharovo in Bulgaria (Bailey 1990). He traced the continuity of specific houses through the twelve building horizons recorded in the stratigraphy of the tell (Todorova et al. 1983) (Fig. 5.8). Much of Bailey's discussion of the importance of the continuity of house and its locus on the land touches on what others would call the home. He suggests, following Bourdieu, that the meaning of the house is different for different actors. But in Bailey's interpretation, the meaning of the house is understood at the scale of the household in which the individual actors are masked. He envisages a world in which there is mounting competition for claims to locus of residence on the mound (tell) and a need to legitimize such claims because of an increasing population. He has an interesting idea that small clay house-models that occur in the archaeological record of the tells are symbolic aids to the legitimization of these claims (Fig. 5.9). To a great extent, the limitations of Douglass Bailey's model were determined by the strategy by which his archaeological data (and therefore his material parameters) were retrieved. At Ovcharovo, as mentioned above, in accord with traditional practice, the house remains were not excavated with a view to constructing individual house-biographies. They were excavated as a stratified sequence of floor-plans, grouped according to building horizon, and Bailey has not questioned this grouping (Todorova et al. 1983).

A crucial limitation to the ability of Douglass Bailey's model to address the question of place and home however, lies, in my opinion, in the distance to which he dares to take his imagination in constructing prehistoric narratives. The unit or actor of his narrative is the household, the driving force is "competition for land" and "need to legitimize the household's claim to land." As Bailey has himself stated, "places" and "homes" are created by boys and girls, young men and young women, old men and

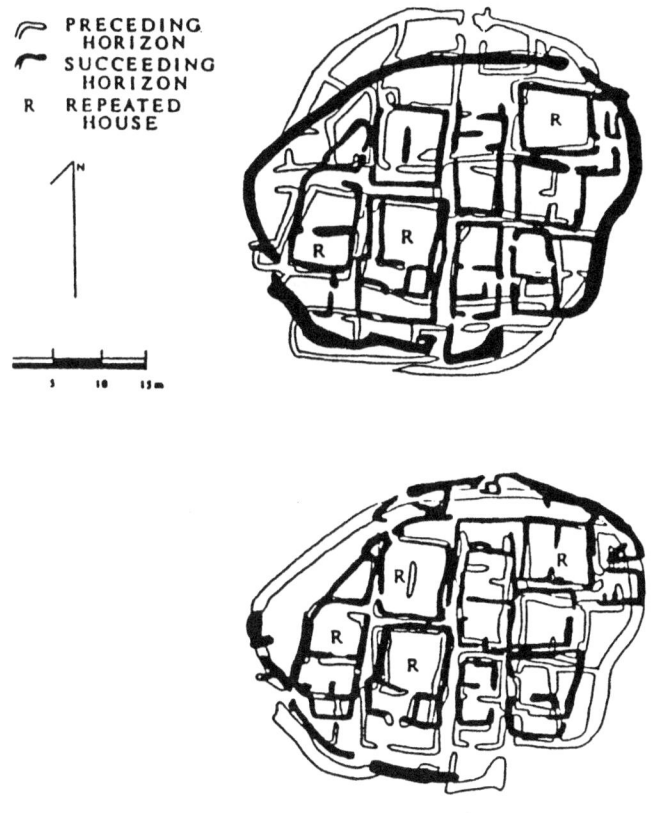

Figure 5.8: Superimposition of floor-plans of houses in various building horizons at Ovcharovo, Bulgaria, showing continuity of certain houses. (After Bailey 1990).

women as individuals, and members of a social group; they are created differently throughout their lives through their experience, perception, and memory of social practice (Boschetti 1986; Porteous 1990; Rodman 1992; Rybczynski 1986; Tuan 1977). But Bailey himself has chosen to normalize these experiences for purposes of comparison and recognizing general trends.

The variable standpoints and experience, as well the breadth of imagination and reading from ethnography and history of the archaeologists who excavate and interpret the materials that generate creations of prehistoric home and place, direct the selection of both the scale and the content of the interpretations. Douglass Bailey is apparently someone who is used to his own space and feels threatened by people crowding in on him. For him, significant social action, such as competition for space, happens *between* groups or families, not between individuals, for example, of different genders, within families.

Figure 5.9 House model found in the settlement mound at Ovcharovo, Bulgaria. (After Todorova 1983).

I see the world very differently. Accordingly, my own narrative of what the world of the Ovcharovo tell was like, and what kind of behavior was generated by the house-models, would have been very different from that of Bailey. According to the theory of structuration to which I am attracted, the variability and transformation of cultural ideologies that we hope to observe at a macroscale are achieved by a process of negotiations and social action by individuals. Thus, at some point in writing prehistory, archaeologists have to dare to interpret their data and imagine (and write narratives about) life at this "microscale." Moreover, gender and age are such powerful dimensions to social life that it seems to me personally essential to consider them in any prehistoric narrative. A growing density of houses on the Ovcharovo tell to me means that there was an organic growth of the households on the mound through the cycles of growth and decline of each household. In this context, negotiation and working around authority is the way that most families and individuals would have run their social practice. A simple correlation of overt symbol (house-model) with power-over (land-claim) legitimation is much less likely in my imagination than personal protective symbol (house-model) with power-to (ability) control one's own fate in, for example, a new husband's house.

An Opovo-Ovcharovo story

One logical extension of my consideration of historically contingent places in prehistory is to write in creative narrative form, incorporating the details of the archaeological record and "macroscale" and "microscale" interpretive models.

The story that I present here is one snippet from a young woman's life or memory. She was born in a large village that might have been Ovcharovo, and is married off to an older man as his second wife. They live in a small village that might be Opovo in the marshlands far away. This story expresses the idea that for her home is the place where she was born. The crowding and competition of her home village is idealized in her memory to mean life, noise, and support for many other women, in stark contrast to the isolation of her life at Opovo (Fig. 5.10).

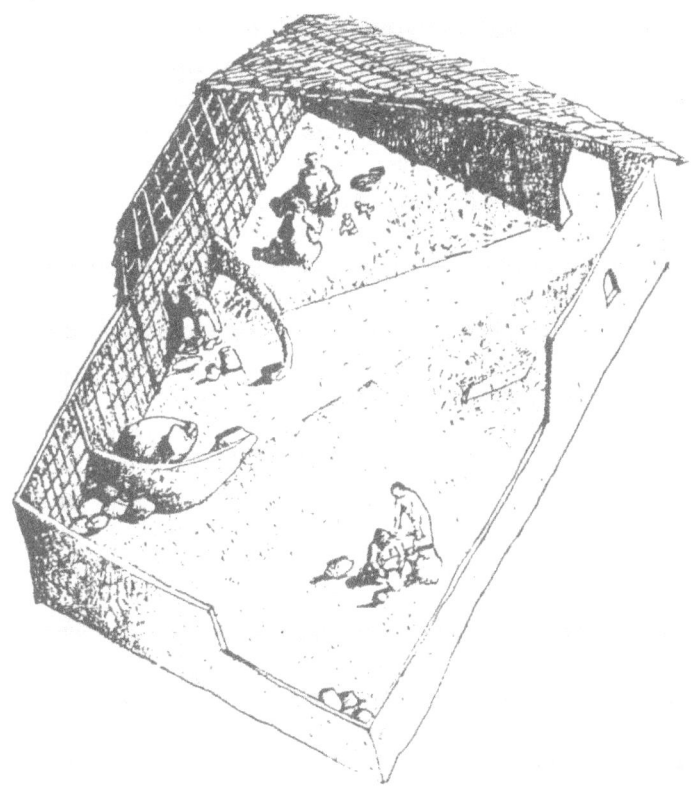

Figure 5.10: Cut-away axonometric view of the interior of House 2 at Opovo (C. Chang).

This house, it's so small. There's no place for anything. He's looking at me. He can see everything. She's watching too. Why doesn't she come in here to keep me company. Tell me what to do. Help me. They're just waiting for me to do something wrong. Have I got to do everything for them? That can't be so. Take their eyes away. Make it dark in here. There's so much light. It's not natural. The oven – at least she's a friend. She looks the same. She must be her. She must be the same one. Where's my little house? I've lost it! Maybe they took it! I need it. I want it. It's my only link with home. ...It's so quiet here. I feel so alone. Except those flies. No they're not flies. Flies don't suck your blood, and make ugly sores on your face. Where is everyone? It's so quiet. There's nothing to do here, no one to talk to. And it smells. You can't get away from it. Inside. Outside. You can't get away.

This is not a story written for its own sake as an escapist novel. Nor, by writing, and through the accompanying illustration, visualizing the places such as Opovo and Ovcharovo, have I produced any true facts or picture of prehistoric social action. I have followed through an interpretation of the significant change in the archaeological pattern of settlement described at Opovo at the end of the Neolithic in Southeast Europe – the dispersal of settlement onto agriculturally marginal lands.

I think however, that I have dramatically expanded the scope in which the architectural context of prehistory (house, artifacts, furniture) can be used to construct a prehistory – many prehistories! Artifacts, such as an undecorated hearth, become more significant potentially, rather than forgotten in the depths of some archaeological report. The significance of a house-model has multiple possibilities, rather than one true interpretation. The invisible arena of the most dramatic social action – housework – takes on a more visible and important role. A house, or a site, becomes important in its own historical trajectory, rather than as a sample from which the whole is to be extrapolated.

Why/How the ancient home - modern internationalized home?

The archaeological materials that constrain my imagination and the interpretive narratives about the prehistory of southeast Europe concern how a place or a home might have been created by the men and women of that historically specific time and place. That specific time is 6000 years and 2000 kilometers distant from the modern Scandinavian home. My last question in this paper is whether there is any connection between the two – the "Ancient Home and Modern Internationalized Home." That is, what lesson is to be learned from an archaeological consideration of home?

My answer would be that an ahistorical (i.e., non-historically contingent) place or home cannot be created. All places and homes are created by their actors on the basis of their past and present context. The archaeologists who create stories about the ancient home each have their own history and emotions about home and place. What I am advocating, if anything, is that you listen to your own history and prehistory before you appropriate the ancient home of other places and other times: other heres and nows.

Endnote

1. For a fuller bibliographic referencing to back up this generalized statement, see (Tringham 1991a, b).

References

Bailey, Douglass. 1990. The Living House: Signifying Continuity. In *The Social Archaeology of Houses*, ed. R. Samson. Edinburgh: Edinburgh University Press.

Banning, E.B., and Brian F. Byrd. 1989. Renovations and the Changing Residential Unit at 'Ain Ghazal, Jordan. In *Households and Communities*, ed. S. MacEachern, D. Archer, and R. Garvin. Calgary: Chacmool.

Binford, Lewis, R. 1981. *Bones: Ancient Men and Modern Myths*. N.Y.: Academic Press.

———. 1982. The Archaeology of Place. *Journal of Anthropo-logical Archaeology* 1 (1).

———. 1983. *In Pursuit of the Past*. London: Thames and Hudson.

Bogucki, Peter. 1988. *Forest Farmers and Stockherders: Early Agriculture and its Consequences in North-Central Europe*. Cambridge: Cambridge University Press.

Boschetti, Margaret. 1986. Emotional Attachment to Homes Past and Present: Continuity of Experience and Integrity of Self in Old Age. In *Architecture in Cultural Change: Essays in Built Form and Culture Research*, ed. D. Saile. School of Architecture and Urban Design, University of Kansas.

Bourdier, Jean-Paul. 1989. Reading Tradition. In *Dwellings, Settlements and Traditions: Cross-Cultural Perspectives*, ed. J.-P. Bourdier and N. AlSayyad. Lanham, MD: University Press of America.

Bourdieu, P. 1990. *The Logic of Practice*. Cambridge: Polity Press.

Brukner, Bogdan. 1980. Naselje Vincanske Grupe na Gomolavi (neolitski ranoeneolitski sloj). In *Rad Vojvodjanskih Muzeja* 26.

———. 1988. Die Siedlung der Vinca-Gruppe auf Gomolava (Die Wohnschicht des Spätneolithikums und Frühäneolithikums-Gomolava Ia-b und Gomolava va Ib) und der Wohnhorizont des äneolithischen Humus (Gomolava II). In *Gomolava: Hronologija i Stratigrafija u Praistoriji i Antici Podunavlja i Jugoistocne Evrope*, ed. N. Tasic and J. Petrovic. Novi Sad: Vojvodanski Muzej and Balkanoloski Institut SAN.

———. 1990. Typen und Siedlunges Modellen und Wohn-Objekte der Vinca-Gruppe in der Panonischen Tiefebene. In *Vinca and its World*, ed. D. Srejovic and N. Tasic. Belgrade: Serbian Academy of Sciences and Arts.

Chapman, John. 1989. The Early Balkan Village. In *Neolithic of Southeastern Europe and its Near Eastern Connections*. Varia Archaeologica 2 (Budapest.

———. 1990a. *Regional Study of the North Lumadija Region*. In *Selevac: a Prehistoric Village in Yugoslavia*, ed. R. Tringham and D. Krstic. Monumenta Archaeologica 15. Los Angeles: UCLA Institute of Archaeology Press.

———. 1990b. Social Inequality on Bulgarian Tells and the Varna Problem. In *The Social Archaeology of Houses*, ed. R. Samson. Edinburgh: Edinburgh University Press.

Cosgrove, Denis. 1984. *Social Formation and Symbolic Landscape*. London: Croom Helm.

Coudart, Anick. 1987. Tradition, Uniformity, and Variability of the Architecture in the Danubian Neolithic. Paper read at the International Seminar of the Neolithic Site of Bylany. Prague: AUCSAV.

Davidson, D. A. 1976. Processes of Tell Formation and Erosion. In *Geoarchaeology: Earth Sciences and the Past.*, ed. D. A. Davidson and M. Shackley. London: Duckworth.

Donley-Reid, Linda. 1990. A Structuring Structure: the Swahili House. In *Domestic Architecture and the Use of Space*, ed. S. Kent. Cambridge: Cambridge University Press.

Giddens, Anthony. 1979. *Central Problems in Social Theory: Action, Structure, and Contradiction in Social Analysis*. Berkeley: University of California Press.

———. 1984. *The Constitution of Society*. Berkeley: University of California Press.

Gimbutas, Marija. 1991. *Civilization of the Goddess.* San Francisco: Harper and Row.
Harris, E. C. 1979. *Principles of Archaeological Stratigraphy.* London: Academic Press.
Hayden, Brian, and Aubrey Cannon. 1983. Where the Garbage Goes: Refuse Disposal in the Maya Highlands. In *Journal of Anthropological Archaeology* 2.
Hodder, Ian. 1986. *Reading the Past.* Cambridge: Cambridge University Press.
———, ed. 1987. *The Archaeology of Contextual Meanings.* Cambridge: Cambridge University Press.
———. 1991. Interpretive Archaeology and its Role. *American Antiquity* 56(1).
Isaac, Glynn. 1976. The Activites of Early African Hominids: A Review of Archaeological Evidence from the Time Span Two and a Half to One Million Years Ago. In *Human Origins: Louis Leakey and the East African Evidence.* ed. G. L. I. Isaac and E. R. McCowan. Menlo Park, California: Staple Press.
Kaiser, T., and B. Voytek. 1983. Sedentism and Economic Change in the Balkan Neolithic. *Journal of Anthropological Archaeology* 2.
Kalicz, N., and P. Raczky. 1987. The Late Neolithic of the Tisza Region. A Survey of Recent Archaeological Research. In *The Late Neolithic of the Tisza Region,* ed. L. Talas, P. Raczky, et al. Budapest: Szolnok.
Kent, Susan. 1990. A Cross-Cultural Study of Segmentation, Architecture and the Use of Space. In *Domestic Architecture and the Use of Space,* ed. S. Kent. Cambridge: Cambridge University Press.
———. 1991. Partitioning Space: Cross-Cultural Factors Influencing Domestic Spatial Segmentation. *Environment and Behavior* 23 (4).
Kirk, Paul. 1969. *Fire Investigation.* N.Y.: John Wiley & Sons Inc.
McGuire, Randall, and Michael Schiffer. 1983. A Theory of Architectural Design. *Journal of Anthropological Archaeology* 2.
Moore, Henrietta. 1986. *Space, Text, and Gender.* Cambridge: Cambridge University Press.
Patrik, Linda. 1985. *Is there an Archaeological Record?* Advances in Archaeological Method and Theory 8, edited by M. Schiffer. N.Y.: Academic Press.
Porteous, Douglas. 1990. *Landscapes of the Mind: Worlds of Sense and Metaphor.* Toronto: University of Toronto Press.
Pred, Allan. 1984. Place as Historically Contingent Process: Structuration and the Time-Geography of Becoming Places. *Annals of the Association of American Geographers* 74(2).

———. 1990. *Making Histories and Constructing Human Geographies.* Boulder, Co.: Westview Press.

Rapoport, Amos. 1976. Sociocultural Aspects of Man-Environment Studies. In *The Mutual Interaction of People and Their Built Environment*, ed. A. Rapoport. The Hague: Mouton Publishers.

———. 1990. Systems of Activities and Systems of Settings. In *Domestic Architecture and the Use of Space*, ed. S. Kent. Cambridge: Cambridge University Press.

Rodman, Margaret. 1992. Empowering Place: Multilocality and Multivocality. *American Anthropologist* 94 (3).

Rybczynski, Witold. 1986. *Home: a Short History of an Idea.* N.Y.: Viking Penguin.

Schiffer, Michael. 1987. *Formation Processes of the Archaeological Record.* Albuquerque: University of New Mexico Press.

Shanks, Michael. 1991. *Experiencing the Past: on the Character of Archaeology.* London: Routledge.

Shanks, Michael, and Christopher Tilley. 1987. *Re-Constructing Archaeology.* Cambridge: Cambridge University Press.

Soja, E. 1989. *Postmodern Geographies: The Reassertion of Space in Critical Social Theory.* London: Verso.

Stalio, Blazenka. 1968. Naselje i Stan Neolitskog Perioda. In *Neolit Centralnog Balkana.* Beograd: Narodni Muzej.

Stea, David, and Mete Turan. 1990. A Statement on Placemaking. In *Vernacular Architecture*, ed. M. Turan. Aldershot, UK: Avebury.

Todorova, Henrietta. 1978. *The Eneolithic Period in Bulgaria in the Fifth Millenium B.C.* International Series 49. Oxford: British Archaeological Reports.

Todorova, Henrietta, Vasil Vasiliev, I. Ianusecic, M. Koracheva, and P. Valev, eds. 1983. *Ovcharovo.* Sofia: Archaeological Institute of the Bulgarian Academy of Sciences.

Todorovic, Jovan, and Aleksandrina Cermanovic. 1961. *Banjica. Naselje v Ncanske Kulture.* Belgrade.

Tringham, Ruth. 1978. Experimentation, Ethnoarchaeology and the Leapfrogs in Archaeological Methodology. In *Explorations in Ethnoarchaeology*, ed. R. Gould. Albuquerque: University of New Mexico Press.

———. 1990. Conclusion: Selevac in the Wider Context of European Prehistory. In *Selevac: a Prehistoric Village in Yugoslavia*, ed. R. Trinhham and D. Krstic. Monumenta Archaeologica 15. Los Angeles: UCLA Institute of Archaeology Press.

———. 1991a. Households with Faces: the Challenge of Gender in Prehistoric Architectural Remains. In *Engendering Archaeology: Women and Prehistory,* ed. J. Gero and M. Conkey. Oxford: Basil Blackwell.

———. 1991b. Men and Women in Prehistoric Architecture. *Traditional Dwellings and Settlements Review* 3 (1).

———. Engendered Places in Prehistory. Forthcoming.

Tringham, R., B. Brukner, T. Kaiser, et al. 1992. The Opovo Project: A Study of Socio-Economic Change in the Balkan Neolithic. 2nd preliminary report. *Journal of Field Archaeology* 19 (3).

Tringham, R., B. Brukner, and B. Voytek. 1985. The Opovo Project: a Study of Socio-Economic Change in the Balkan Neolithic. *Journal of Field Archaeology* 12 (4).

Tuan, Yi-Fu. 1977. *Space and Place: The Perspective of Experience.* Minneapolis: University of Minnesota Press.

6

House and Home in Viking Age Iceland: Cultural Expression in Scandinavian Colonial Architecture

Neil S. Price

Introduction

One of the most pressing problems facing archaeologists working in the Viking Age is the recognition of manifestations of personal, cultural, and ethnic identity in the archaeological record. In the archaeology of the Scandinavian overseas colonies in the north Atlantic, England, the Celtic West, north-west France and Russia, this is usually expressed in its most basic form of simply trying to isolate anything at all in the surviving material culture which could be interpreted as specifically Scandinavian. The true nature of the question is, of course, much more complex. Its reflections may be found in numerous aspects of human activity, from the built environment (settlement form, building traditions), to portable material culture and its semiotic content (artefact types, artistic motifs, symbolism), through social action (negotiations of power, religious practice, mortuary behaviour), and communication (place-names, linguistic material), to mention only the most obvious.

In the Scandinavian colonial sphere, these problems are sharpened by the sheer complexity of the cultural range involved: in the West, interaction between the Anglo-Saxon English, Celts, and Franks; in the East, between Slavs, Balts, Finns, and Sámi. Each of these groups in turn contain many levels of social, ethnic, and political affiliations and variations. Most importantly, the Scandinavians with whom these people came into contact were not themselves a homogenous group. Among them we meet merchants, adventurers, mercenaries, settlers, soldiers, pirates, exiles, not to mention the range of social classes and above all the individual women and men that we perceive in the excavated evidence. Nor must we forget the Vikings themselves (the word is not synonymous with contemporary Scandinavians), whose precise attributes and identities are regrettably beyond the scope of this paper.

One specific area of this debate in which dramatic archaeological inroads may be made is the study of identity as expressed in domestic architecture: one aspect of this may be called the concept of the *home*. In this paper I want briefly to discuss the preliminary results of a study which may go some way towards the recovery of such concepts from the material record. Although the technique is based on a system of spatial analysis originally designed for architectural studies, it can also be applied in a variant form to building design in the Viking Age. The primary focus will be on structures from the early settlement period in Iceland, but the results presented below have implications beyond Iceland and other areas of colonial expansion to the Scandinavian homelands themselves.

Archaeology and architecture: Spatial analysis

To date, most comparisons between early Medieval buildings have been made in an attempt to examine any kind of personal or cultural expression on the basis of building style, size, shape, constructional technique, and appearance. With the exception of stylistic embellishment, it would seem that these factors are all largely functional by-products of local resources, topography, available building space, climate, environment, and technical skill, all of which are quite independent of cultural background, and therefore unsuitable as indicators of social practice. This paper will argue that a more profitable area of enquiry in a search for an identifiable Scandinavian concept of the home is the possible existence of a culturally diagnostic *spatial pattern*, expressed in architecture and reproduced over a wide geographical area. Spatial pattern is here used to mean the spatial configuration or layout of buildings, and their contingent properties.

Studies of many cultures – principally in an ethnographic context, and notably the Inuit, Sámi. Native Americans, and Siberian nomads – have demonstrated the cultural constitution of building design and spatial form, and the potential for its articulation as a means of expressing personal, cultural, and ethnic identity.[1] (The Sámi *kåhte* with its principal spatial and symbolic oppositions is shown as an example in Fig. 6.1)

This social organisation of space has been studied through many forms of spatial analysis, most often developed by architects and geographers (see Hodder and Orton 1976; Hietala 1984; Kent 1990; Samson 1991, for general reading). Among the most recent archaeological applications of these, have been the attempts to isolate abstract generative principles which may be analyzed and quantified in the morphology of buildings, as typified in the "shape grammars" of Stiny and Gips (1978) and the pattern languages of the Berkeley school (Alexander, Ishigawa and Silverstein 1977); it is notable that the recognition of the archaeological value of these studies has often come more than a decade after their adoption (and sometimes rejection) by the architectural community.

Despite this barrage of work, the central problem of deducing process from form has remained (a given spatial pattern may be produced by many different spatial processes), but spatial analysis has now begun to explicitly consider the constant factors which may underpin (and perhaps explain) a spatial pattern, rather than studying it in isolation.

Spatial patterning carries social information and content, for just as the form of a building assembles empty spaces into a pattern (in both functional and stylistic contexts), the specific way in which space is ordered is also the purpose of the building. Similarly, while the positioning of boundaries and access points across these boundaries (i.e., walls and doors) transform space through the medium of objects, this spatial ordering also structures the relations between the people who use the buildings; the spatial form "provides the material preconditions for the patterns of movement, encounter and avoidance which are the material realisation [and]...sometimes the generator...of social relations" (Hillier and Hanson 1984, ix).

A noticeable feature of most earlier techniques of spatial analysis was that they contained implicit notions of distance and location within their methodologies. What seemed to be missing was a purely descriptive means of measuring and comparing the morphological features of settlement space that could be determined by social processes and structures (accepting the concept of socially organised space mentioned above). In the early 1980s, two scholars from the Bartlett School of Architecture and Planning in London, Bill Hillier and Julienne Hanson, began developing such a descriptive system with what they have called "a structural anthropological approach to the pattern-forming dimensions of society" (ibid., 5). After its initial testing stages, this system – known as "space syntax" – was published in 1984 in their book *The Social Logic of Space*.

Hillier and Hanson's theories rested on the complete rejection of earlier territorially deterministic ideas of spatial organisation, which assumed constant links between individual social groups (in a biological sense) and recognizable spatial domains. The alternative, they suggested, was a link between spatial order and individual cultural groups: the primary influence of social structure on space. (While arguing for this primacy, Hillier and Hanson acknowledged that the degree of influence was culturally variable.)

Similarly rejected were theories that took an environmental or geographical approach, in which spatial order was conditioned by climatic factors or in which social structure was itself dictated by spatial organization. In essence, their work was an elaboration on that of architectural semiologists, in which the built environment was seen as expressing social meaning through systems of signs – "a systematics of appearances" (Hillier and Hanson 1984, 6–8). Their development of this was to demonstrate how spatial organization does not just represent social patterns, but is actually the physical embodiment and constitution of them. They argued that buildings could be defined as "objects whose spatial form is a form of spatial ordering," and that through this ordering of space, the human-constructed world is already a form of social behavior (ibid., 9). This creation of a particular spatial order for social purposes may take place by a combination of design or accumulation, and through this pattern a given society or culture may be both constrained and – most importantly from an archaeological perspective – recognizable.

Laying their emphasis on describing and analyzing spatial patterns prior to examining their causative external agencies, Hillier and Hanson developed a form of "syntactic grammar" – a kind of basic architectural vocabulary for the ordering of space within a building or settlement. In terms of practical methodology, this went through many phases of development (mostly by statistical and computer manipulation), but all the techniques used focused especially on the inter-relationships of different defined spaces, and on the routes of access between them (i.e., transitional spaces: corridors, entrance complexes, etc.). The methods used, in their most pared-down form, revolve around the permeability of buildings – the sequential access possible to different parts of the overall structure from given points within it, or more usually, from outside the structure. This is expressed visually by means of accessibility or *gamma maps*, in which symbols representing separate defined spaces (rooms, passages etc.) are linked by lines showing paths of access between them. In this way, the different routes by which an individual can negotiate the rooms and passageways of a building can be accurately charted and displayed.

An example of the basic method is shown in Fig. 6.2, depicting a hypothetical one-storey house with front and back yards. In Hillier and Hanson's analysis, any structure is surrounded by a carrier space, which contains it and from which it is entered; in physical terms, this carrier space may be the street which fronts a house, the open countryside around a rural dwelling, or any other surrounding space. The carrier space is represented by an encircled cross on the gamma maps, and other symbols may be used to denote defined and transitional spaces. In the example of the

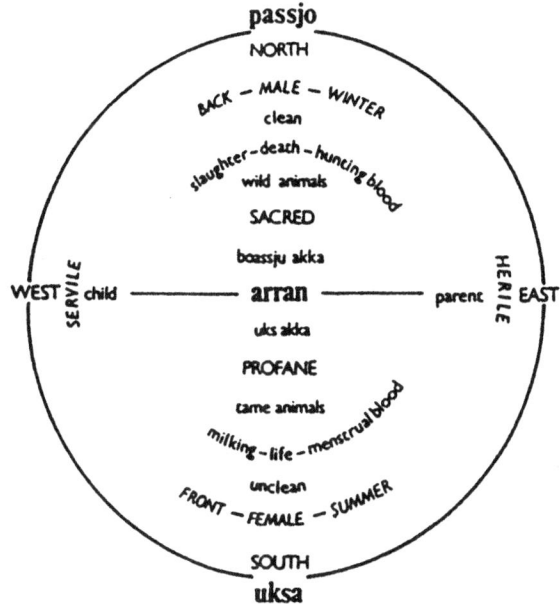

Fig. 6.1. Social meaning expressed in spatial terms: the principle oppositions found in the groundplan of a Sámi *káhte* tent (after Yates 1989).

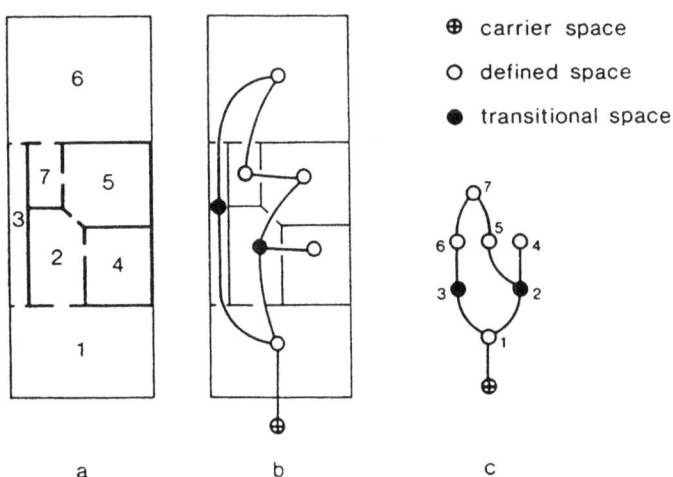

Fig. 6.2. Hillier and Hanson's access analysis: an example of a hypothetical one-storey house (after Hillier and Hanson 1984; Foster 1989).

house, the permeability map is first superimposed on the plan of the building; it may be seen how each space is indicated by a symbol, and is connected to its neighbours by an access line. Finally, the map is taken separately and justified into a series of successive levels or shells. These shells represent the position of each defined space as its "depth" within the structure, moving from the carrier space to the most inaccessible space. Each space is number-coded so its position on the house-plan can be identified; in more sophisticated maps, such as those presented below, more symbols can be used to indicate precise room function. The method of gamma mapping provides an objective tool of spatial description for building design, and can be applied not just to individual structures but to whole settlements. Its great advantage is that the maps are in no way related to physical appearance (especially the size and shape of rooms), only to relative spatial positioning. This means that structures with the same permeability map may appear quite different when visually compared as building plans, or conversely, that very similar-looking buildings may have totally different spatial patterns.

An example of this is shown in Fig. 6.3, which illustrates three houses designed by the architect Frank Lloyd Wright. Although the buildings differ in their proportions and style, we find that they all have exactly the same permeability map.

There are, however, a number of drawbacks to the concept of space syntax as formally defined by its designers. The main problem centers on their insistence that spatial form is a direct function of social relationships, and in particular that these social patterns can be inferred from studying building organization. That an element of social information and context is encoded within spatial ordering is beyond doubt (and the authors admit that its predominance as a guiding principle is variable), but some critics have argued that Hillier and Hanson have gone too far in their interpretation of the social use of space (cf., Leach 1978). Hillier and Hanson illustrate their gamma maps and related techniques of spatial analysis with reference to a wide range of archaeologically — and anthropologically — recorded structures, and it is clear that they have recognized the potential of their methods for archaeological research.[2] With this in mind, we must acknowledge a degree of caution. If the techniques of gamma mapping are to be effective in the study of excavated buildings and settlements, it is clearly necessary to possess the complete plan of a structure, including all doorways and boundaries. The extent to which a knowledge of room function is also necessary for the system to work, or whether in fact it is this very information and its corresponding social patterns that the maps will provide, is at the heart of debate on the subject. It must be emphasized

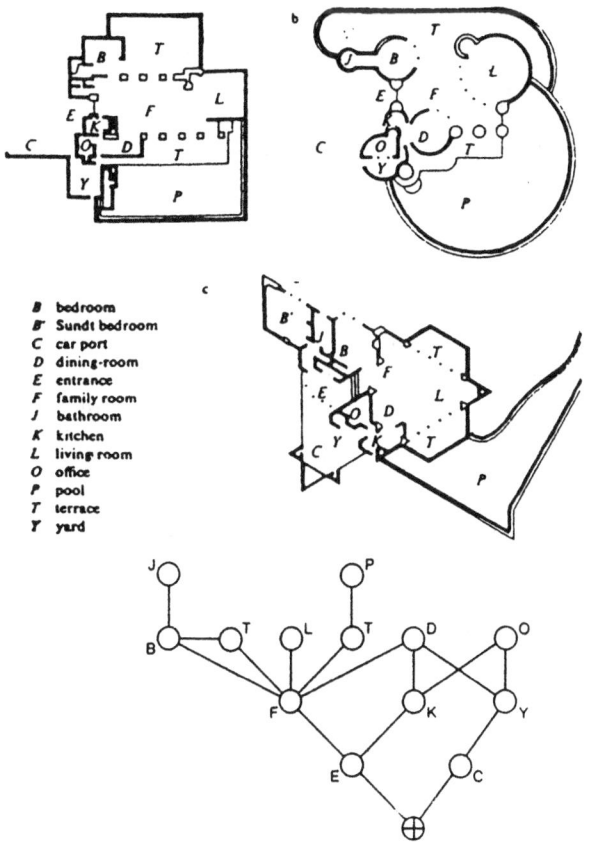

Fig. 6.3. Access analysis and floor-plans:
although different in physical form and style, the three examples of Frank Lloyd Wright houses shown here all have the same access map (after Lawrence 1990).
  a. *Life* 'House for a family of $ 5,000-6,000 income,' 1938.
  b. Ralph Jester House, Palos Verdes, California, 1938.
  c. Vigo Sundt House, near Madison, Wisconsin, 1941.

that in this paper, Hillier and Hanson's methods are used purely as mapping techniques, and as useful tools for the analysis and display of spatial information.

Form, space and function in Viking Age Iceland

We can now examine these issues with practical reference to Icelandic buildings in the Viking Age.[3] It should be noted that Iceland is an area of Scandinavian colonial settlement with no indigenous building tradition to influence the architecture of the early settlers (the presence of Irish monks in the ninth century and a possible Celtic element among the first colonists may be discounted in this context – see Stefán Aðalsteinsson 1987, for a recent discussion).

In the last 55 years, over thirty major sites of Viking Age and Medieval settlements have been excavated in Iceland, with several buildings often being found at each site. As with most archaeological work, the quality of the surviving remains is highly variable, with many structures poorly preserved; the number of intact building plans is therefore quite low. The foundation for this work was laid by the Nordic Archaeological Expedition to Iceland in 1939, which excavated several sites but used rather primitive techniques (Stenberger 1943). Since then, the principle work has included urban excavations in Reykjavík (Nordahl 1988), digging at the ecclesiastical sites of Viðey (Margrét Hallgrímsdóttir 1989) and Skálholt (Hörður Ágústsson 1988), a study of Þing assembly sites (Guðmundur Ólafsson 1987), programmes of environmental research,[4] and numerous excavations at isolated farm sites.[5] In recent years, Hörður Ágústsson (1982a, 1983) has published a number of studies of early Icelandic architecture which have greatly illuminated the building traditions of the early settlers, and which have been of vital importance to the present study . As yet, the geographical coverage of sites is concentrated in the South-West, but a picture is slowly being built up for the North and East through continued excavation. Dating remains a constant problem, since Iceland is culturally homogenous in terms of artefact types from the initial settlement to the Middle Ages, and methods such as radiocarbon dating are insufficiently precise for such a small time period. Icelandic scholars have therefore specialized in tephrachronological dating methods, which analyse deposits of volcanic ash found either as layers on the site or else incorporated within the walls of buildings. The ash is recorded by natural color, refraction index, chemical composition and spectra, and it is possible to link the ash to individual volcanoes and to particular dated eruptions, thus providing a series of dating horizons for the site (Sigurður Þórarinsson 1944; Shelf and Sparks 1981).

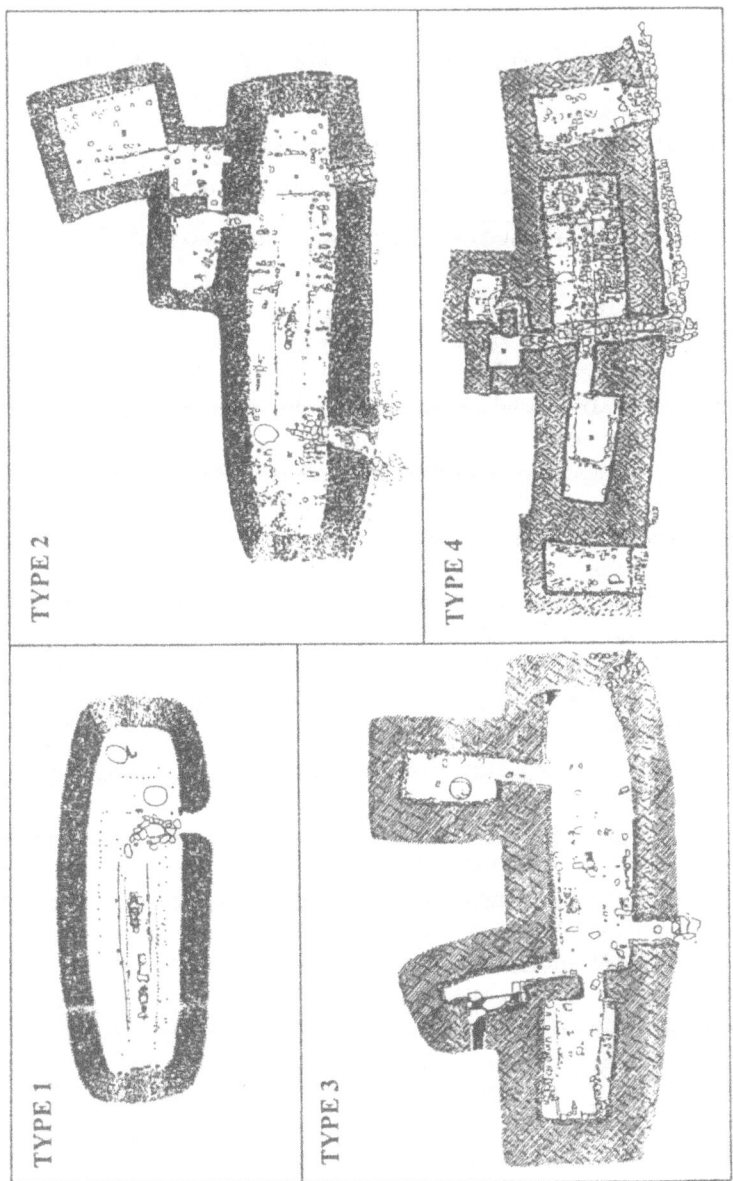

Fig. 6.4. The Hallgrímsdóttir Typology: the four principle types of longhouse found in early Medieval Iceland. Based on Margrét Hallgrímsdóttir 1987, 31; examples shown from Ísleifsstaðir (Type 1), Skallakot (Type 2), Gjáskógar (Type 3) and Gröf (Type 4). Not to scale.

The conventional building typology for Icelandic structures has been recently clarified by Margrét Hallgrímsdóttir in her 1987 thesis, with four basic types, defined by broad structural form and general chronological development (Fig. 6.4):

1. Simple longhouse with separate outbuildings – ninth and tenth centuries
2. longhouse with integral outbuildings – tenth century
3. longhouse with lateral projections – eleventh century
4. developed building complex – twelfth and thirteenth centuries

The later type 4 structures will not be covered in the present paper as it is chronologically beyond the range of the study.

Following visits to the sites themselves in 1991, work on the published and unpublished records, and discussion with the excavators, spatial accessibility/permeability maps were drawn up for all of the thirty-three known sites and the results compared with the Hallgrímsdóttir typology. For obvious reasons of space, only a few selected, representative examples will be discussed here (Fig. 6.5). The full study may be found in the final project publication (Price Forthcoming).

We may look firstly at maps of three of the earliest Type 1 structures from the ninth and tenth centuries, from Klaufanes in the North, Ísleifsstaðir in the West, and Hvítárholt I in the South (Fig. 6.6). Here we see a consistent spatial pattern, common over a wide geographical distribution, with comparable organization of the functional areas: in the terms of this study, it is argued that this represents a consistent spatial concept of the house and dwelling.

If we then turn to the Type 2 structures as they develop into the later tenth century – Skallakot in the South, Hvítárholt II, and Grelutóttir in the North-West – we see a slightly changed picture (Fig. 6.7). The house plans appear visually similar but spatially begin to show significant variation in the relative juxtapositioning of functional areas.

By the eleventh century, with the southern Type 3 structures at Þórarinsstadir, Gjáskógar and Stöng (the latter often quoted as the "classic" early Medieval Icelandic hall), this trend toward differentiation has increased dramatically (Fig. 6.8). Although they are all geographically very close, and appear to be almost identical in appearance (especially Gjáskógar and Stöng), they are spatially organized very differently. This developing spatial variation becomes total by the twelfth century and the Type 4 house complexes, with every structure being spatially unique.

HOUSE AND HOME IN VIKING AGE ICELAND

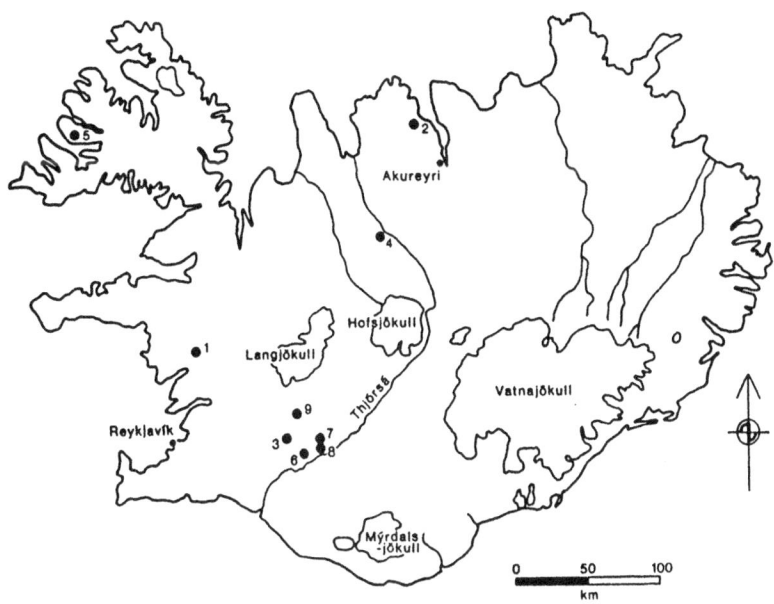

Fig. 6.5. Map of Iceland showing sites mentioned in the text:
1 – Ísleifsstaðir; 2 – Klaufanes; 3 – Hvítárholt I & II; 4 – Hraunþúfuklaustur;
5 – Grelutóttir; 6 – Skallakot; 7 – Sámsstaðir; 8 – Gjáskógar;
9 – Stöng and Þórarinsstaðir

⊕	Carrier space	⊖	Wall panel space (*skot*)
●	Transitional space	⊗	Dairy
○	Defined space of unknown function	⊙	Storage space
│	Path of access	◐	Smithy
┆	Possible path of access	◐	Lavatory
│?	Uncertain path of access	⊗	Barn
▲	Cooking hearth (*stofa*)	⊗	Byre
△	Domestic hearth (*skáli*)	⊖	Stable

Key to room function for Figures 6.6.–6.8.

119

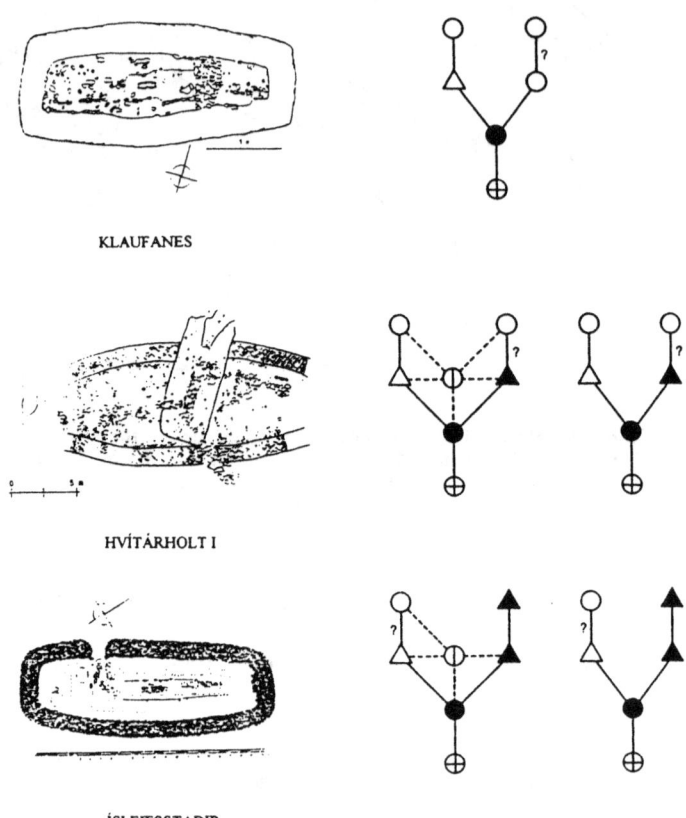

Fig. 6.6. Type 1 structures from Iceland with justified access maps. The alternative maps for Hvítárholt I and Isleifsstadir incorporate the uncertainty as to the presence of a *skot* wall panel space.

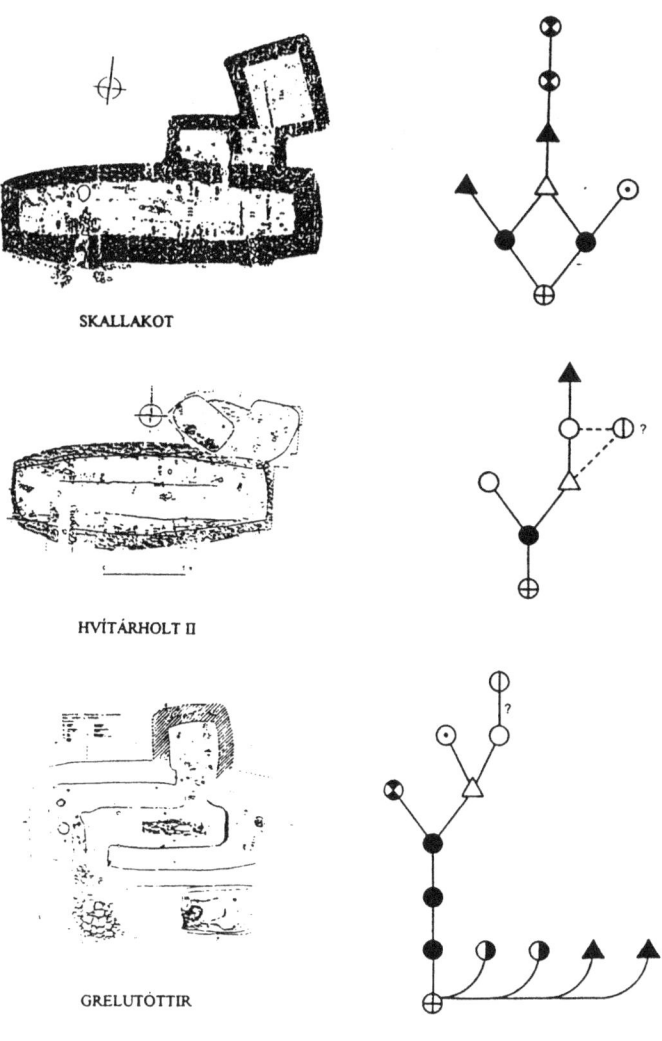

Fig. 6.7. Type 2 structures from Iceland with justified access maps.

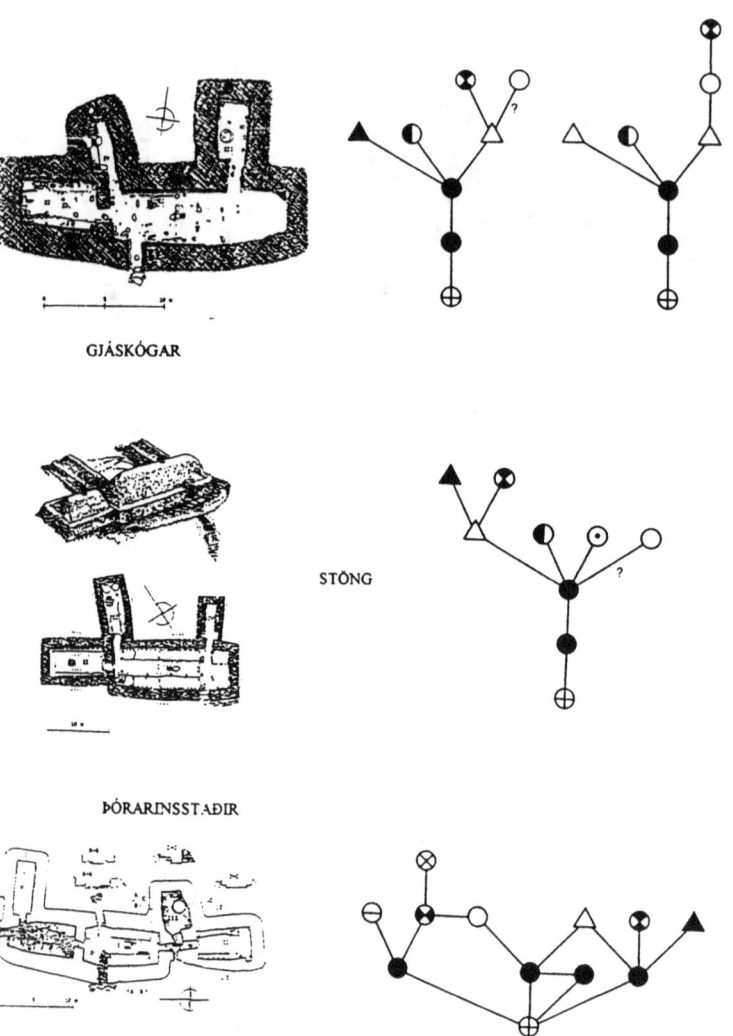

Fig. 6.8. Type 3 structures from Iceland with justified access maps. The alternative maps for Gjáskógar incorporate uncertainty as to the spatial relationship between the eastern end of the hall and the dairy.

This presents a very different picture to that proposed by the conventional building typologies. It must be emphasized that the four types are still valid for the structures' construction and form, but not for their use, i.e., their social organization of space. It seems clear from even this small sample that concepts of the home as it can be spatially articulated – together with its concomitant effects on social action – are changing dramatically in Iceland in the centuries immediately following the settlement. It is especially important to realise the process of choice that is being exercised (though perhaps not by those living in the dwellings, as opposed to other members of Icelandic society) at both levels – the physical design of the buildings and their social use; it is not coincidental that Stöng and Gjáskógar are so visually similar, for example. We see here a set of clearly consensual meanings and differences.

This paper attempts only to demonstrate the differential spatial patterning in these buildings over time; to interpret these changes is a second step (as such, this paper forms an interim report on the project and a full attempt at interpretation will be found in the main publication). We may, however, note that the two most common reasons cited for the changing structure of Icelandic buildings through the Viking period and early Middle Ages – both related to the retention of greater warmth within the structures, either for protection against a worsening climate or to stimulate the production of dairy products by enclosing cattle stalls inside the main complex – do not explain the spatial variations within buildings of the same Hallgrímsdóttir group. When we add other factors to the equation, such as gender division within the structures – many of these rooms can be divided on the basis of gender domains in addition to basic function – and also the different construction techniques with varying turf cuts and wood types used for different parts of the buildings, (for decorative or symbolic reasons rather than structural necessity; see Hörður Ágústsson 1987), it is clear that these buildings contain many levels of social complexity and meaning. We may take this still further and relate changes in the organization of the buildings to the wider social and political situation in Iceland and its relations with mainland Scandinavia in the early Middle Ages.

I would argue that we may see in these buildings the material articulation of the Viking Age colonial concept of the home – how people thought about and structured the spaces which they inhabited. It would seem that the Scandinavian concept of the dwelling was actually located in its particular social use of space, which is consistent in buildings of very different types and appearances in many parts of the Viking world. In essence, this may be seen as an attachment not to a particular style of building, but to a particular arrangement of living environment – a kind of mental template regulating the requirements for a home. When this type of spatial analysis is extended to other parts of the Viking world (see Price Forthcoming for an analysis of English and Russian structures in this context), the conclusions have far-reaching implications for the early Medieval concept of living space and its relationship to contemporary social structure. If such challenging possibilities for future research are taken up, we may be on the verge of a new understanding of the Viking Age mind.

Acknowledgements

I would like to extend particular thanks to David Benjamin and the conference organizing committee for their hospitality in Trondheim and for the financial assistance which made it possible for me to attend the symposium. Accommodation in Trondheim was kindly provided by Riksantikvaren's utgravningskontor, via Ian Reed and Sally Holt; I would also like to thank Aidan Allen for his help in Norway, and guidance around the Trondheim pubs. The Icelandic fieldwork was carried out in 1991, and I would like to thank the staff of Þjóðminjasafn Íslands (the National Museum of Iceland in Reykjavík) and Árbæjarsafn for their assistance. In addition, I would like to thank the following individuals who discussed and assisted with the research on which this paper is based, both in England and Iceland: Roberta Gilchrist, Guðmundur Ólafsson, Guðrún Sveinbjarnardóttir, Richard Hall, Hörður Ágústsson, Roderick Lawrence, Margrét Hallgrímsdóttir, Margrét Hermans-Auðardóttir, Mjöll Snæsdóttir, Steve Roskams, Síf Guðjonsdóttir, Mark Townley and Þór Magnússon. Any errors are, of course, my own responsibility. The access maps and the map of Iceland were drawn by Phillip Emery, for which I thank him. My work in Iceland was financed by generous grants from the Society for Medieval Archaeology, the University of York, and York Archaeological Trust.

Note

While the Chicago reference system has been adopted for this paper, occasional notes have been used to provide general bibliographical surveys of archaeological background material which may be useful for any architectural scholars wishing to follow up points of information. Similarly, notes have been used where long passages of references would otherwise have disrupted the text.

Endnotes

1. In general there has been little attention paid by western archaeologists to the theoretical background of ethnicity and cultural identity studies – including concepts of the home which may be seen as part of this field – in the early Medieval period, with methodology usually derived from prehistoric or ethnographic research (see Austin and Alcock 1990). In this general field, the following studies provide a basic guide to recent research: Hodder 1982; Shennan 1989; Miller, Rowlands and Tilley 1989; Hodder 1989; Layton 1989. For the Viking period specifically, there are almost no publications which deal solely with the question of identity and interaction, though these issues are often mentioned in passing in more general publications. The most recent survey of the Viking Age is by Roesdahl and Wilson (1992), which contains an extensive bibliography; other bibliographies intended to serve as general reviews of Viking studies may be found in Graham-Campbell (1980) and Farrell (1982), of which the former is more comprehensive.

2. Hillier and Hanson's methods have been adopted by a number of archaeologists, but almost always with the primary emphasis on the element of social relations which the designers argue is encoded in the accessibility patterns of structures. The most prominent examples may be found in Gilchrist 1988, 1990 and 1993 (on English Medieval nunneries), Foster 1989 (on Scottish Iron Age brochs) and Brown 1984 (on late Medieval urban planning); a number of examples are also presented in Samson 1990. In addition, Hillier and Hanson's work has been discussed at several recent British conferences, including TAG 1988, 1989 and 1992, and the 1992 Medieval Europe conference in York. The technique has never been archaeologically used before in the context of cultural identity and the concept of the home.

3. A spatial study of Medieval Icelandic buildings was suggested by Ross Samson in his introduction to The Social Archaeology of Houses (1990, 10), presumably unaware that the present survey had already begun.

4. The interpretation of Icelandic structures in the landscape has been massively augmented in recent years by the work of Guðrún Sveinbjarnardóttir (1983a) and the Birmingham University team who carried out palaeoecological studies on Iceland in the early 1980s (Guðrún Sveinbjarnardóttir et al 1981 and 1982; Buckland et al 1986).

5. A number of general surveys of Viking Age Icelandic settlement have recently been completed, and serve as a useful guide to the current state of research (they all contain full bibliographies): these publications form the basic references for the buildings presented in this paper. General surveys include Margrét Hallgrímsdóttir 1987; Guðrún Sveinbjarnardóttir 1976, 1987, 1992 and forthcoming; Morris and Rackham 1992; Hördur Ágústsson 1987 and 1989; Þór Magnússon 1983. Individual site reports of particular significance include Guðmundur Ólafsson 1980; Sveinbjörn Rafnsson 1976 and 1990; Guðrún Sveinbjarnardóttir 1982 and 1983b; Gisli Gestsson 1959; Matthías Þórðarsson 1932; new findings are usually published in the annual *Árbók hins Íslenzka Fornleifafelags*.

References

Abbreviation: *Árbók* = *Árbók hins Islenzka fornleifafelags*

Note: Icelandic authors are cited alphabetically by forename, following Icelandic practice.

Alexander, C., S. Ishigawa, and M. Silverstein. 1977. *A Pattern Language*. N.Y.: Oxford University Press.

Austin, D. and L. Alcock, eds. 1990. *From the Baltic to the Black Sea: Studies in Medieval Archaeology*. London: Unwin.

Brown, F. 1984. *The Spatial Development of the City of London*. Milton Keynes: Open University Press.

Buckland, P. C. et al. 1986. Late Holocene Palaeoecology at Ketilsstaðir in Myrdalur, South Iceland. *Jökull* 36.

Farrell, R., ed. 1982. *The Vikings*. Chichester,U.K.: Phillimore.

Foster, S. 1989. Analysis of Spatial Patterns in Buildings (Access Analysis) as an Insight into Social Structure: Examples from the Scottish Atlantic Iron Age. *Antiquity* 238.

Gilchrist, R. 1988. The Spatial Archaeology of Gender Domains: A Case Study of Medieval English Nunneries. *Archaeological Review from Cambridge* 7(1).

———. 1990. *The archaeology of female piety*. D.phil. diss., York University, U.K.

———. 1993. *Gender and Material Culture*. London: Routledge.

Gisli Gestsson. 1959. Gröf i Öraefum. *Arbók* 59.

Graham-Campbell, J.A. 1980. *Viking Artefacts*. London: British Museum Press.
Guðmundur Ólafsson. 1980. Grelutóttir: landnámsbær á Eyri við Arnarfjörd. *Arbók 79*.
———. 1987. Þingnes by Elliðvatn: The First Local Assembly in Iceland? In *Proceedings of the Tenth Viking Congress*, ed. J. E. Knirk. Oslo: Universitetets Oldsakssamling.
Guðrún Sveinbjarnardóttir. 1976. *Settlements and Buildings of the Scandinavians in the North Atlantic Region 800–1150*. Masters thesis, University of London.
———. 1982. Byggðaleifar vid Einhyrningsflatir í Fljótshlíð. In *Eldur er í Nordri*, ed. Sigurður Þórarinsson. Reykjavík: Sogufelag.
———. 1983a. Palæologiske undersøgelser på Holt i Eyjafjallasveit, Sydisland. In *Hus, gård og bebyggelse*, ed. Guðmundur Ólafsson. Reykjavík.
———. 1983b. Byggðaleifar á Þórsmörk. *Arbók 82*.
———. 1987. *Settlement Patterns in Medieval and post-Medieval Iceland: an Inter-Disciplinary Study*. PhD diss., University of Birmingham, U.K.
———. 1992. *Farm Abandonment in Medieval and post-Medieval Iceland*. Oxford: Oxbow.
———. Forthcoming. *Domestic architecture in Iceland from the Late 9th Century to c. 1100*.
Guðrún Sveinbjarnardóttir, et al. 1981. Excavations at Stóraborg: A Palaeoecological Approach. *Arbók 80*.
Guðrún Sveinbjarnardóttir, et al. 1982. Landscape Change in Eyjafjallasveit, Southern Iceland. *Norsk Geografisk Tidsskrift 36*.
Hietala, H., ed. 1984. *Intrasite Spatial Analysis in Archaeology*. Cambridge: Cambridge University Press.
Hillier, B. and J. Hanson. 1984. *The Social Logic of Space*. Cambridge: Cambridge University Press.
Hodder, I. 1982. *The Present Past*. London: Routledge.
Hodder, I. and C. Orton. 1976. *Spatial Analysis in Archaeology*. Cambridge: Cambridge University Press.
Hörður Ágústsson 1982a. Den indre opbygning af det islandske torvehus. In *Vestnordisk byggeskikk gjennom to tusen år*, ed. B. Myhre, B. Stoklund, and P. Gjærder. Stavanger: Stavanger Arkeologisk Museum.
———. 1982b. Den islandske bondegards udvikling fra landnamstiden indtil det 20. århundrede. In *Vestnordisk byggeskikk gjennom to tusen år*, ed. B. Myhre, B. Stoklund, and P. Gjærder. Stavanger: Stavanger Museum.

———. 1983. Rekonstruktionen af Stöng. In *Hus, gård och bebyggelse*, ed. Guðmundur Ólafsson. Reykjavík.

———. 1987. Islenski torfbærinn. In *Islensk þóðmenning I. Uppruni og umhverfi*, ed. Frosti Jóhansson. Reykjavík.

———. 1988. *Skálholt.* Reykjavík.

———. 1989. Húsagerð á Síðmiðöldum. *Saga Islands* 4.

Layton, R., ed. 1989. *Conflict in the Archaeology of Living Traditions.* London: Unwin.

Leach, E. 1978. Does space syntax really 'constitute the social?'. In *Social Organisation and Settlement: Contributions from Anthropology*, ed. D. Green, C. Haselgrove, and C. Spriggs. Oxford: British Archaeological Reports.

Lawrence, R.L. 1990. Public Collective and Private Space: A Study of Urban Housing in Switzerland. In *Domestic Architecture and the Use of Space*, ed. S. Kent. Cambridge: Cambridge University Press.

Margrét Hallgrímsdóttir 1987. *Gårdar och ekonomi på Island under Vikingatid och Medeltid.* University of Stockholm. Mimeo.

Mattías Þórðarsson. 1932. Bólstadur vid Alftafjörd. *Arbók* 32.

Miller, D., M. Rowlands, and C. Tilley, eds. 1989. *Domination and Resistance.* London: Unwin.

Morris, C. and J. Rackham, eds. 1992. *Norse and Later Settlement and Subsistence in the North Atlantic.* Glasgow: Glasgow University Press.

Nordahl, E. 1988. *Reykjavík from the Archaeological Point of View.* Uppsala: Uppsala University Press.

Roesdahl, E. and D. M. Wilson, eds. 1992. *From Viking to Crusader: Scandinavia and Europe 800–1200.* Uddevalla: Council of Europe.

Samson, R., ed. 1990. *The Social Archaeology of Houses.* Edinburgh: Edinburgh University Press.

Shelf, S. and R. Spark, eds. 1981. *Tephra studies.*

Shennan, S. ed. 1989. *Archaeological Approaches to Cultural Identity.* London: Unwin.

Sigurður Þórarinsson. 1944. *Tefrokronologiska studier på Island.* Copenhagen.

Stefán Aðalsteinsson. 1987. Líffræðilegur uppruni Islendinga. In *Islensk þódmenning I. Uppruni og Umhverfi*, ed. Frosti Jóhansson. Reykjavík.

Stenberger, M., ed. 1943. *Forntida gårdar i Island.* Copenhagen: Munksgaard.

Stiny, G. and J. Gips. 1978. *Algorithmic Aesthetics.* Berkley: University of California Press.

Sveinbjörn Rafnsson. 1976. Sámsstadir í Thjórsárdal. *Arbók* 75.

———. 1990. *Byggdaleifar í Hrafnkelsdal og á Brúardölum.* Reykjavík.

Þór Magnússon 1983. Isländska boningshus under Vikingatid och Medeltid. In *Hus, gård och bebyggelse*, ed. Guðmundur Ólafsson. Reykjavík.

Yates, T. 1989. Habitus and Social Space: Some Suggestions about Meaning in the Saami (Lapp) Tent ca. 1700–1900. In *The meanings of things*, ed. I. Hodder. London: Unwin.

7
Identity, Intimacy and Domicile
– Notes on the Phenomenology of Home

Juhani Pallasmaa

Homo Faber and the existential vacuum

Identity was the recurrent theme in the literary work of Max Frisch, who, incidentally, was an architect by training. In his book *Homo Faber* (1961) Frisch portrays a Unesco expert, an engineer – the symbol of Modern Man – who continuously travels around the world on his missions. He is a rational and realistic man whose life seems to be under perfect rational control. However, gradually he looses contact with locality and home, and finally, with his own identity. He ends up falling in love with his own daughter whom he does not recognize as the tragic consequence of his loss of home and roots. Their indecent love ends violently in the daughter's death.

Homo Faber's grave mistake was his conviction that man can exist without a domicile and that technology can transform the world so that it need not any longer be experienced through emotions.

Many of us in the consumer world today are suffering from Homo Faber's alienation. We have become homeless in our culture of abundance.

The architect and the concept of home

We architects are concerned with designing dwellings as architectural manifestations of space, structure, and order, but we seem unable to touch upon the more subtle, emotional, and diffuse aspects of home. In schools of architecture we are taught to design houses and dwellings, not homes. Yet it is the capacity of the dwelling to provide domicile in the world that matters to the individual dweller. The dwelling has its psyche and soul in addition to its formal and quantifiable qualities.

The titles of architectural books invariably use the notion of house – *The Modern House, GA-Houses, California Houses*, etc. – whereas books and magazines that deal with interior decoration and celebrities are engaged with the notion of home – *Celebrity Homes, Artist Homes*, etc.. Needless to say that the publications of the latter type are considered sentimental entertainment and kitsch by the professional architect.

Our concept of architecture is based on the idea of the perfectly articulated architectural object. The famous court case between Mies van der Rohe and his client, Dr. Edith Farnsworth, concerning the Farnsworth House, is an example of the contradiction between architecture and home. As we all know, Mies had designed one of the most important and aesthetically appealing houses of our century, but his client did not find it satisfactory as a home. The court, incidentally, decided in Mies's favour. I am not underrating Mies's architecture, I am simply pointing out the distancing from life and a deliberate reduction of the spectrum of life that this architectural work displays.

When we compare designs of early Modernity at large and of today's avant-garde, we can immediately observe a loss of empathy for the dweller. Instead of being motivated by the architect's social vision or an empathetic view of life, architecture has become self-referential and autistic.

Many of us architects seem to have developed a kind of a split personality; as designers and as dwellers we apply different sets of values to the environment. In our role as architects we aspire for a meticulously articulated and temporally one-dimensional environment, whereas as dwellers ourselves, we prefer a more layered, ambiguous, and aesthetically less coherent environment; the instinctual dweller seems to emerge through the role values of the professional.

Architecture vs. home

The question arises: can a home be an architectural expression? Home is not, perhaps, at all a notion of architecture, but of psychology, psychoanalysis, and sociology. Home is an individualized dwelling, and the means of this subtle personalization seem to be outside of our concept of architecture. Dwelling, or the house, is the container, the shell for home. The substance of home is secreted, as it were, upon the framework of the dwelling by the dweller. Home is an expression of the dweller's personality and his unique patterns of life. Consequently, the essence of home is closer to life itself than an artefact.

The architectural dimension of the house and the personal and private dimension of life have become totally fused in our time of excessive specialization and fragmentation only in special cases such as Alvar Aalto's Villa Mairea. This was a product of an exceptional friendship and interaction between the architect and his client, an "opus con amore," as Aalto (1963) himself has confessed. Equally importantly, this residential masterpiece is an expression of a mutually shared utopian vision of a better and more humane world. Villa Mairea is archaic and modern, rustic and elegant, regional and universal at the same time. It refers simultaneously to the past and the future, it is abundant in its imagery and, consequently, provides ample soil for individual psychic attachment.

In *The Poetics of Space* (1969), which deals with the psyche of space, Gaston Bachelard deliberates on the essence of the oneiric house, the dream house of the mind. He is undecided about the number of floors of this archetypal house; it has either three or four floors. But the existence of an attic and a cellar are essential, because the attic is the symbolic storage place for pleasant memories that the dweller wants to return to, whereas the cellar is the final hiding place for unpleasant memories; both are needed for our mental well-being.

It is evident that the characteristics of the oneiric house are culturally conditioned, but on the other hand, the image seems to reflect universal constants of the human mind. Modern architecture however, has forcefully attempted to avoid or eliminate this oneiric image. Consequently, it is not surprising that modern man's arrogant rejection of history has been accompanied by the rejection of psychic memory attached to primal images. The obsession with newness, the non-traditional, and the unforeseen, has wiped away the image of the oneiric house from our soul. We build dwellings that satisfy, perhaps, most of our physical needs, but which cannot house our mind.

The essence of home

It is evident that home is not merely an object or a building, but a diffuse and complex condition, which integrates memories and images, desires and fears, the past and the present. A home is also a set of rituals, personal rhythms and routines of everyday life. And a home cannot be produced at once; it has its time dimension and continuum, and it is a gradual product of the dweller's adaptation to the world.

Thus, a home cannot become a marketable product. Current advertisements of furniture shops offering a chance "to renew one's home at once" are absurd – they amount to a psychologist's advertisement to renew the mental contents of the patient's mind at once.

Reflection on the essence of home takes us away from the physical properties of house into the psychic territory of the mind. It engages us with issues of identity and memory, consciousness as well as the unconscious, and biologically motivated behavioral remnants as well as culturally conditioned reactions and values.

Poetics of home – refuge and terror

The description of home seems to belong more to the realms of poetry, novel, film, and painting than architecture. "Poets and painters are born phenomenologists," as J.H. van den Berg has remarked (see Bachelard 1969). And so, in my view, are also novelists, photographers, and film directors. That is why the essence of home, its function as a mirror and support of the inhabitant's psyche, is often more revealingly pictured in these art forms than in architecture. The filmmaker Jan Vrijman (1994) has made the thought provoking remark: "Why is it that architecture and architects, unlike film and filmmakers, are so little interested in people during the design process? Why are they so theoretical, so distant from life in general?"

The artist is not concerned with the principles and intentions of the discipline of architecture and, consequently, he directly approaches the mental significance of images of the house and the home. Thus, artworks dealing with space, light, buildings, and dwelling, can provide valuable lessons to architects on the very essence of architecture itself.

Jean-Paul Sartre (1978) has written perceptively about the authenticity of the artist's house: "(The painter) makes them (houses), that is, he creates an imaginary house on the canvas and not a sign of a house. And the house, which thus appears preserves all the ambiguity of real houses."

As well as being a symbol of protection and order, home can, in negative life situations, become a concretization of human misery: loneliness, rejection, exploitation, and violence.

In the beginning chapter of *Crime and Punishment* (Dostojevsky 1866), Raskolnikov visits the home of the old usurer woman, his future victim, and Dostojevsky gives a laconic but haunting description of the home, which eventually turns into the scene of a brutal murder. Home turns from the symbol of security to an image of threat and violence.

Home is an intra-psychic and multi-dimensional experience, which is difficult to describe objectively. Thus an introspective and phenomenological survey of images, emotions, experiences, and recollections attached to home seem to be a fruitful approach in analyzing this notion that we all constantly use, but rarely stop to analyze.

The home of the memory

The word *home* makes us immediately and simultaneously remember all the warmth, protection, and love of our entire childhood. Perhaps our homes of adulthood are only an unconscious search for the lost home of childhood. But the memory of home also wakens all the distress and fear that we might have experienced in our childhood.

Bachelard (1969, 17) writes: "A house constitutes a body of images that give mankind proofs or illusions of stability," and, "It is an instrument with which to confront the cosmos." And he is speaking about home, a house filled with the essence of personal life.

Home is a collection and concretization of personal images of protection and intimacy, which help one recognize and remember who one is. "I am the space, where I am," in the words of the French poet Noel Arnaud (see Bachelard 1969, 137).

Home is a staging of personal memory. It functions as a two-way mediator – personal space expresses the personality to the outside world, but equally importantly, it strengthens the dweller's self-image and concretizes his world order. In their influential book *Community and Privacy* (1963), Christopher Alexander and Serge Chermayeff identified six spatial mechanisms between the polarities of private and public. Thus home is also a complex mediator between intimacy and public life.

The image of home

Before reaching high school age, my family moved several times due to my father's job, and consequently, I lived in seven different houses during my childhood. In addition, I spent my childhood summers and most of the war years in my farmer grandfather's house. Regardless of having lived in eight houses, I have only had one experiential home in my childhood; my experiential home seems to have travelled with me and constantly transformed into new physical shapes as we moved.

I cannot recall the exact architectural shape or lay-out of any of the eight houses. But I do recall vividly the sense of home, the feeling of returning home from a skiing trip in the darkness of a cold winter evening. The experience of home is never stronger than when seeing the windows of one's house lit in the dark winter landscape and sensing the invitation of warmth warming your frozen limbs. "Light in the window of the home is a waiting light," as Bachelard (1969, 34) has observed. An authentic home has a soul.

I cannot recall the shape of the front door of my grandfather's house either, but I can still sense the warmth and odour of air flowing against my face as I open the door in my dreams.

In an essay entitled *The Geometry of Feeling* (1985), I dealt with the properties of lived space as compared to common notions of architecture. It seems to me that emotions deriving from built form and space arise from distinct confrontations between man and space. The emotional impact is related to an act, not an object or a visual or figural element. Consequently, the phenomenology of architecture is founded on verbs rather than nouns: The approach to the house, (not the facade); the act of entering, (not the door); the act of looking out of the window, (not the window itself); or the act of gathering around (rather than the hearth or the table as such), seem to trigger our strongest emotions.

Nostalgia of home

I also remember the sadness and secret threat of leaving behind the home as we moved to another town. The most tragic experience was the fear of facing an unknown future and loosing one's childhood friends.

It is clear that the experience of home consists of and integrates an incredible array of mental dimensions from that of nationality and being a subject in a specific culture to those of unconscious desires and fears. No wonder sociologists have found out that the sorrow for a lost home among slum residents is very similar to the mourning for a lost relative.

There is a strange melancholy in an abandoned home or a demolished apartment house which reveals traces and scars of intimate lives to the public gaze on its crumbling walls. It is touching to come across remains of foundations or the hearth of a ruined or burnt house, half buried in the forest grass. The tenderness of the experience results from the fact that we do not imagine the house, but the home, life, and faith of its members.

Andrei Tarkovsky's film *Nostalgia* is a touching record of the loss and grievance of home (Pallasmaa 1992). It is a film about the nostalgia for an absent home which is typical for the Russian sentiment from the times of Dostojevsky and Gogol, to Tarkovsky himself. Throughout the film the central figure, the poet Andrei Gorchakov, keeps fingering the keys to his home in Russia in the pocket of his overcoat as an unconscious reflection of his longing for home. All of Tarkovsky's films, in fact, seem to deal with the nostalgia of the absent domicile (Volkova 1992). In the Communist state, home changed from a refuge into a place of surveillance, a concentration camp. Yet, home also turned into a mystical dream that countless Russian artists have described in their works.

Home and identity

The interdependence of identity and context is so strong that psychologists speak of a situational personality. The notion is based on the observation that the behaviour of an individual varies more under different conditions than the behaviour of different individuals under the same conditions.

The psycho-linguistic studies of the Norwegian born Finn, Frode Strömnes (1976; 1981, 7–29; 1982) have brought out further dimensions of the interdependence of psyche and context. In his research on imagery as the basis of linguistic operations, he has shown that language conditions our conception and utilization of space. Consequently, our concept of home is founded in language; our first home is in the domicile of our mother tongue. And language is strongly tied to our bodily existence, so that the geometry of our language articulates our being in the world.

Home is a projection and basis of identity, not only of an individual but also of the family. But in homes, the mere secrecy of private lives concealed from the public eye also structures social life. Homes delineate the realms of intimacy and public life.

It is frustrating to be forced to live in a space which one cannot recognize or mark as one's personal territory. An anonymous hotel room is immediately personalized and taken into possession by subtly marking the territory, laying out clothes, books, objects, opening the bed, etc.. The minimum home of a child or a primitive [*sic* –Ed.] is the mascot or the personal idol which gives a sense of safety and normality. My five-year old daughter cannot go anywhere without her scratching pillow, my American architect assistant travelled to Finland with four books (Joyce's *Ulysses*, T.S. Eliot's *Four Quartets* and two books on American poetry), while an American architect woman friend travels with her set of kitchen knives, which are her magical instruments to recreate a sense of home.

The Finnish poet Jarkko Laine (1982, 323–324) writes of the things on his window ledge: "I like looking at these things. I don't seek aesthetic pleasure in them…nor do I recall their origins: that is not important. But even so they all arouse memories, real and imagined. A poem is a thing which arouses memories of real and imagined things…. The things in the window act like a poem. They are images which do not reflect anything.... I sing of the things in the window."

Intimacy and home

We have private and social personalities; home is the realm of the former. Home is the place where we hide our secrets and express our private selves. Home is our place of resting and dreaming in safety. More precisely, the role of home as delineator or mediator between the realms of public and private, the transparency of the home, as it were, varies greatly. There are ways of life in which home has become a public showcase and the public gaze penetrates the secrecy of home.

Generally however, the intimacy of home is almost a taboo in our culture. We have a feeling of guilt and embarrassment if we, for some reason, are obliged to enter someone's home uninvited when the occupant is not at home. To see an unattended home is the same as seeing its dweller naked or in his/her most intimate situation.

In *The Notebooks of Malte Laurids Brigge,* Rainer Maria Rilke (1992, 47–48) gives a powerful description of the marks of intimacy, the lives in a house that had already been demolished but which could still be seen in traces left on the wall of its neighbouring building. These traces of life enabled Brigge to recreate his own past. Rilke describes with staggering force how life penetrates dead matter; here the history of life can be traced in the most minute fragments of the dwelling.

Fig. 7.1:Home as a manifestation of life. Vincent van Gogh, The Bedroom, 1888. (From Walter, Ingo F., and Rainer Metzger. 1990. Vincent van Gogh: L'oeuvre Complete-Peinture. Cologne: Benedikt Taschen. Courtesy of Vincent van Gogh Foundation, van Gogh Museum, Amsterdam)

In its emotional power Rilke's description reminds one of Heidegger's (1977, 163) famous description of the epic message of van Gogh's *Peasant's Shoes* (Fig. 7.1). The later questioning of the relevance of Heidegger's interpretation by Meyer Shapiro does not diminish the poetic power of his words; Shapiro has pointed out that van Gogh actually painted his own shoes, and besides, he made the painting during his short stay in Paris. What is important, however, is the artist's extraordinarily dense imagery that reflects an authentic form of life.

In its intimate polarity, Bachelard (1969, xxxiv) points out a bodily experience of the home: "Indeed, in our houses we have nooks and corners in which we like to curl up comfortably. To curl up belongs to the phenomenology of the verb to inhabit, and only those who have learned to do so can inhabit with intensity." Home seems to be an extension of both our bodily and mental existence.

The fascination of the world of personal intimacy is so great that I recall Architectural Design Magazine in the late 1960s having reported on a minute theater in New York where the audience watched through a one-directional mirror-window the daily life of a normal American family living in a flat they had rented unaware of being on stage. The theater was open 24 hours a day and continuously sold out until it was closed by the authorities as inhuman.

The recent four-volume book entitled *A History of Private Life* (Aries and Duby 1987) traces the evolution of the private realm from pagan Rome to the Great War in nearly 2800 pages and makes the reader understand the cultural relativism of even the most personal and intimate life. Not much can be taken as given in human reality.

Ingredients of home

Home seems to consist of three types of mental or symbolic elements:

1. elements which have their foundation at the deep unconscious, bio-cultural level (entry, hearth)

2. elements that are related with the inhabitant's personal life and identity (memorabilia, inherited objects of the family)

3. social symbols intended to give certain images and messages to outsiders (signs of wealth, education, social identity, etc.)

It should be clear by now, that the structuring of home as a lived institution differs from the principles of architecture. A house as composed by the architect is a system of spatial hierarchies and dynamics, of structure, light, colour, etc., whereas home is structured around a few foci consisting of distinct domestic functions and objects. The following types of elements may function as the foci of behaviour and symbolization: front (front yard, facade, the urban situation), entry, window, hearth, stove, table, cupboard, bath, bookcase, television, furniture, family treasures, and finally memorabilia.

The poetry of the wardrobe

The meaning of each element can be phenomenologically analyzed. Bachelard's analysis of the essential task of drawers, chests, and wardrobes in our mental imagery sets an inspiring example. He gives these objects – rarely considered as having architectural significance – an impressive role in the world of fantasy and daydream. "In the wardrobe there exists a center of order that protects the entire house against uncurbed disorder" (1969, 79).

Wardrobes, cupboards, and drawers represent the functions of putting away and taking out, storing and remembering. The inside of a cupboard is an intimate and secret space, and it is not supposed to be opened by just anybody. Little boxes and caskets are hiding places for intimate secrets and as such are of significance for our imagination. Our imagination fills out compartments of rooms and buildings with memories and turns them into our own personal territories. We have just as great a need to keep secrets as we have to reveal and understand them.

One of the reasons why contemporary houses and cities are so alienating is that they do not contain secrets; their structure and contents are conceived at a single glance. Just compare the labyrinthian secrets of an old medieval town or an old house which can stimulate our imagination, and fill it with expectation and excitement to the transparent emptiness of our new cityscape and blocks of flats.

Marcuse's *One-Dimensional Man* (1964) considers that buildings of our time are unerotic compared with the erotic imagery conjured up by an environment of nature or traditional buildings. One can compare for instance, the fantasies provoked by a meadow outside ancient town walls or by an old attic, to the numbing no-man's-land of a new housing area or the anonymity of a contemporary flat cramped between concrete walls and floors. Marcuse believes that the flagrant and violent sexuality of our time is a result of the absence of erotic imagery in today's built environment.

Hearth and fire

The significance of hearth or stove for the sense of home is self-evident. The image of fire in the home combines the sense of the most archaic to the most present. The power of the symbolism of the hearth is based on its capacity to fuse archaic images of the life-supporting fire of the primitive [*sic* – Ed.], experiences of personal comfort, and symbols of togetherness and social status.

Maurice Vlaminck (see Bachelard 1969, 91), the Fauve painter, has written: "The well-being I feel, seated in front of my fire, while bad weather rages out-of-doors, is entirely animal. A rat in its hole, a rabbit in its burrow, cows in the stable, must all feel the same contentment that I feel."

The fireplace is a bourgeois symbol of the separation of fire for pleasure from the fire for preparing food, whereas the image of the stove has peasant-like connotations. Having spent my childhood in a farmer's home, I can still vividly recall the role of the stove in structuring family life, in marking the rhythm of the day and in defining the male and female roles.

The power of the image of fire is so vivid that hearths are often built solely as symbols, in the form of mere mantles without any possibility of actual fire. The image of the hearth carries also immediate erotic connotations. No wonder Lewis Mumford discusses the influence of the invention of the oven on sexual behaviour in his *The Culture of the City*.

In the modern home the hearth has been flattened to an object with a distant and decorative function. Fire itself has been tamed and turned into a framed picture devoid of its essential quality to give warmth and to sustain life. We can speak of the cold fire of the modern home.

Functions of the table

The structuring function and symbolic role of the table has also largely been lost in contemporary architecture. The significance of the table, however, is powerfully expressed in painting and poetry.

Again, I vividly recall the heavy, unpainted wooden table of my farmer grandfather. The remembrance of the table is stronger than of the room itself. Everyone had his or her place at the table, my grandfather sitting at the inner end. The opposite end of the long table, closer to the entry, was left empty and was occupied only when there was an occasional guest. The table was the stage for eating, sewing, playing, doing homework, and socializing with neighbours and strangers, etc.. The table was the organizing center of the farmer's house. The table marked the difference between weekday and Sunday, work day and feast.

Dilution of the images of home

I want to add a remark on the dilution of the image of the bed from being a miniature house, a house within the house, symbolizing privacy, to being a mere neutral horizontal plane, a stage of privacy, as it were. This makes one recall Bachelard's (1969, 27) observation that the house, and consequently, our lives have lost their vertical dimension and become mere horisontality. Again, innumerous images in historical paintings and drawings reveal the essence of the bed as the intimate core of home.

A less self-evident, but powerfully poetic and essential experience of home is the window and, in particular, the act of looking out of the window of the home to the yard or to the garden. Home is particularly strongly felt when you look out from its enclosed privacy. The tendency of contemporary architecture to use glass walls eliminates the window as a framing and rationing device, and weakens the essential tension between the home and the world. The ontology of the door has been lost in the same way.

Lack of concreteness

I live in an attic flat under a tin roof. The strongest and most pleasurable experience of home occurs during a heavy storm when rain beats the roof, magnifying the feeling of warmth and protection. At the same time, the beating of rain just a foot away from my skin puts me in direct contact with primal elements. But these sensations are lost for the dweller of the standard flat.

Cooking by fire is immensely satisfying because one can experience a primal causality between the fire and the hearth. Again, this causality is lost with the electric stove or even more so with the microwave oven.

In the contemporary home, the function of the hearth has been taken over by television. Both seem to be foci of social gathering and individual concentration, but the difference in quality is however, decisive. The fire ties us back to our unconscious memory, to the archaeology of images. Fire is a primal image, and it reminds us of the primary causality of the physical world. At the same time that flames stimulate meditative dreaming, they reinforce our sense of reality. The television alienates us from a sense of causality and transports us into a dream world which weakens our sense of reality, of ourself and the ethical essence of togetherness. Instead of promoting togetherness, television forces isolation and privatization. The most shocking experience of the negative impact of the television was the Gulf War, which was telecast in real time around the globe as dramatized entertainment.

An analysis of television as a structuring device of the contemporary home is, of course, essential for the theme of this Symposium, but I do not have time to elaborate on it.

Altogether, the weakening of the sense of causality threatens modern life. The menace represented by our brave new world lies in its lack of concreteness. Even fear is acceptable as long as it has its understandable cause or it symbolizes something, and as long as it is not cloaked in apparent order and wellbeing. The irrational fear in our cities grows out of the meaninglessness of the environment to our reason, and its incomprehensibility to our senses. We are loosing the primary causality in our sensory experience of the world.

The psychologist Edward Edinger (1973) writes that "Symptoms (of an illness) are, in fact, degraded symbols, degraded by the reductive fallacy of the ego. Symptoms are intolerable precisely because they are meaningless. Almost any difficulty can be borne if we can discern its meaning. It is meaninglessness which is the greatest threat to humanity."

This meaninglessness, a hypnotizing emptiness and absence of locality and focus, the existential vacuum, has become a recurring motif of contemporary art. It is alarming, indeed, that the favourite theme of art today is the total isolation of man, disrobed of all signs of individual identity and human dignity.

The architecture of tolerance

If architecture and home are conflicting notions, as it seems, what then is the architect's possibility of facilitating homecoming, that Aldo van Eyck has so emphatically demanded?

In my view, architecture can either tolerate and encourage personalization or stifle it. We can make a distinction between an architecture of accommodation and an architecture of rejection. The first one facilitates reconciliation, the second attempts to impose by its arrogant and unchangeable order. The first is based on images that are deeply rooted in our common memory, that is, in the phenomenologically authentic ground of architecture. The second manipulates images, striking and fashionable, perhaps, but which do not incorporate the personal identity, memories, and dreams of the inhabitant. It is likely that the latter attitude creates architecturally more imposing houses, but the first provides the condition of homecoming.

Furthermore, there is a significant difference in the nature and quality with which different architectural designs can allow and absorb aesthetic deviation without resulting in undesirable conflict. The architecture and furniture designs of Alvar Aalto are an encouraging example of design which has a great aesthetic tolerance, yet it is artistically uncompromising.

The virtue of idealization

My acknowledgement of a conflict between architecture and the intrinsic requirements of home, could perhaps be interpreted as advocacy of the view that the architect should faithfully fulfill the explicit requirements and desires of the client. I want to say very firmly that I do not believe in such a populist view. Uncritical acceptance of the client's brief only leads to sentimental kitsch; the architect's responsibility is to penetrate the surface of most often commercially, socially, and momentarily conditioned desire. The authentic artist and architect consciously or unknowingly engage in an ideal world. Art and exhilarating architecture are lost at the point that this vision and aspiration for an ideal is lost.

The South-African writer J.M. Coetzee (Coetzee 1987) has said that taking the reader into consideration when writing is a deadly error for the writer. Umberto Eco (1985) has distinguished between two types of writers; the first type writes what he expects the reader to want to read, the second creates his ideal reader as he writes. In Eco's view, the first writer will write mere kiosk literature, whereas the second writer is capable of writing literature that timelessly touches the human soul.

In my view, only the architect, who creates his ideal client as he designs, can create houses and homes that give mankind hope and direction instead of mere superficial satisfaction. Without Frank Lloyd Wright's *Fallingwater*, Gerrit Rietveld's *Schröder House*, Le Corbusier's *Villa Savoye*, Pierre Chareau's *Glass House* and Alvar Aalto's *Villa Mairea* our understanding of modernity, and of ourselves, would be considerably weaker than now because these masterpieces concretize the possibilities of human habitat.

Feasibility of a homecoming

Authentic architecture is always about life; man's existential experience is the prime subject matter of the art of building. To a certain degree great architecture is also always about architecture itself, about the rules and boundaries of the discipline itself. But today's architecture seems to have abandoned life entirely and changed into a pure architectural fabrication.

Authentic architecture represents and reflects a way of life, an image of life. It is thought provoking that today's buildings frequently appear instead empty; they do not seem to represent any real and authentic way of life.

Today's architectural avantgarde has delibetately rejected the notion of home. Peter Eisenman (1987) stated that "Architecture must dislocate... without destroying its own being, while a house today must still shelter, it does not need to symbolize or romanticize its sheltering function, to the contrary: such symbols are today meaningless and merely nostalgia."

Beyond the rejection of issues of domicile, today's avant-garde architecture has all but abandoned the problems of mass-housing, which was a core issue of the Modern project. Our post-historical era has ended historical narratives and the notion of progress, and closed our view of the future. This loss of horizon and sense of purpose, and shortening of perspective, has turned architecture away from images of reality and life into an autistic and self-referential engagement with its own structures. At the same time, architecture has distanced itself from other sense realms and become a purely visual artform.

I may believe in groundless nostalgia, but I also believe in the feasibility of an architecture of reconciliation, an architecture that can mediate man's homecoming. The art of architecture can still produce houses that enable us to live with dignity. And, we still need houses that reinforce our sense of human reality and the essential hierarchies of life.

Fig. 7.2: The Living Room by Balthus. (Courtesy of The Minneapolis Institute of Arts.)
The home interiors of Balthus reflect strange sexual tensions –
the home has become eroticized – a necessary component for modern man.

A friend of mine, the Finnish poet Bo Carpelan, has written a number of powerful poems that deal with the poetics of the house and the home. His poems, I feel, condense the essence of home and give a lesson to us architects:

> There are still houses with low roofs,
> window bays where children climb
> and crouch, chins pressed to their knees,
> watching the damp snow falling peacefully
> into the dark, crowded yard.
> There are still rooms that tell of life,
> cupboards full of clean linen, passed down.
> There are quiet kitchens where someone sits
> and reads, book propped against the loaf.
> Light has the sound of white curtains.
> Shut your eyes, and see
> that you await the morn, even impatiently,
> that its warmth mixes with the warmth herein
> and that each falling snowflake
> is a sign of homecoming
>
> – Bo Carpelan, 1989

References

Alvar Aalto: *Vol. 1. 1922–1962*. 1963. Zurich: Les Editions d'Architecture Artemis.

Alexander, Christopher, and Serge Chermayeff. 1963. *Community and Privacy*. Garden City, N.Y.: Doubleday & Company.

Aries, Phillippe, and Georges Duby, eds. 1987. *A History of Private Life*. 4 vols. Cambridge, Mass.: Harvard University Press.

Bachelard, Gaston. 1969. *The Poetics of Space*. Boston: Beacon Press.

Carpelan, Bo. 1989. *Vuodet Kuin Lehdet*. Translated by Micheal Wynne-Ellis. Helsinki: Otava.

Coetzee, J. M. 1987. Interview in *Helsingin Sanomat*.

Eco, Umberto. 1985. *Postcript to The Name of the Rose*. In Journey to Hyperreality. WSOY.

Eisenman, Peter. 1987. Interview with Carsten Juel-Christiansen. *Skala* 12.

Edinger, Edward. 1973. *Ego and Archetype*. Baltimore: Penguin Books.
Frisch, Max. 1961. *Homo Faber*. Helsinki: Otava.
Heidegger, Martin. 1977. The Origin of the Work of Art. In *Basic Writings*. N.Y.: Harper & Row.
Laine, Jarkko. 1982. Tikusta Asiaa. *Parnasso 6* (Helsinki).
Marcuse, Herbert. 1964. *One Dimensional Man*. Boston: Beacon Press.
Olofsson, Anders. 1986. *Nostalgia. Tanken på en Hemkonst*. Stockholm: Alfa Beta Bokförlag.
Pallasmaa, Juhani. 1985. The Geometry of Feeling: a Look at the Phenomenology of Architecture. *Arkkitehti 3* (Helsinki). With English translation.

―――. 1992 Space and Image in Andrej Tarkovsky's Nostalgia. In *Focus*. Helsinki: The Faculty of Architecture, Helsinki University of Technology.

Rilke, Rainer Maria. [1949] 1992. *The Notebooks of Malte Laurids Brigge*. Reprint. Translated by M. D. Herter. N.Y.: W.W. Norton & Company.
Satre, Jean-Paul. 1978. *What is Literature?* Gloucester, U.K.: Peter Smith.
Strömnes, Frode. 1976. *A New Physics of Inner Worlds*. Tromsö: Institute of Social Science, University of Tromsö.

―――. 1981. On the Architecture of Thought. In *Abacus, Yearbook of the Museum of Finnish Architecture*. Helsinki: Museum of Finnish Architecture.

―――. 1982. The Externalized Image. A Study Showing Differences Correlating with Language Structure between Pictorial Structure in Ural-Altaic and Indo-European Filmed Versions of the Same Plays. *Reports from the Planning and Research Department, The Finnish Broadcasting Company*, no. 21. Helsinki: The Finnish Broadcasting Co.

Volkova, Paola. 1992. Interview with Mikael Fränti. In *Helsingin Sanomat* September 12, 1992.
Vrijman, Jan. 1994. Filmmakers Spacemakers. *The Berlage Papers* 11, January. Amsterdam: The Berlage Institute.

Part Three

Home as Reflection of
Societal Contention and Change

8

Domicide: The Destruction of Home

J. Douglas Porteous

> Old stone to new building, old timber to new fires,
> Old fires to ashes, and ashes to the earth
> Which is already flesh, fur and faeces,
> Bone of man and beast, cornstalk and leaf.
> Houses live and die....
>
> — T.S. Eliot, *East Coker*

Houses live and die. So do villages and city neighbourhoods. It seems a natural process. T.S. Eliot, anyway, was far less interested in people's attachment to houses than in their search for God. Unfortunately, individuals continue to develop attachments to buildings, communities, and places generally. I say unfortunately because so often these attachments come to grief when the objects of attachment – places – are destroyed in the name of progress.

We are then left lamenting, as Morris Berman does over his former home in the Bronx, lost to an expressway, in the aptly titled *All that is Solid Melts into Air* (Berman 1982). Modern novels are replete with evocations of homes lost to planning, development, and urban renewal in enterprise cultures. In David Lodge's *Nice Work* (1989, 31):

> Every morning Vic drives over the flattened site of his Gran's house and passes at chimney-pot level the one in which he himself grew up, where his widower father still stubbornly lives on in spite of all Vic's efforts to persuade him to move, like a sailor clinging to the rigging of a sinking ship – buffeted, deafened and choked by the thundering torrent of traffic thirty yards from the bedroom window.

For survivors like Vic's father, life is a matter of clinging to the wreckage until that, too, is destroyed. Lodge's words resonate with me, personally, for through the broken window of the bedroom in which I slept for many years I can see the docks whose expansion threatens not only my former home but the whole village in which I grew up (Porteous 1989).

Topocide and domicide

Literature on the nature of home is usually quite upbeat. Many of the papers in this volume stress the support given by home-making to personal identity and suggest that home plays an important role in the phenomenology of being. In contrast, this paper takes a gloomier view, confronting the normal practises of architecture, planning, business, and bureaucracy, all of which are implicated in the destruction of homes and communities (Porteous 1977).

First, some definitions. Initially it is important to distinguish between *locations* (which exist as coordinates in space, as in central place theory, and have characteristics but little character), *places* (which have character, via the process whereby love makes space place) and *home* (the individual's central place). Home is the landscape of the heart.

The concept of *destruction* must also be entertained. To destroy: to eradicate, obliterate, abolish, annihilate, efface, erase, expunge, remove, wipe out. When this happens to places, I call it *topocide*, the murder of place (a more mellifluous neologism than such purer locutions as *lococide* or *topothanasia*). When it happens to homes we may speak of *domicide*, the murder of a home.

After a small surge of interest in the 1960s, mainly induced by the topocide of Boston's West End (Fried 1963), geographers and planners have tended to ignore this downbeat theme. Generally, these professions have been too preoccupied with concepts such as growth, top-down hierarchies, and urban dominance, and have failed to investigate the effects of such dominance:

> We recognize, of course, that places "die" but there seems to have been an unwritten assumption that the places to which this happens are no longer important, that they no longer serve a useful purpose – an urban systems application of Darwinian doctrine. Yet there is abundant evidence that these places often continue to have real value to their residents, as witnessed by the passionate protests that attend the threat of extinction and by the way that people will cling on in the most daunting circumstances.... And when "death" is a consequence

of public policy...the implications have to be addressed as a matter of social responsibility. (Smith 1992).

Here I attempt to look under this as yet unturned stone. One problem, of course, is that we are dealing with environmental intangibles – attachment, grief, loss – which are immeasurable, difficult to articulate, and thus easy to ignore by the cost-benefit brigade. Moreover, certain planners and social philosophers actually celebrate topocide – one thinks of Melvin Webber's "nonplace urban realm" (1964) and "community without propinquity" (1963), wonderful no doubt, for white collar professionals jetting through the one-way streets of the so-called global village, but less charming to those who retain pre-enterprise culture values.

The issue, therefore, is not merely loss and change (Marris 1974) but deliberate change and enforced loss, actions committed by corporations and governments against ordinary people, and, at the world scale, by the North against the South. I am, therefore concerned with who does what to whom, and why and how and to what effect. Specifically, the premises of this discussion are: that individuals and groups may be strongly attached to home; that home is a component of personal and group identity; that homes are being destroyed at a vast and accelerating rate, at all geographical scales, in peace and war, legally, and in all parts of the world; and that this domicide has negative social and psychological effects on its human victims. To illustrate these points in more detail, I will now discuss domicide in the context of general topocide, create a tentative typology as a framework for further study, and give brief examples based on my research in Canada, Chile, and Britain.

Towards theory

Planning studies include a significant amount of research on the "planned relocation" of groups of residents or even of whole communities. Most emphasis has been placed on the relocation of agriculturalists or the elimination of urban neighbourhoods. There is overwhelming evidence that grandiose modern planning projects, from Third World "resettlement" schemes to World Fairs, have deleterious effects on impacted social groups. Change almost invariably means loss. Marris (1974) specifically included slum clearance and other planning-related issues along with mourning and bereavement in his general study of loss. Yet his emphasis on the response to loss means that he largely ignores the political and economic causes of loss. In my *Planned to Death* (1989) this emphasis is reversed, although some degree of balance has been aimed for.

Place destruction occurs at all times and in many regions. It may be due to natural causes, as with the destruction of whole towns by volcanic eruption. Or it may occur because of deliberate human agency. The destroyed unit may vary in size from a house (Israel), a neighbourhood (Boston's West End), or a city (*delenda est Carthago*), through the loss of integrity of provinces and counties (the loss of Rutland and other entities during British county-level administrative reorganization in 1974) to whole countries (Poland) and even empires (as after 1918).

The most spectacular efforts at 'place annihilation' (Hewitt 1983) may be the least effective; Dresden, Hamburg, Hiroshima and Nagasaki have risen from the ashes, an astounding manifestation of place loyalty. Physical deconstruction, using crowbars, bulldozers, explosives, and fire can be effective, as with many cases of cities laid waste by Babylonians, Assyrians, and Romans to the American destruction of the Japanese-Micronesian town of Koror, in Palau, towards the end of World War II. Perhaps the most effective method is drowning, as innumerable valley villages now below the surface of reservoirs bear witness.

The destruction of places by modern bureaucratic and political fiat is more common than might be supposed. During the 1970s I chronicled the efforts of left-wing Chilean governments to rid their land of American built company towns, hated symbols of economic dependence (Porteous 1972, 1973, 1974). In the United States small towns have commonly been relocated because of resource-extraction demands; one example involved a decision by the US Army Corps of Engineers that the best location for a second power-house at the Bonneville Dam on the Columbia River would be the site of the town of Bonneville itself (Comstock and Fox 1982). George Mackay Brown's *Greenvoe* (1972) chronicles in compelling detail, albeit in novelistic form, the destruction of a Scottish island community when external authorities decide that the island is the best location for a military installation. The inhabitants of numerous islands in the Pacific and Indian oceans – notably those of Bikini, Eniwetak, Kwajalein, Banaba, and Diego Garcia – have been removed wholesale to less viable environments and reduced to misery and penury because of the political, economic and military "needs" of Britain and the United States.

Company towns, or, as they are known more euphemistically, single-industry settlements, are particularly vulnerable to destruction due to resource depletion or changes in market forces. As there are approximately 700 such towns in Canada, the problem has been addressed most frequently in that country. Bowles' *Little Communities and Big Industries* (1982) draws some attention to the issue of community death, including a study of the arbitrary closing and re-opening of the town of Elliot Lake with changes in the world uranium market. Another book by the same author (Bowles 1981) raises the questions of possible, probable, and plausible futures for company towns in terms of social impact assessment methodology.

Bradbury and St. Martin (1983) have investigated the "winding-down" process in relation to the town of Schefferville, Quebec, whose iron mine was closed down in 1982. Their analysis points to the parallel processes of decreasing company involvement (withdrawal from public service provision and from municipal affairs; disinvestment) and community winding-down (emigration, instability, rumours, social dislocation). Of most interest for "topocide" research are the authors' assessments that:

1. Corporations, especially conglomerates, feel no compunction in opening or closing plant (and thus destroying or reviving the raison d'être of a one-industry town) for a "variety of reasons directly related to the nature of centralized management and control." Effectively, this means that although decisions taken on an international or national basis have profound repercussions at local level, these effects are of little account in the corporate world view.

2. The prevailing atmosphere among the inhabitants of declining or dying one-industry communities is one of rumour, uncertainty, and anxiety. This is often due to failure of communication on the part of the company, which merely emphasizes residents' feelings of neglect, as well as their feelings of impotence in the face of changing circumstances resulting from changes in the company's structure [and] "the absence of local participation in decision making."

Within Britain, studies of place destruction have tended towards the historical, with an emphasis on the annihilation of early modern villages in favour of sheep pasture and parkland. The study of historic deserted villages in England has become an academic growth industry since the development of extensive and accurate aerial photography. Contemporary studies of place annihilation more commonly concentrate on Third World locales (Sutton 1977). Military coercion is only infrequently investigated, but has clearly led to the destruction of places through both bombing and the relocation of millions of peasants to resettlement areas, from Afghanistan and Algeria to Vietnam and Zimbabwe. Places have been destroyed or fundamentally reshaped by military policy throughout the Arab-inhabited areas of Israel. I have witnessed the loss of place experienced by Israeli Bedouin concomitant upon increasing military demands in the Negev subsequent to the Israeli withdrawal from Sinai. Coercive political and economic policy underlay the "villagization" policies in Tanzania and Mozambique.

Surprisingly, it was not until 1976 that any significant attempt was made to generate a comprehensive theory of place destruction (Gallaher and Padfield 1980). The "dying community" seminars held at the School of American Research in Santa Fe, New Mexico, in the 1970s brought together anthropologists, archaeologists, sociologists, psychiatrists, and members of departments of English and Social Work. Although little theory emerged, several insights are important for topocide study. First, the emphasis on the small community; little settlements are clearly more vulnerable than cities. Second, the affirmation that community death is perhaps less common than community persistence in the midst of decay. Third, that the metaphor of death can be appropriately applied to communities; although sociologists and economists may debate this issue, "few archaeologists or historians will have any reservations on this score" (Adams 1980, 23). Fourth, we may profitably distinguish between communities which die a more lingering "natural" death and those which are "killed" by the violence of man or nature. Fifth, the two most interesting and pertinent questions are: why communities die; and how they die. These questions form the stuff of my *Planned to Death* study (Porteous 1989).

More specifically, Gallaher (1980, 93) provides context for the case-study of Schefferville, reported above, as well as for many other cases of topocide by confirming the dependence of small communities on external authorities. Addressing himself to the deaths of communities which come about as a by-product of corporate policy change, he asserts that:

> The basis for such decisions is not the desire to destroy a community but rather relates more to company production, profits, or changes in technology. Thus, decisions made in distant boardrooms, involving variables not addressing human needs per se, have the incidental effect of destroying a human community.

Dependence on external authority, further, often breeds a "culture of dependence" which encourages co-optation of community inhabitants and discourages protest or reaction.

This emphasis on local powerlessness is confirmed by Padfield (1980, 173) who affirms that:

> Clearly, *local* applies to the boundaries of small communities' political power and not to the boundaries of the political ties enjoyed by the industries which dominate them. The effective environment of industry...has grown continually larger, while the effective environment of the local community...has grown smaller. Clues to the mystery of the

small community's demise are not to be found locally, but in far away places, like the central headquarters for multinational corporations, and regulatory agencies.

One's geographic sense of community relates to the area over which one feels a sense of control. In small communities dominated by big industries, especially those in which the company controls much of the housing and public services, the individual controls very little. When the individual sense of control is missing it diminishes the general sense of community.

Significantly, the "dying community" seminar series involved no geographers or planners. Little effort was made, therefore, to investigate the effects of normal planning decisions on the life of small communities. Nor have planners themselves paid much attention to this issue. Indeed, the dying community receives less attention in frontier Canada and Australia than future-orientated "boom-town" studies. Clearly, the boom end of the "boom and bust cycle" in frontier zones is deemed more exciting and lucrative. Yet the growth of scholarly concern for those whose lives are disrupted by either growth or decay renders it imperative that planners and academics alike both provide data on, and interpretations of, such ongoing processes. Too often, despite the growth of social impact assessment, the reactions of the impacted population are simply neglected.

A tentative typology

A tentative typology of topocide/domicide can best be grasped in terms of the total range of place-unmaking, levels of power, causal agents, and scale.

Topocide, defined as the physical destruction of place, is not the only way in which places lose their integrity and identity. The character of a place may be effaced by the extremely rapid growth associated with boom conditions. More generally, the spatial homogenization associated with global capitalism promotes feelings of placelessness in existing settlements (Relph 1976). Topocide, in contrast, is a more violent process. In terms of power, it is clear that smaller places in the settlement hierarchy are generally at the mercy of the larger. In other words, global interests, often transnational corporations, dominate national interests, national interests in turn dominate regions, and all the above impact upon the local level where most of us live.

In terms of causal agents, topocide/domicide can best be conceptualized as a tree-diagram. The first distinction is between natural topocide (acts of God such as earthquakes, tsunamis, and the volcanic eruption which recently destroyed Clark Air Force Base in the Philippines) and topocide caused by human agency. The latter dichotomizes into war-time (Lidice, Dresden, Hiroshima, Sarajevo etc.) and peace-time topocide. This in turn branches into accidental (the Chernobyl region) and planned topocide. It is curious that so little attention has been paid to planned topocide, given that it is usually possible to identify the perpetrators.

Planned topocide occurs when powerful agencies, such as governments or corporations, deliberately choose to delete a place from the landscape. At the smaller scale, such deletions are physical, as when dwellings, neighborhoods, villages, and even whole valleys are bulldozed or flooded. At the larger scale, deletions are more likely to be conceptual, as when entities which command the loyalties of major communities lose their names, power, or identity. Poland is a celebrated example, and the current upheavals in the former USSR and Eastern Europe are cases where submerged identities are reasserting themselves in spatial terms. At the regional level, there has been much protest against the 1974 administrative reorganization of Britain which involved the total loss of several historic counties and the dismembering of others.

Finally, it is clear that from the individual's viewpoint, domicide can occur at every spatial level from one's bed, through room, dwelling, and neighbourhood, to landscape, region, nation, and perhaps the earth itself. Ecological thinking is beginning to convince us that the whole earth is our home. To continue to foul this nest beyond recovery is to commit the ultimate act of domicide.

Three brief case-studies

I will discuss the three case-studies chiefly from the viewpoints of motives for domicide and its effects on former residents.

Socioeconomic motives are most prevalent in Canada. Here topocide commonly involves the abandonment of remote single-enterprise communities (often "company towns") as the resource-base declines or social demands grow (Porteous 1975). Currently, attention is being focused on the choice between "towns" (a purpose built town in a remote location), "wheels" (commuting by land from established centres), and "wings" (weekly or longer-term commuting by airplane).

Politico-economic motives are more common in Britain. The Thatcherite enterprise culture has resulted in the loss of the raison d'être of several towns. In other cases, entire villages are erased to accommodate new industrial plant. My book *Planned to Death* (Porteous 1989) outlines this process.

In Chile, before 1973, socio-political motives were paramount (Porteous 1972). Christian Democrat and Popular Unity governments, in nationalizing the copper industry, sought to abandon American-owned company towns and resettle their populations in established centres "in the Chilean mainstream." This process was brought to an abrupt halt by General Pinochet.

My research in these regions emphasizes not only the motives for and mechanisms of domicide but also the effects of this violent process upon the uprooted inhabitants of destroyed settlements. Change almost invariably involves loss, and bereavement-like symptoms of grief are common among those uprooted and relocated. Resistance is usually ineffectual. Relocatees often improve their living standards dramatically, but pay for this in terms of considerable social and psychological disruption.

Conclusion

In conclusion, there is considerable evidence that grandiose modern planning projects involving domicide have severely deleterious affects on impacted populations. Much research is required on the effects of past, current, and imminent projects, especially in the Third World, where vast valley-drowning schemes are on line in India and China. And mechanisms for both prevention and mitigation demand the attention of planners and citizen groups.

Attachment to place is a common human trait. Recent work in France (Burgel 1992) suggests that attachment is strongest at the extremes of the spatial spectrum, i.e., the dwelling and the nation, and next strongest at neighbourhood and regional levels. These are the spaces people fight for and grieve over. They certainly complain that changes brought about without consultation drastically reduce their self-esteem, feelings of control, and the ability to make choices. Domicide is not democratic at the grass-roots level. Yet land-use theory continues to speak of the "invasion and succession" of urban land-uses as if dealing with plant rather than human communities. Theorists still subscribe to the notion of the "highest and best use'" of land, expressing this chiefly in financial terms. Ideas about land-use efficiency rarely focus on social efficiency and have little to say about intangibles such as the psychic relationships between people and place.

Domicide is extremely common throughout the world and is probably increasing. It is euphemistically explained away as "progress" or "development" or as being "in the interests of the nation" (which often means in the interests of plutocrats and professionals). And thus topophilia becomes topophobia, and domicile becomes domicide.

References

Adams, W.Y. 1980. The Dead Community: Perspectives from the Past. In *The Dying Community,* ed. A. Gallaher and H. Padfield. Albuquerque: University of New Mexico Press.
Berman, M. 1982. *All that Is Solid Melts into Air.* N.Y.: Simon and Schuster.
Bowles, R.T. 1981. *Social Impact Assessment in Small Communities.* Toronto: Butterworths.
———. 1982. *Little Communities and Big Industries.* Toronto: Butterworths.
Bradbury, J.H. and I. St. Martin 1983. Winding down in a Quebec Mining Town: a case-study of Schefferville. *Canadian Geographer* 27.
Brown, G.M. 1972. *Greenvoe.* Harmondsworth, U.K.: Penguin.
Burgel, G. 1992. The Big City: Audacity and Necessity. Keynote address, IAPS conference, Marmaras, Chalkidiki, Greece, July.
Comstock, D.E. and R. Fox. 1982. Participatory Research as Critical Theory. Paper presented at 10th World Conference of Sociology, Mexico City, August.
Fried, M. 1963. Grieving for a Lost Home. In *The Urban Condition,* ed. L.J. Duhl. N.Y.: Simon and Schuster.
Gallaher, A. 1980. Dependence on external authority and the decline of the community. In *The Dying Community,* ed. A. Gallaher and H. Padfield. Albuquerque: University of New Mexico Press.
Gallaher, A. and H. Padfield, eds. 1980. *The Dying Community.* Albuquerque: University of New Mexico Press.
Lodge, D. 1989. *Nice Work.* Harmondsworth, U.K.: Penguin.
Morris, P. 1974. *Loss and Change.* N.Y.: Pantheon.
Padfield, H. 1980. The Expendable Rural Community. In *The Dying Community,* ed. A. Gallaher and H. Padfield. Albuquerque: University of New Mexico Press.
Porteous, J.D. 1972. Urban Transplantation in Chile. *Geographical Review* 62
———. 1975. Quality of Life in B.C. company towns. *Contact* 7.
———. 1977. *Environment & Behavior.* Reading, Mass.: Addison-Wesley.
———. 1989. *Planned to Death.* Manchester: University of Manchester Press/Toronto: University of Toronto Press.
Relph, E. 1976. *Place and Placelessness.* London: Pion.
Smith, P. 1992. *Personal Communication.* University of Alberta, Edmonton.

Webber, M.M. 1963. Order in Diversity: Community without Propinquity. In *Cities and Space,* ed. L. Wingo. Baltimore: Johns Hopkins Press.
———. ed. 1964. The Urban Place and the Non-Place Urban Realm. In *Explorations into Urban Structure.* Philadelphia: University of Pennsylvania Press.

9
Ethnoarchaeology and the Concept of Home: A Cross-Cultural Analysis

Susan Kent

Introduction

To most westerners, *home* is a concept that gives symbolic meaning to a house that goes beyond its architecture. Home represents a refuge of personal space, which is all-important to westerners. This is one reason for the intense feelings of violation among people who have been burglarized (e.g., Korosec-Serfaty 1985). The concept of home also varies according to an individual's past experiences, particularly those concerned with family. In other words, the concept of home to westerners is an individual psychological, and often emotional, one. In the United States, depending on one's experience, home can be a castle or a dungeon – a place to escape to or to escape from. That is, home can symbolize security and warmth or gender roles and domesticity, or even tyranny through domination or abuse. Whatever the concept of home, it is an individual meaning, often concerned with family, that is expressed in culturally recognizable ways. Rapoport (this volume) points out the ambiguity of the concept in scholarly discourse.

The concept of home leads to several interesting questions. For example, do non-western societies endow architecture with meaning above and beyond the functional properties of a building and, if so, do they do it in the same ways and for the same reasons that westerners do? Specifically, do people with different mobility strategies, such as nomadism, also have a concept of home? And can the answers to these questions lead us to insights regarding the ontological nature of dwellings and the use of space?

I use cross-cultural ethnoarchaeological data I have collected in order to answer these questions. Before we can address them however, we need to define what ethnoarchaeology is. If you ask five ethnoarchaeologists to define ethnoarchaeology, you are likely to get five different answers! I will not detail the sometimes heated debates over definitions, but will instead summarize them. There are primarily two groups of ethnoarchaeologists, those who believe ethnoarchaeology is simply a form or extension of ethnographic analogy and those, including myself, who consider ethnoarchaeology to be quite distinct from ethnographic analogy, (for a detailed discussion see Kent 1987, 1992a).

Ethnoarchaeology beyond analogy

Ethnoarchaeology is a method to collect data on material culture, architecture, and use of space in contemporary societies that often are not part of an ethnographer's realm of interest, but are vital for understanding the past (as well as the present and future). How does it differ from ethnographic analogy? Basically, ethnographic analogy is the use of contemporary data to identify objects in the archaeological record. Ethnographic analogy attributes the modern function or meaning of an object, art style, or architecture to archaeological data. It is not a means for discerning patterning and relationships. Rather, ethnographic analogy is the attempt to assign a function to a usually non-western artifact. An example of the use of ethnographic analogy is the line of thinking that because Eskimos (Inuits) use an object of a particular shape for a specific activity, the same function may be inferred for a similar-looking object uncovered at a prehistoric hunter-gatherer site.

There is nothing intrinsically wrong with using ethnographic analogy. As long as comparisons are actually analogous, ethnographic analogy is a necessary part of archaeological inferences; if not, we would end up with classifications of object morphologies without function or meaning, a very sterile enterprise. How else would we be able to identify a pointed object as a projectile point unless we used modern analogies? Even here we sometimes mistake a pointed object for a piercing hunting tool when use-wear analyses indicate it was used as a hafted knife with a cutting function. One major difficulty in the use of ethnographic analogy is the underlying assumption that there has been little or no change in the function of an object, building, or space through time. Another difficulty is that ethnographic analogy is based on the implicit assumption that similar morphologies of modern objects necessarily denote similar functions or meanings in the past.

Problems arise when ethnographic analogy is confused with ethnoarchaeology. As noted by Rapoport (1990, 18) some archaeologists have used Naroll's (1962) formula for the number of people per dwelling square meter to estimate populations for a site or a region. Naroll's formula is an example of ethnographic analogy where the analog, or in this case, formula, is indiscriminately applied to very different societies in different environments with different mobility strategies. Such a simple formula for population estimates would, indeed, be convenient, but is unfortunately not very meaningful because it is based on the number of people per square meter of floor space from a number of disparate societies. On the other hand, Ethnoarchaeological research conducted in a variety of similar and dissimilar societies indicates that the size of dwellings depends on cultural principles that were not examined when Naroll's formula was calculated. Specifically, dwelling size appears to be more dependent on how long people plan to occupy a structure and/or site, (an issue of mobility), than on the number of people who actually inhabit it (Kent 1991a).

Unlike ethnographic analogy, ethnoarchaeology is most productive for discerning and understanding patterns and relationships. In several publications, Amos Rapoport (1990a, b) has referred to the need to analyze such patterns and relationships, which he regards as a concern with systems of settings rather than with buildings alone. In my opinion, elucidating patterning (that is similarities) as well as diversity (that is differences), constitutes the heart or essence of ethnoarchaeology. As an anthropologist, I want to know *why* patterning does or does *not* exist in my data. Ethnoarchaeology allows me to do precisely that by emphasizing links between material culture (such as architecture, which is sometimes ignored by ethnographers), behavior (such as the use of space, also often ignored by ethnographers), and culture (such as the socio-political organization of a society, frequently ignored by archaeologists). Ethnoarchaeology can be conducted from a very ecological or materialistic perspective (e.g., Binford 1979, 1983a,b 1989; O'Connell, Hawkes, and Blurton Jones 1988; Yellen 1977) or from a social, symbolic, or other more cultural orientation (e.g., Blanton 1994; Kent 1992b, 1993a,b).

"Be it ever so humble, there's no place like home"

"Be it ever so humble, there's no place like home" is a line from a well-known American song. We can say that in Western society the concept of home is more symbolically charged than that of house. How widespread, temporally or geographically, is the home concept? Does home have a similar connotation in non-Western societies? Answering these questions requires that we understand architectural and spatial patterning among diverse groups. I will elaborate on three vastly different societies in which I have conducted research:

1. sedentary Euro-Americans from different socio-political classes who live primarily in western Oklahoma and eastern Colorado in the United States

2. formerly semi-sedentary Navajo Indians who, at the time of my research, were living in one of the most remote and traditional parts of their Reservation located on the border of Utah and Arizona

3. formerly nomadic *Basarwa* (Bushmen or *San* as they have been called), who live in the Kalahari Desert of Botswana.[1]

These three groups provide a useful continuum of mobility patterns, from recent sedentism to long-term sedentism, with Euro-Americans being the most sedentary for the longest period of time and the Basarwa being the least sedentary for the shortest period of time. The Euro-Americans I studied occupied their dwellings for many years. Some Navajo families with whom I lived were year-round sedentary but occupied a dwelling for only a few years at a time. Other Navajo families practiced a more transhumant pattern of mobility wherein they moved at least twice a year if not more.

The Basarwa traditionally were nomadic, usually living in five or more different camps a year. Although my work has been with Basarwa who have been relatively sedentary for the past 15 to 20 years, I can compare their ways with the excellent ethnographies that span the 1950s to the mid-1970s written about the same linguistic groups as those who occupy Kutse when they were still nomadic (Silberbauer 1981; Tanaka 1980).

Because environmental or ecological explanations are so popular in anthropology, I deliberately selected groups to study which inhabit semi-arid regions (even for the Euro-Americans). As a result, I was able to factor out environment as a variable. Had I examined societies located in disparate environmental zones, it would have been most difficult to delineate variability resulting from differences in the environment from variability resulting from the differences in mobility.

While I acknowledge that the environment exerts very gross limitations on architecture and the use of space, I am more interested in non-environmental factors. For instance, why is there so much diversity within relatively similar, or sometimes even the same, geographical areas? As a specific example, why do some people, such as the tropical rainforest farmers of Central Africa, build rectangular houses constructed of mud and thatch, while their Pygmy neighbors build round houses constructed of leaves and wood (i.e., both are in the identical environment)? In other words, I find the social, political, organizational, and other behavioral and cultural factors more directly influential in shaping architecture and the use of space than is the affect of the physical environment, which in this case is minimal.

With one notable exception, one of whom is a contributor to this volume (Amos Rapoport), many scholars tend to focus on one society and often imply either that their conclusions can be generalized to different groups or time periods or that the study group is unique in some way. I think it is essential to ultimately test all hypotheses with cross-cultural data. It is one of the best ways to determine whether or not interpretations are valid only in the specific context in which a researcher happens to study. We need to be able to differentiate culturally idiosyncratic behavior from generalizable cross-cultural behavior. Cross-cultural research suggests that while Westerners place individual, psychological symbolism on domestic architecture, Navajo Indians place culture-wide, religious symbolism on their round dwellings. The Basarwa, I suggest, do not attach any symbolism to their domiciles. Had I studied only one of these groups, instead of all three, I would have probably reached very different conclusions about the nature of home and houses.

An example of what can happen if hypotheses are *not* tested cross-culturally is the very reasonable sounding proposition made by Hillier and Hanson (1984). They wrote that British houses are segmented into numerous rooms, particularly individual bedrooms that are gender-specific, because of the strong incest taboo among the British. However, had this proposition been tested cross-culturally, the authors would have found non-western groups with as strong, if not stronger, incest taboos who do *not* physically partition their dwellings at all (Kent 1990b). In these latter cases, everyone, regardless of gender or age, all sleep, eat, and perform a wide range of activities in a single room.

Among Navajo Indians, mating with anyone from the same clan no matter how remote the biological relationship, if any relation at all, is considered an act of incest. This includes the mating of individuals who Western society would not classify as kin. Incestuous matings are thought to cause insanity in the practitioners and severe birth defects in any offspring (Frisbie and McAllester 1978; Kluckhohn and Leighton 1962; Reichard 1974; Shepardson and Hammond 1970). Further, Navajos believe that, by definition, incest is practiced only by witches (Kluckhohn 1962). These are strong sanctions to discourage incest and yet the Navajo sleep and live in, depending on the season, either a one-room round *hogan* or a one-room rectangular *ramada* (shade).

Other cross-cultural examples show that there is little correlation between the strength of the incest taboo and the number of physical partitions in a house.[2] However, there are facets of culture other than the incest taboo that explain why Navajos all sleep together in one room, despite their abhorrence of incest, and why westerners and other societies tend to physically segregate their sleeping space within separate rooms partitioned by walls. On a cross-cultural level, we find that culturally segmented (or complex) societies tend to construct dwellings with more interior divisions. Elsewhere I have referred to this phenomenon as the principle of segmentation which underlies architectural and spatial organization (Kent 1990a, 1991b).

There appears to be a consistent relationship between behavior, culture, and architecture. The more socially, politically, and economically complex a society (or culturally segmented), the more architectural and spatial segmentation occurs (Kent 1990a). Complexity or segmentation is expressed in the presence or absence of stratification, hierarchies, and specialization. We can examine complex Western societies, such as Europe or North America, and see that houses are partitioned more than they are in some societies but the same amount as others; we are not unique in other words. Similar architectural segmentation occurs in culturally segmented non-Western societies as well. These include the state societies of Asia or West Africa, among others. It is equally instructive to compare societies that do not have much cultural segmentation, such as the Pygmies or Basarwa. These societies are characterized by an absence of spatial or architectural segmentation. Culturally non-segmented groups do not partition their architecture or use of space as much as culturally segmented societies do, which is isomorphic with their social, political, and economic organization that also lacks segmentation. In other words, there is an absence of stratification, specialization, or hierarchies in any realm – be it culture, behavior (e.g., use of space) or material culture (e.g., architecture). Tribal and chiefdom groups that lay between the extremes of cultural segmentation also tend to have an intermediate amount of architectural and spatial partitioning.

Observations of formerly nomadic peoples who have been relatively sedentary for only the past 20 to 30 years reveal the role of sedentism in promoting architectural and spatial segmentation or partitioning. Baka African Pygmies, for example, have enlarged their traditional huts and partitioned off rooms. One sedentary Pygmy camp I very briefly visited in Cameroon had a separate covered kitchen area, additional evidence of an increasing segmented use of space in conjunction with the partitioned hut. Basarwa living near Ghanzi or the Nata River in the Kalahari Desert have been sedentary for generations (Guenther 1986; Hitchcock 1982). They also partition their use of space more than still-nomadic groups in terms of both the activity function and the sex of the person performing the activity (e.g., Hitchcock 1987).

I suggest that it is not mobility itself conditioning the segmentation of the built environment. Concomitant with the shift to sedentism in these societies has been the development of socio-political segmentation in the form of formal leaders, which indicates an increase in political stratification or, in other words, cultural segmentation or complexity (e.g., Hitchcock and Holm 1985; Guenther 1975, 1976). In ways too complicated to detail here, I suggest that mobility and cultural segmentation or complexity are interrelated (Kent 1989). It is difficult to untangle mobility patterns from socio-political segmentation because they are interrelated on one level. Whereas both occur in the ethnographic record, highly egalitarian sedentary societies or highly *non*-egalitarian nomadic societies are not common (although both do occur as discussed below).

Is home for everyone?

As mentioned previously, home is an individual psychological concept for most westerners that gives meaning to a house that goes far beyond its architecture. In contrast, Navajo Indians imbue their conception of the *hogan*, their winter dwelling, with symbolic religious meaning that is collective or culture-wide rather than individual. Navajo *hogans*, whether constructed of wood, cement, or tar and plaster board, are thought to represent the cosmos. Both the *hogan* (by definition) and the cosmos are round and lack physical partitioning. In addition, both the *hogan* and cosmos are spatially partitioned through use by gender. So, whereas home can have different meanings for individual westerners, the sacredness of the *hogan* is a concept shared by all traditional Navajos. Here we can see that although the Navajo *hogan* and western house both have symbolic meaning beyond the architecture or use of the structure, the meaning is on very different levels – individual and psychological in contrast to collective or culture-wide and religious. Confusion of these two levels can lead to a misunderstanding of the nature of the use of space and architecture, as well as the concept of home.

How can we know if a symbolic attachment to a dwelling is a collective, culture-wide phenomenon or individual phenomenon? A number of people have conceptually outlined the necessary steps (e.g., see Binford 1983a, b, 1989, and elsewhere; Rapoport 1990b). The actual steps I took were to live with different Navajo families who ranged from traditional to semi-nontraditional (Kent 1984). More traditional Navajos segregated male space from female space through use in their one-room *hogans*. However, none of the Navajo families physically or through use partitioned their living space into function-specific activity areas or multiple rooms.

Many Navajo myths, legends, and healing chants specify what the *hogan* represents; that is, the cosmos, and how *hogan* space should be used by males and females. They dictate that the northern half be used by females and the southern by males. They also reveal that the Navajo concept, use, and partitioning of dwellings, or lack of partitioning, is based on collective or culture-wide ideology. Religious belief, which mandates that many ceremonies be performed only in round *hogans* because of their sacred status, also indicates that the symbolism of the *hogan* is on a cultural level (Kluckhohn and Leighton 1962; Reichard 1974).

Examining the variability in the use of space, particularly in reference to partitioning, also allows us to distinguish individual from group symbolism. The rectangular *ramada*, which is occupied during the summer, is used by the same people for the same exact activities conducted in the same way as in the *hogan*. The *ramada*, however, is *not* considered to be a representation of the cosmos (because it is not round). Therefore, the family which observes a spatial division in the *hogan* does not observe a similar division in the rectangular *ramada* (Kent 1984). Rectangular dwellings are not sacred to the Navajos and are not imbued with meaning above and beyond their utilitarian function.

As Navajos begin to adopt a new cosmology, or at least no longer believe in the traditional one, the circular *hogan* has begun to lose its sacredness and its status as a representation of the cosmos. As a result of this change, many Navajos today no longer adhere to the traditional male-female division of space within the *hogan*. Despite this change, even the less traditional Navajos living in three-bedroom Euro-American style rectangular houses built by the Bureau of Indian Affairs used fewer partitions than any western family from any socio-economic class that I have observed. Lower class Euro-Americans occupying houses with fewer rooms often physically, or through use, partition off parts of rooms to create more spatial segmentation (Kent n.d.). In contrast, Navajos occupying large, three-bedroom houses often do not use all the rooms available and perform a variety of activities in multi-purpose and non-gender specific areas. In other words, despite some variability attributable to the rapid transformation of Navajo society, through which many traditions are changing or lost, the way the Navajos as a group use space and architectural partitioning is more similar to one another than to any Western society's use; that is, intra-group variation, though present, is less than inter-group variation.

Although for different reasons, dwellings have meaning for both Navajos and westerners that is above and beyond mere habitation. Because the symbolism of the cosmos for round Navajo dwellings is on the cultural level, rather than on the individual level, the meaning attached to the *hogan* is the same for all traditional Navajos and is not subject to personal past experiences. It would be completely inappropriate to ascribe the Navajo partitioning of *hogan* space, into male and female halves, to the same factors that influence gender and activity partitioning in western houses. It would be equally inappropriate to attribute the symbolic importance and meaning of the *hogan* to Navajos to the same factors that make a house a home to westerners.

What about the recently sedentary, non-culturally segmented Basarwa? What is their relationship to their dwellings and do they attach meaning to their abodes on either an individual or culture-wide level?

The Basarwa and their fellow Bakgalagadi (Bantu-speaking), residents at Kutse, are primarily, though not exclusively, hunters and gatherers. Previously they were nomadic, following the availability of wild plants. When nomadic, they did not wander aimlessly around the landscape. The Basarwa and Bakgalagadi occupied large territories with localities, such as a *pan* (a seasonal pond), that were "owned" by a family but not in the western sense of ownership (Silberbauer 1981). Owners and their families are not politically, socially, symbolically, or otherwise different from people who are not owners. Usually ownership is assigned to the family thought to have first arrived at a location. Whereas etiquette requires one to ask permission to stay at a locality owned by someone, etiquette also requires that an owner never refuse such a request. The Kutse Basarwa can be classified as culturally non-segmented because they lack permanent formal leaders, economic specialization, or socio-political hierarchies or stratification (Kent 1993c).

Interestingly enough, Kutse residents basically live out-of-doors unless there is rain. They sleep outside, eat outside, work outside, and entertain outside. They construct windbreaks next to a focal hearth and conduct most of their activities in camp there. Windbreaks are also used to keep possessions out of the reach of children and dogs. Huts are built during the hot, rainy season, but they are used more for storage and for temporary escape from the rain and oppressive heat of the season rather than for a living space in the western sense of the term.

Traditionally, Basarwa constructed huts only at summer camps; winter camps traditionally contained only a windbreak. Today at Kutse, year-round camps typically have both a hut and a windbreak. Huts are used for year-round storage and many even have an interior storage platform, a feature that is directly associated with increasing sedentism and not found in huts when Basarwa were more mobile. People who plan a short occupation at a camp tend to build more ephemeral windbreaks and huts than those who plan a long occupation. This tendency occurs regardless of the number of inhabitants. More substantially constructed windbreaks and huts are often built at camps where a long occupation is anticipated (Kent and Vierich 1989).

There is no spatial or architectural partitioning either by sex or by activity function at Kutse camps. Unmarried friends of the same sex often share a windbreak or hut, whereas nuclear families usually occupy their own. Group composition at Kutse camps today is variable. People visit other camps at and away from Kutse for a few hours, a few months, or even a few years. In the latter cases, a hut and/or windbreak is constructed at the host camp. Camp membership is very fluid. Individuals or entire families move in and out of camps.

Unlike the more sedentary Navajo Indians and westerners, mobile peoples, or newly sedentary peoples like those at Kutse, do not appear to attach symbolism to their dwellings. In other words, there is no symbolic or emotional attachment to a dwelling or a particular locus. I suggest attachments may, instead, be with other people with whom they live or visit, rather than with their dwellings, i.e., more social and less materialistic. Even so, Kutse residents do not want to be relocated by the government as was once planned. Their resistance to moving is not, however, because individual houses or windbreaks are particularly meaningful to them, as might be the case for westerners. Their reasons for wanting to remain in their current community include their ties to the general area, convenience for visiting family and friends residing in the Central Kalahari Game Reserve, plentiful wild game and wild plants in the area for hunting and gathering, good opportunities to sell curios to passing tourists, the availability of year-round water and firewood, easy access to transportation to and from towns provided free of charge by game reserve and mining employees who pass through their current community, and so on.

Houses, homes, and work

Comparisons of different societies reveals that not all people differentiate between living areas and work areas. In western society, people often work outside the house (in an office or other building or in fields on a farm, etc.).

This separation of activities reinforces the distinction between work and home; separate buildings are used for non-domestic activities. The separation of domestic versus non-domestic buildings is consistent with the amount of cultural segmentation present in western society. Westerners tend to divide their cultural universe into segments (as is visible by the amount of stratification in their socio-political organization, such as classes, etc.). They do the same with architecture and use of space. In contrast, the Basarwa do not recognize such segments in their built environment because they are not present in their culture. Activity areas are multi-purpose and non-sex-specific in use. There is no separation between home and non-home buildings because all activities can and do occur at any locus.

It is interesting that as more Westerners begin to work in their houses, many still retain a spatial distinction between areas of non-domestic activities or work and areas of domestic activities. A study of British workers revealed they conceptually and/or physically partition work areas (e.g., offices in the house) from non-work areas, i.e., separate from home (Mars and Mars 1992: personal communication). By keeping the two loci clearly delineated and differentiated, westerners are perpetuating the symbolism of the house as home. From this perspective, the phrase "home office" is somewhat misleading. More accurate is "house office" which is distinct from "house home."

Navajos occasionally separate work space from domestic or house space, but not to the same extent as do westerners. For example, work activities which require much space, such as butchering, sheering sheep and goats, and weaving rugs on a loom, tend to be conducted out-of-doors (weaving can also be done indoors). Unlike westerners, many activities, including food preparation and consumption, sleeping, and entertaining are not spatially differentiated inside their abodes.

Kutse residents do not differentiate between work areas and domestic or dwelling areas, unless an activity requires a large open work space in which case they locate it away from the areas in use. As mentioned above, they do not separate activities physically or through area usage. Kutse residents also do not divide sacred space from profane space as the Navajos do. Dances for entertainment or for healing occur around any focal hearth located in a fairly open space (dancers need a large area to move in). This absence of segregated areas is directly related to the absence of segmentation (stratification and hierarchies) in Basarwa culture. Nor do formerly nomadic Basarwa attach psychological significance to their houses. They do not elevate them to individually important concepts as more culturally segmented and sedentary Euro-Americans do. To them a domestic dwelling is a house, not a home.

The Bedouin are a good example to illustrate the principle that mobility enhances or inhibits segmentation in the built environment (enhancing it in the following), but does not cause it. Cultural segmentation causes spatial and architectural segmentation.

Bedouins are nomadic as Kalahari peoples traditionally were, and yet they assign symbolic meaning to different areas in their tents. That is, they cognitively partition living space into male and female space, into activity-specific areas inside and outside the tents, and into high status space (the sheik's tent which is often larger than the others and partitioned into four or five rooms; Layne 1987). Although Bedouins are nomadic, the tent travels with them. In a sense they retain the same residence as do sedentary groups; they simply set up in different locations. They do not occupy and then abandon a tent, as the Basarwa occupy and abandon forever a windbreak and/or hut, because the tent has importance and permanence that the Basarwa structures lack. The other significant difference between Bedouin and nomadic groups like the Basarwa, is the former's highly complex, segmented social and political system, which translates into status hierarchies, specialization, and political stratification. These are visible in their segmentation of tent space by an individual's gender and status and by activity function.

It is interesting to see the increase in architectural and spatial segmentation as Bedouins become stationary (Layne 1987). Sedentism enhances the segmentation already present in the Bedouin dwellings and space, whereas the amount of cultural segmentation influences the presence or absence of spatial or dwelling segmentation, some of which was present when Bedouins were still nomadic. Culturally, Bedouins are as dissimilar to non-culturally segmented nomadic peoples as are sedentary, culturally segmented societies which have status hierarchies and other stratification in their culture. Only in their mobility are Bedouins similar to nomadic, but less culturally segmented, groups.

Now that they are sedentary, Basarwa tend to not segregate places of rest for the dead from the living (this was not the traditional pattern). At Kutse, corpses are buried at a currently occupied camp, next to a hut or windbreak, or under a nearby tree. How different this pattern is from the more sedentary Navajo Indians, who traditionally permanently abandoned the dwelling in which a death occurred, and often abandoned an entire camp (they occasionally burned a *hogan* in which a death occurred to prevent the dangerous ghost from returning to the locale; Kent 1990c). In the Navajo case, a distinction between space for the dead and space for the living is made through the abandonment of an otherwise acceptable camp. Westerners do not generally abandon houses in which a death has occurred, but they have specific areas designated exclusively for the dead – that is, cemeteries.

It is important to realize that we can no more ignore a society's culture (in this case cultural segmentation and organization) when studying its architecture or use of space than we can ignore its patterns of mobility. We need to study the context of buildings and their meaning within the cultural system, as Rapoport (1990a, b) has advocated for a long time. I have tried to illustrate how one can go about doing so using ethnoarchaeology.

Discussion

A house consists primarily of walls with a roof and floor; a home is much more. The concept of home is embedded in individual meaning for many westerners. *Hogans* are symbolically charged for Navajos, but for different reasons and at a different level: that of shared cultural meaning rather than individual meaning. Many non-Western societies, particularly sociopolitically noncomplex ones, do not segment their culture, use of space, and architecture, especially in terms of domestic and non-domestic work areas. This fact does not make the concept of home any less valid or less important to westerners. Highly egalitarian, mobile groups do not have the psychological, personally meaningful concept of home or attachment to house as a result of the way their culture, behavior, and material culture are organized.

Ethnoarchaeology is a method for acquiring data on the built environment. It provides a way in which to understand how and why people elevate architecture into something that has meaning above and beyond a structure's functional properties. Some scholars see the relationships as primarily ecological while others, such as myself, see the relationships as primarily cultural. Either way, ethnoarchaeology can be used as a methodological bridge linking the built environment to the meanings (be they ecological, symbolic, or other), that people attribute to it. Ethnoarchaeology's forte is linking patterning to underlying relationships. Understanding these relationships allows us to predict in which cultures we can expect to find a concept similar to that of the Western home, where we might find less individualistic meanings associated with domestic dwellings, such as the Navajo *hogan,* and when we will probably not find a symbolically significant meaning attached to a group's dwellings, as with the Basarwa huts and windbreaks.

The human species has been highly egalitarian and nomadic for a majority of its existence. Many groups have made the transition to sedentism and have become culturally segmented with stratification and hierarchies common, including Western society. Understanding the impact and influence of both mobility patterns and cultural segmentation is therefore crucial to our understanding of past, contemporary, and future patterns of architecture and the use of space. This presents a challenge to architects to take into account the culture of a society for which they are designing buildings, to archaeologists to take into account the settlement patterns and cultural segmentation and organization of the prehistoric societies they study, and to ethnographers to take into account the relationships linking the use of space and architecture to mobility and cultural segmentation in the groups they study. The need for close interaction between archaeologists, ethnographers, and architects has been recognized by a number of people, as exemplified by this very volume. Such an interdisciplinary approach, whether accomplished by an individual or by a team, is, in my opinion, the most productive avenue to the understanding of the form, context, and meaning of the built environment.

Conclusions

We can delineate general patterns which are linked by cross-culturally consistent relationships among cultural segmentation, mobility patterns, and partitioning of the built environment. Whereas sedentism may intensify architectural and spatial differentiation, cultural segmentation causes it. The more culturally segmented a society, with more stratification and hierarchies in the socio-political, economic, religious, and other facets of culture, the more stratification of space and architecture into gender, status, age, or activity-specific areas or rooms. Sedentary societies, which are culturally segmented, will tend to be more architecturally and spatially segmented as well. In such societies, domestic (i.e., home), and non-domestic work will be spatially, and whenever possible physically, partitioned. In the example presented here, ethnoarchaeologically collected data was a tool used to elucidate patterns in an attempt to understand the relationship among cultural segmentation, mobility, and architectural and spatial partitioning.

Acknowledgements

This paper is dedicated to Amos Rapoport, whose work continues to be an inspiration to my research. I would like to sincerely thank David Benjamin and the University of Trondheim for inviting me to the conference on the meaning of home held in Trondheim, Norway, and for providing the funding which allowed me to participate. I am grateful to the diverse groups of people who have shared a part of their lives with me, including the Kutse residents, Navajos, and Euro-Americans. I greatly appreciate the permission granted by the Botswana Office of the President, Ministry of Local Government and Lands, and the National Museum and Art Gallery to allow me to work in Botswana and the permission granted by the Navajo Nation that allowed me to work on the Reservation. Funding throughout the years has been provided by the Fulbright Foundation, Swan Fund, Wenner Gren, and Old Dominion University. I thank all the funding agencies for making the research possible.

Endnotes

1. Originally the Basarwa lived in and near the Central Kalahari Game Reserve. Today they live at a community called Kutse located just outside the Khutse Game Reserve (alternate spelling of Kutse is used to differentiate the community from the game reserve). Along with Basarwa who speak different Central Kalahari dialects there are Bakgalagadi, or Bantu-speakers, who make up between 20 to 30 per cent of the community. Kutse residents represent the most mobile sedentary people I know! They are clearly in a transitional state that is, in and of itself, a very interesting topic, but one that cannot be persued here.

2. The strength of the incest taboo is difficult to measure because the definition of who is appropriate to mate with is not universally agreed upon. For example, it was not considered to be incestuous for Egyptian pharaohs to marry their sisters any more than it was incestuous for European royalty to marry close cousins.

References

Altman, Irwin, and Carol Werner, eds. 1985. Home Environments. Vol. 8 of *Human Behavior and Environment. Advances in Theory and Research*. N.Y.: Plenum Press.

Binford, Lewis. 1979. *Nunimut Ethnoarchaeology*. New York: Academic Press.

———. 1983a. *In Pursuit of the Past*. London: Thames and Hudson.

———. 1983b. *Working at Archaeology*. N.Y.: Academic Press.

———. 1989. *Debating Archaeology*. Orlando, CA: Academic Press.

Blanton, Richard. 1994. *Houses and Households: A Comparative Study*. N.Y.: Plenum Press.

Frisbie, Charlotte and David McAllester, eds. 1978. *Navajo Blessingway Singer*. Tucson: University of Arizona Press.

Hillier, B. and J. Hanson. 1984. *The Social Logic of Space*. Cambridge: Cambridge University Press.

Guenther, Mathias. 1975. The Trance Dancer as an Agent of Social Change among the Farm Bushmen of the Ghanzi District. *Botswana Notes and Records* 7.

———. 1976. "From Hunters to Squatters: Social and Cultural Change among the Farm San of Ghanzi, Botswana." In *Kalahari Hunter-Gatherers*, edited by Richard Lee and Irven DeVore. Cambridge: Harvard University Press.

———. 1986. *The Nharo Bushmen of Botswana: Tradition and Change*. Hamburg: Helmut Buske Verlag.

Hitchcock, Robert. 1982. The Ethnoarchaeology of Sedentism: Mobility Strategies and Site Structure Among Foraging and Food Producing Populations in the Eastern Kalahari Desert, Botswana. PhD diss., University of New Mexico.

———. 1987. Sedentism and Site Structure: Organizational Changes in Kalahari Basarwa Residential Locations. In *Method and Theory for Activity Area Research: An Ethnoarchaeological Approach*, ed. S. Kent. N.Y.: Columbia University Press.

Hitchcock, Robert, and John Holm. 1985. Political Development Among the Basarwa of Botswana. *Cultural Survival Quarterly* 9(3).

Kent, Susan. 1987. Understanding the Use of Space – An Ethnoarchaeological Perspective. In *Method and Theory for Activity Area Research. An Ethnoarchaeological Approach*, ed. S. Kent. N.Y.: Columbia University Press.

———. 1989. Cross-Cultural Perceptions of Farmers as Hunters and the Value of Meat. In *Farmers as Hunters – The Implications of Sedentism*, ed. S. Kent. Cambridge: Cambridge University Press.

———. 1990a. A Cross-Cultural Study of Segmentation, Architecture, and the Use of Space. In *Domestic Architecture and the Use of Space. An Interdisciplinary Cross-Cultural Study,* ed. S. Kent. Cambridge: Cambridge University Press.

———. 1990b. Activity Areas and Architecture: An Interdisciplinary View of the Relationship Between Use of Space and Domestic Built Environments. In *Domestic Architecture and the Use of Space. An Inter-disciplinary Cross-Cultural study,* ed. S. Kent. Cambridge: Cambridge University Press.

———. 1991a. The Relationship Between Mobility Strategies and Site Structure. In *The Interpretation of Spatial Patterning within Stone Age Archaeological Sites,* ed. E. Kroll and T. D. Price. N.Y.: Plenum Publishing Corporation.

———. 1991b. Partitioning Space: Cross-Cultural Factors Influencing Domestic Spatial Configuration. *Environment and Behavior* 23(4).

———. 1992a. The Current Forager Controversy: Real Versus Ideal Views of Hunter-Gatherers. *Man* 27(1).

———. 1992b. Studying Variability in the Archaeological Record: An Ethnoarchaeological Model for Distinguishing Mobility Patterns. *American Antiquity* 57(4).

———. 1993a. Influence of Hunting Success and Skill, Sharing, Mode of Cooking, and Dogs on Faunal Remains at a Sedentary Kalahari Community. In *Journal of Anthropological Archaeology* 12(4).

———. 1993b. Models of Abandonment and Material Culture Frequencies. In *Abandonment Processes: Seasonal Variation and Regional Mobility,* ed. C. Cameron and Steven Tomka. Cambridge: Cambridge University Press.

———. 1993c. Sharing in an Egalitarian Kalahari Community. *Man* 28.

———. n.d. *Rich Houses, Poor Houses – Architectural and Spatial Micro-Variation in American Society.* Mimeo.

Kent, Susan, and Helga Vierich. 1989. The Myth of Ecological Determinism – Anticipated Mobility and Site Spatial Organization. In *Farmers as Hunters – The Implications of Sedentism,* ed. S. Kent. Cambridge: Cambridge University Press.

Kluckhohn, Clyde. 1962. *Navaho witchcraft.* Boston: Beacon Press.

Kluckhohn, Clyde and Dorothea Leighton. 1962. *The Navaho.* Rev. ed. Garden City, N.Y.: Doubleday and Company.

Korosec-Serfaty, Perla. 1985. Experience and Use of the Dwelling. In *Home environments.* Vol. 8 of *Human Behavior and Environment. Advances in Theory and Research,* ed. I. Altman and C. Werner. N.Y.: Plenum Press.

Layne, Linda. 1987. Village-Bedouin: Patterns of Change from Mobility to Sedentism in Jordan. In *Method and Theory for Activity Area Research: An Ethnoarchaeological Approach,* ed. S. Kent. N.Y.: Columbia University Press.

Naroll, R. 1962. Floor Area and Settlement Population. *American Antiquity* 27.

O'Connell, James, Kristen Hawkes, and Nicholas Blurton Jones. 1988. Hadza Hunting, Butchering, and Bone Transport and their Archaeological Implications. *Journal of Anthropological Research* 44(2).

Rapoport, Amos. 1990a. Systems of Activities and Systems of Settings. In *Domestic Architecture and the Use of Space. An Interdisciplinary Perspective,* ed. S. Kent. Cambridge: Cambridge University Press.

―――. 1990b. *History and Precedent in Environmental Design.* N.Y.: Plenum Press.

Reichard, Gladys. 1974. *Navaho Religion: A Study of Symbolism.* Princeton: Princeton University Press.

Shepardson, Mary and Blodwen Hammond. 1970. *The Navajo Mountain Community: Social Organization and Kinship Terminology.* Berkeley: University of California Press.

Silberbauer, George. 1981. *Hunter and Habitat in the Central Kalahari Desert.* Cambridge: Cambridge University Press.

Tanaka, Jiro. 1980. *The San Hunters-Gatherers of the Kalahari.* Tokyo: University of Tokyo Press.

Yellen, John. 1977. *Archaeological Approaches to the Past.* N.Y.: Academic Press.

10

House and Home: Identity, Dichotomy, or Dialectic? (With Special Reference to Mexico)[1]

David Stea

Introduction

The title of this session is "The Home and Personal Identity," and I am billed as coming from psychology. I was once an experimental psychologist and, I suppose, one of the grandfathers of environmental psychology, but I confess to having become an outspoken and, hopefully, constructive critic of both fields in recent years. This criticism stems from the evolving perspective on western behavioral science of someone born and raised in the United States, but who has spent much of his life in the developing world. From this evolving perspective, and in relation to issues of built environment, the program of Anglo-American experimental psychology has come to seem, first, tautological, and second, culture-bound.

The program of psychology is tautological, in my view, in that it claims to study the universals of human behavior while implicitly assuming that the behavior it studies is universal. It is culture-bound, largely within Euro-American society, in its overwhelming concern with the *individual*. However, a critical examination of the ideological and philosophical roots of both psychology and environmental psychology are beyond the scope of this presentation. Thus, I hope that I will be forgiven for trying to adopt a view different than that usually associated with the label psychologist, a view based more upon experience than upon academic degrees conferred a long time ago.

This different viewpoint should ideally be encompassed within the sub-field of cross-cultural psychology. Unfortunately, cultural considerations in this potentially rich area have been distorted by subordination to the conceptual framework of western psychology, including the perennial search for consistent variation in a lawful universe. But cultures are not consistent. Buber (1965) correctly, I believe, has characterized culture as a merger of contrasts. Deductive schools might sub-sume these contrasts under complementarities, while dialectics would label them contradictions. In truth, cultures are probably composed of both complementary and contradictory elements: the latter, the presence of conceptual opposites within the same reality, are the most difficult to comprehend. The important point is that since cultural cores (Steward 1955; Rapoport 1987) and their peripheries cannot be expected to be rigidly consistent, neither can their correlates in domestic architecture: the presence of a certain element in a society also implies its opposite. The contrast between the Mexican home interior, in the example introduced later, and the street, is such a contradiction.

Within the originally assigned theme of "home and personal identity," I should like to consider the words *home, personal,* and *identity* separately. First, concerning home in a broad sense, some differences between *house,* as a physical artifact, and home as place identity and social construct, will be explored. Second, I will try to break the usually assumed equation of personal and individual: thus, the individual who was once the sole concern of environmental psychology is seen as only one of many social units whose behavior gives identity to home and to which home gives identity. Because individual and social behavior are also related to value systems, house form expresses *values identity,* as well. Third, identity will be examined in two senses: first, in the above house-home relationship; second, in the plural form identities, reflecting the sometimes complementary and often contradictory complexes of social and individual roles that characterize societies.

Fourth, in an attempt to bridge the universality and particularity of behavior, three concepts of global interest will be considered: family, social hierarchy, and mode of activity, and in some examples drawn from Mexico, how both are expressed and related to household and social identity. Finally, the foregoing will be related to certain broader issues concerning the relation between identity, home, and society.

House and home: Place identity and attachment to place

The first part of this presentation is directed to the nature of the relationship between house as a physical cultural artifact and *home base* as identification with a defined portion of space or spaces, of particular places on earth. The relation of these two terms to the concept *dwelling* has been adequately treated by Lawrence (1987). The fundamental question of this first segment is: when is a house a home, and when not, and what is the relation between this conjunction or disjunction and the forms of houses/housing? Our concern here is not with the pristine, unchanging vernacular house, but with transition, and with transitional societies en-route from *traditional* forms to approximations of what we call *modern*.

Our ideal – often our assumption – is the identity of house and home. This reflects a sedentary, agrarian set of values, and a particular concept of "rootedness." Usually ignored is the fact that one's abilities to maintain an identity between house and home – that is, actually to dwell in the place one regards as home – are strongly related to the socio-political economy of the country in question.

Many environmental psychologists, however, are so firmly rooted in the mythology of ubiquitous personal choice that we often fail to recognize that the choice of home base is limited for most people: the failure to exercise the "choice" to maintain house-home identity is taken as evidence of the equally mythological "culture of poverty" (Stea, 1991). Rapoport's (1985) concept of choice allows for its absence as well as its presence, both being related to "homeless:"

> ...*choice*...is central regarding home environments. It seems characteristic of those...that *they are chosen*. One could almost argue that *if they are not chosen they are not home*. An imposed setting is unlikely to be a home environment...(Rapoport 1985, 256).

A case of clear non-choice is that of forced or "involuntary" resettlement (Cernea, 1988; Cummings, 1990), a phenomenon clearly typical of (but no longer confined to), peasants and indigenous people displaced by large-scale hydroelectric projects and extractive industries. Paradoxically, because individual needs are subordinated to the international political economy, people who would like to move (nomads), are forced to settle, and those who would like to remain settled (no longer just the poor), are often forced to move.

Among the latter, house and home are thus separated: the house becomes more of a dormitory for people (temporarily, they imagine), separated from their true homes. They see themselves as exiles rather than settlers, thus establishing a dichotomy between house and home. Other resettlers retain strong ties to their "former" (real) homes, often to the extent of maintaining "dual households." The relationship between a house in one place and a home in another – the establishment of separate identities with "house" and "home" – then becomes dialectical.

Failure to express identity through a house seems to result when: (1) identity with the home base is much stronger than with the place where the house is located, and (2) perceived control over the house is absent or much attenuated – e.g. American Indian Reservation housing.[2] Yet a third factor, repugnant to those of us who see houses as the prime form of personal expression, is that, among those with very limited means, other life priorities may be so much higher that the house is of little importance except as mere shelter. Thus, the outward appearance of housing in otherwise well-planned urban "squatter" settlements in Latin America is a result neither of innate slovenliness nor the operation of a "culture of poverty;" rather, it indicates the low priority of the house relative to other needs.

Both industrialized and developing societies, for differing but increasingly convergent reasons, have become highly mobile. The effects of this mobility upon the house have much to do with its effects upon home, ranging from reduction in the importance of the house to mere shelter, as in the case of the irregular urban settlements mentioned above, to the opposite extreme, where the house is expected to fulfill most of the functions once fulfilled by the larger settlement, or "home ground" (Sennett 1977), and from houses expected to perform all the functions of home (and often more), to houses expected to form very few of these.

The spatial aspects of home transcend conventional concepts of territoriality and home range; they are related to, but are by no means identical with "home ground," or *tierra,* or "sense of place" (Ralph 1984). Being involuntarily separated from one's home is "placelessness;" the modern internationalized house, associated with no particular place, is also "placeless." Dovey (1985) equates this placelessness with one kind of homelessness:

> The dream of the modern movement in architecture and planning was that technology and industrialized housing would be able to provide high-quality housing for everyone, mass-produced in high-rise blocks set in a garden landscape. Housing was regarded rationally in terms of universal requirements, applicable internationally and cross-culturally. The house was conceived as a "machine-for-living-in," a piece of technology. The result, we have since learned, was homelessness. (Dovey 1985, 59)

Economic conditions in the U.S.A. of the past 12 years have resulted in a second kind of homelessness: being forced out of one's home. Ironically, those with too strong a "sense of place," initially unwilling to leave their homes under economic pressure of the current crisis (or to "vote with the feet"),[3] have often lost both house and home thereby, becoming "houseless" as well as homeless. (Fried 1963; Dovey 1985)

An important aspect of this argument involves the nature of ties between the inhabitants of the house and what they conceive as home, between the house and home ground, and the spatio-temporal separations between these. What is necessary, in a transitional society, for a house to become a home? One consideration is the adaptiveness of a given house form to cultural necessities: modern internationalized housing is particularly poor at this. Then there is the element of forced non-adaptiveness, or *coercive housing*: the use of housing as a means of acculturation, to forcibly break the tie between house and traditional home, to establish new concepts of the "proper house," (Perin 1977) and to force the establishment not just of new houses, but often unsuccessfully, of new homes.

Cognitive maps and intercultural perspectives

Socio-cultural constructions of communities (Suttles 1972) are translated into cognitive maps of spaces appropriate to accommodate these constructions, forming "templates" with which to judge the appropriateness of dwelling places. Such maps may be detailed or general. As a general social dimension, consider separation vs. aggregation, represented, on a social level by social units, by families and neighbors, and values of spatial privacy, and on a physical level by connected or disconnected dwellings. Most of us are familiar with the interestingly enormous value placed by American society on the free-standing house: an extreme form is indicated by Rapoport (1985):

> The...narrow lots of Milwaukee allow (buildings at) densities as high as townhouses (to look) like single-family dwellings. The spacing of 3-4 feet is not "useful" in instrumental terms and even was disadvantageous...(in) a Pittsburgh example...the spacing is only 18 inches. (Rapoport 1985, 275)

There are tens of thousands of examples of what might be called the "detached rowhouse" in Brooklyn, New York, some with lateral spacings as narrow as in Rapoport's example, so narrow that cleaning is rendered extremely difficult and snow removal nearly impossible. But there is another aspect to these houses, whose dimensions, in the Brooklyn example, are usually 4-5 meters by 20 or 25 meters. Because they are even narrower than townhouses on equivalent-sized lots, there is no space for corridors or passageways on ground level: the result is what apartment dwellers refer to as the "railway flat," where social, dining, and food-preparation spaces are coupled as in a train. There is simply no way of getting from one space to another without passing through all the spaces in between. Expressively, these houses connote dense within-family linkages and strong separation from those outside: they happily accommodate highly interactive groups and clearly frustrate spatial privacy.

Understandably, much research in the environment-behavior realm has focused upon built form as a primary datum, then upon behavior as a set of abstract labels, and finally upon the relationship of these abstract labels to built form. Here, the opposite is proposed: to focus first upon the manifestation of psychological universals in socio-cultural particulars, and then how these, in turn, are related to dwelling. In other words, the task is to find out what people most value and how this is related to domestic behavior, a procedure not unlike that advocated by Kent (1990b). This approach is applicable to a variety of cultural regions, including Scandinavia.

House and Home in Mexico:
Mexican and Scandinavian perspectives

The descriptions that follow are based, first, upon five years of participant observation by the author and numerous interviews with expert informants; second, on in-depth interviews with three families resident in Mexico whose members are either Scandinavian or have lived in Scandinavia.

Mexican homes

In the case of Mexican houses, the above model directs us to examine basic value structures (Bonfil Batalla 1990; Condon 1980, 1985; Paz 1950; Riding 1989), as evidenced in both traditional and transitional areas. "Transition" refers, in Mexico, much more to material culture than to the cultural core, which has proven remarkably resilient to change in the face of enormous external pressures and devastating crises. Primary among Mexican values – so far in front that it often eclipses all others – is the family. To consider personal identity apart from family identity in the Mexican house would be utterly meaningless:

> The family's survival as a powerful and deeply conservative institution has been crucial to maintaining Mexico's...stability.... In reality, society reflects the family...the paternalistic and authoritarian structure of the family also seems to prepare Mexicans to accept the hierarchical social arrangements that prevail in the country at large.

The continuing strength of the family is all the more remarkable in a country that has been convulsed by social change over the past forty years...yet the family has changed less than the country. For most Mexicans the family remains the pivot of their lives. It is not a matter of choice: it is simply the way society is organized.... Closed to outsiders, the family is enormously self-sufficient.... Social life involves being with relatives, children have no reason to play with anyone but siblings and cousins.... Mexicans need few friends because they have many relatives...the very insularity of the family teaches Mexicans to distrust society as a whole and they feel safer...if surrounded by relatives. (Riding 1989, 238–239)

But the Spanish word *familia* has a very different meaning in Latin America in general, and Mexico above all, than does family in the U.S.A., or many parts of Northern Europe: the nuclear family has four or five members, the extended *familia*, which exists in symbiotic relationship with the Church, has hundreds. The *familia* is extended beyond grandparents, uncles, aunts, and cousins, in many parts of Latin America, through first, the system of *compadrazgo*, the incorporation into the *familia* of another set of god parents at each of many ceremonies, and second, the incorporation of *cuates* (literally twins), or best friends. The resulting enormous conglomerate is an "insurance umbrella" encompassing nearly everything of importance to traditional rural Mexicans: members of such extended families live close-by and often constitute entire neighborhoods. But the importance of the *familia* to *urban* Mexicans is not markedly less.

Urban Mexican houses give little hint of the foregoing. Free-standing or attached, they incorporate, primarily, nuclear families. A cursory inspection of the urban Mexican house, coupled with the hasty attachment of environment-behavior labels, therefore leads to the very misleading conclusion that the extended family has been weakened and the separation of nuclear elements somehow strengthened. Nothing could be further from the truth. In fact, linkages in this matrifocal world have been spatially lengthened but not markedly strained, and the ties of these nuclear family dwellings to other *familia*-related dwellings is, in general, still infinitely stronger than to neighbors.

Let's consider concepts of "public and private." In the traditional Mexican town or village, houses of the middle-class and above are divided from the street by continuous walls. The gradient is hard and abrupt, and there is no exterior semi-public space as such. Unless the street is also an extended family domain, the street is familially non-territorial; this may contribute to some observers' impression of incredible contrasts between littered streets and spotlessly clean, compulsively ordered house interiors. It is also part of a dialectical relationship: certainly, compulsivity is not a general part of Mexican psychology: in fact, it is both sex-linked and place-specific. Inside, the house is the responsibility of the mother; the outside is the responsibility of something nebulous, ill-understood: "the government." We shall return to this later.

The hard walls define a boundary between the private and public realm, but private and public to whom? In brief, as with the Maori (Linzey 1987) but in a very different way, hospitality is all-important. In the Mexican case, this hospitality must be available to any member or members of the extended *familia* at any time. All members of the *familia* have access to all parts of the house but food preparation and laundry areas – these are the only ones that can be considered semi-private. They are semi-permeable alien territories, related to a gender-divided hierarchical society: In brief, they are the servants' territory, and accessible only to the women of the *familia*, who supervise, but do not engage in, the demeaning manual labor they represent, (see Diaz-Plaja 1975, 277, for Cervantes' marvelous *Trato de Angel,* mocking this scorning of manual labor, which is Arabic as well as Hispanic).

Important objects are always conspicuously displayed, in an array that strikes the careless observer as clutter, but is in fact a highly ordered, closely packed, often museum-like collection having, in most homes, almost no relation to traditional Mexico (Bonfil Batalla 1990). As there is little physically private space, so there are few private objects. The early internationalized homes even incorporated the automobile as part of this conspicuous display: designs which opened garages onto living rooms were extremely popular just a few years ago.

Indeed, the closest equivalents to the English word "privacy" in the Spanish language are intimacy, isolation, and solitude, of which two are connotatively negative and the other sexual.[4] Octavio Paz' (1950) *labyrinth of solitude* exists on psychological and philosophical levels, but not in the physical environment.

Because all non-servant spaces are public to all *familia* members, they must be kept in perfect order at all times: Room doors must be open except when sleeping or dressing and all closet doors closed (although closet interiors must be as ordered as the rooms). As Gorden (1974) indicates for Colombia, and which is true as well of Mexico, bedrooms are also where women often entertain. A mother refers to the bedroom in which she sleeps with her husband not as *nuestro cuarto* (our room) but as *mi cuarto* (my room): some women allow female friends or relatives to enter, but not their maids (Seiersen 1992). The entire house is clearly female territory, and the kitchen exclusively so.

In households such as the above, there is a relatively high tolerance for noise, time is difficult to plan, and "action chains" (Hall and Hall 1987) can rarely be completed. In terms of Goffman's (1966) theater model, "front stage" and "back stage" shift with time: bedrooms which serve as dressing rooms ("back stage") upon arising in the morning become entertainment spaces ("front stage") during the day.

The nuclear family is always subordinate, in both form and function, to the *familia,* and the duties of husband and wife to both their *familias* transcend duties to each other. It is said that "in Mexico, one does not marry an individual; one marries a family." Therefore, while the house is occupied by a nuclear family, it is identified with the extended *familia.*

Social reproduction of the *familia* implies many nested ceremonies: these involve extensive preparation and considerable expense at various significant points in the life of the developing child. They are also replicated by others that occur more frequently. The Sunday *comida* (afternoon lunch) at grandmother's house is further replicated by the daily *comida* in the nuclear family dwelling. The ceremonial quality of this is reflected in the observation that the most important elements not just of traditional Mexican society, but everywhere apart from the largest cities, are still "mother and lunch." Even in large cities, nearly all mothers eat lunch with their children at home; this is the only time, until late at night, that the father is likely to be home. Thus, the space devoted to dining is large and central for two reasons: behaviorally, it must accommodate not just the nuclear family, but members of the *familia* on many weekends; symbolically, it is the formal representation of the society's most important value.

Kent (1990b), quoting Hillier and Hanson, has also noted that domestic space use replicates, on a family level, entire social systems. What this means, astonishingly, is that "eating lunch" can have repercussions at the metropolitan, national, and international levels. The cultural press to return home for *comida* in one of Mexico City's internationalized homes means four rush hours instead of two: astonishingly, "lunch" is thus a major contributor to the greatest urban pollution problem on earth.

What do these "modern internationalized homes," encapsulated in buildings externally distinguished from office high-rises only by the presence of balconies, look like? As example of such a home, constructed for upper middle-class families in 1960, is indicated in Figure 10.1. The first thing to note about this example is that it is not one apartment, but two, with separate entrances: one for the family, and one for the maid or maids. These sub-apartments represent social hierarchy in both spatial and accommodation terms; interpenetration is minimal, and the treatment of the two is very different.

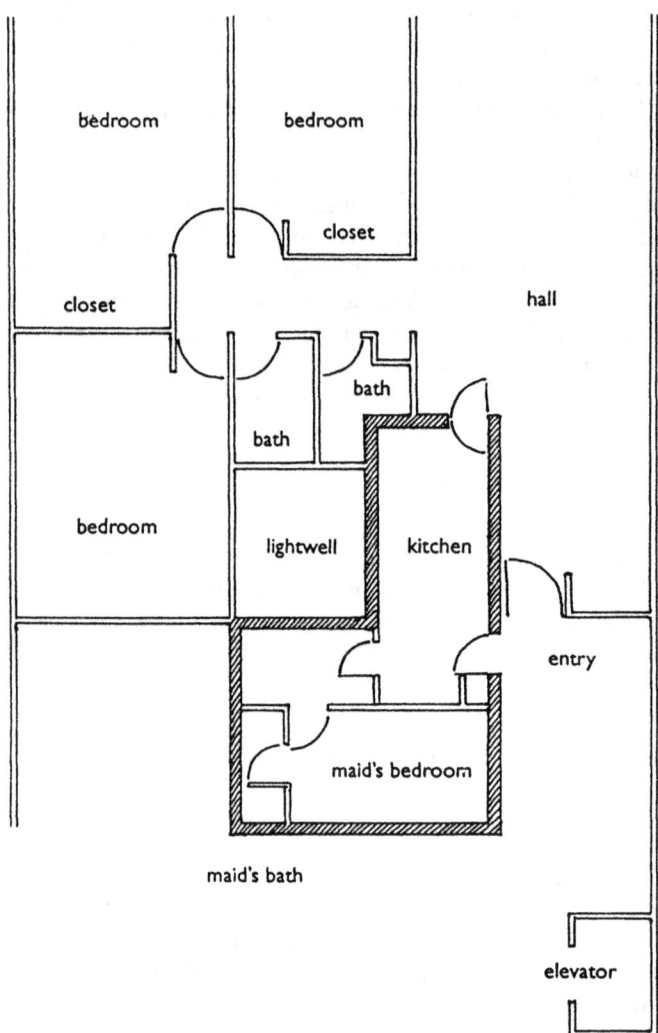

Figure 10.1. Floor plan of a Mexican apartment, constructed in 1960. The "servant's territory" is outlined more darkly. As originally designed, the apartment consisted of the *recamera* (bedroom), *cocina* (kitchen), *bano* (bath), *cuarto de servicio* (maid's bedroom), and *cubo de luz* (light well: the symbolic remains of the open patio at fifth-floor level). *B.S.* is the maid's bath. The hall, largely devoted to dining, was later enlarged through annexation of the adjacent bedroom.

Such apartments worked well during the middle-class "servant era;" after the economic crisis of the early 1980s, however, the middle class was forced in large part to give up its servants. Apartments such as that illustrated prove to be extremely difficult to accommodate to a servantless era. The proportions of the long, narrow kitchens, for example, are suited to the preparation of food but not to its consumption – in most cases only to a lone worker – and cannot accommodate labor-saving informal eating arrangements (a maidless mother can more easily serve her children in the kitchen, but its shape precludes this). The servant quarters – cold, institutional and windowless, with the most rudimentary bath facilities – cannot be easily converted into other uses, such as guest quarters.

A note of caution: in no way is it suggested that the kitchen in such internationalized homes is either a direct physical representation of traditional values or isomorphic to a traditional kitchen, but simply that it is intended to accommodate a set of hierarchically segregated behaviors related to a particular value system.

One architect friend of the author suggested demolishing the upper part of the wall separating the kitchen from the dining area, opening it to the remainder of the apartment, as in many contemporary U.S. homes. A few Mexicans whom the author queried concerning this suggestion reacted with utter horror, indicating that such an alteration would make the apartment essentially unrentable and unsuitable for sale. They pointed out that neither future occupants nor their Mexican servants would tolerate breaking down the hard barrier between each other's territories, and that while Mexicans love the smell of food, many Mexican men detest cooking odors. It appeared from these comments that food preparation, far from being a source of fascination, is now regarded by many as a somewhat repulsive, "backstage," activity. Although The word *hogar* in Spanish means both home and hearth, food preparation and consumption became separated at some point in Mexican history.[5]

Territoriality has been a popular area of study in environmental psychology (e.g., Sebba and Churchman, 1983) and we have already stated that the house is primarily the mother's territory, (the children have "their" spaces as well). But Mexico remains a rigidly patriarchal society: "The idea of a strong family is inseparable from that of a family controlled by a paternalistic figure of authority." (Riding 1989, 242). How then does this all-powerful male figure relate to the home?

I am indebted to a Danish architect, a 35-year resident of Mexico and a favorite student of Steen Eiler Rasmussen, for another hypothesis (Seiersen, 1992). The adult male, who occupies the top of the familial "pecking order," has no domestic territory. My observations confirm this: in the provinces, the man exists in two worlds, but his realm, (social rather than individual territory), is the street and the *cantina*; in middle-class urban Mexico it is often the office. A few Mexican men have offices "at home," these are either in a separate building on the same lot or in a separate wing of the house. In either case, it usually has no access from the house and is entered only from the outside. Thus, in the domestic sphere, territory and hierarchy do not coincide.

Scandinavian views of the modern Mexican home.

As noted in endtnote 4, Rybczynski (1986) identifies early examples of intimacy (in the non-sexual sense), privacy, and individualization of domestic environments within northern Europe of the seventeenth century, and draws a detailed and fascinating example from Kristiania, the old name of present-day Oslo. This sense of, and concern with, privacy appears to have typified much of Scandinavia – but not Latin America. Let us then examine a few contemporary Scandinavian impressions of Mexican domestic life.

These impressions of cultural contrast in domestic life were obtained, as earlier indicated, in interviews with several families with extensive Scandinavian experience, either as natives or long-term residents of the area. The harvest of data was not a rich one, largely because diplomatic and expatriate families are usually placed in houses designed especially for foreigners: thus, those in Mexico City rarely experience living in a Mexican home. This may account for the paucity of observations on living space. Most comments by non-architects concerned the micro-level of materials and the macro-level of inside-outside relations.

Concrete is the "new traditional" building material almost everywhere in timber-poor Mexico, (with the exception of certain upland areas of Chihuahua and Michoacan). Although adobe houses are still common in many rural places, most residents of Mexico City experience only concrete on all interior and exterior surfaces. Swedish respondents commented on the contrast between the ubiquitous rough stucco walls and the smooth surfaces which they were used to at home. But most alienating, to people accustomed to wood, were the concrete floors. The Scandinavian wood floors were equally strange to the Mexicans: One Mexican woman volunteered that when the front door of her future husband's Norwegian home opened, she knew that she could never live there: "My son would ruin the wood floors in a day." Seiersen (1992) included wood kitchen floors in his design for a wealthy Mexican couple: the material was rejected as being inappropriate for servants.

Some of the most interesting observations, however, from the perspective of this paper, concerned contrasts between the nature of family in Scandinavian and Latin American cultures, and between the care devoted to domestic spaces and the condition of public areas. These observations emphasized organization of modern Scandinavian domestic life around the single person (a third of Swedish households), and the nuclear family, along with their relatively weak extended families – similar to the U.S.A. In addition, they noted a puzzling contradiction between the scrupulously neat Mexican home interior and what seemed to the, in contrast to their homelands, garbage-strewn unmaintained streets outside.

Discussion

At this point, I am forced to qualify the title of today's session: it is my firm belief that any attempt to resolve the dichotomy or dialectic between traditional and internationalized homes in solely formal terms, or even in formal terms related to (individual) personal identity, is doomed to failure. While dealing solely with isolated individuals, at one extreme, can be misleading, I have not found abstract cultural analysis, at the other extreme, terribly helpful either. If psychology has anything at all to offer to this debate, it consists in contributions from community psychology, in relating systems of values to behavior (Kent 1990, 1991) and in exploring the nature of the nested social units which characterize many societies.

Nested social units, also called hierarchical nesting, refer to the various levels of social grouping that range from the individual through the nuclear family, extended family, sub-tribe or neighborhood, tribe or municipality, though higher levels of social and governmental aggregations. Clearly, not all levels are present in all societies: advanced semi-nomadic peoples in their nomadic phase, for example, have little need for socio-physical organization above that of the mobile unit that provides security and constitutes an economic unit. Sebba (1991, 1992) in her studies of Israeli Bedouin, remarks on the absence of a socio-physical phenomenon called replication by Vogt (Stea and Wood 1971):

> The total control of the family, in Bedouin society, is expressed by the structural fabric of the village and the internal fabric of the household. In the same manner as in the house, *it is impossible to find expressions of individual organization, it is impossible to find expressions of public organization on a communal basis in the village.* (Sebba 1991, 233)

The isolated individual is an absurdity and public organization an anomaly in Bedouin or Australian Aboriginal society: one is suicidal and the other unnecessary in traditional existence. But the "crunch" comes in the transition to settled, even urban society. With regard to the Bedouin:

> The village houses, which seem to be a random cluster of houses in various stages of building, testify to the lack of common planning in the entire village. The lack of overall planning in the village is accompanied by the lack of infrastructure, roads and lighting.... All of this testifies to the absence of a social entity (with real power or symbolic representation), that represents the link between all of the inhabitants. Such a social entity (which is meant to develop on the basis of communal living over time), could not have developed with the Bedouin's nomadic lifestyle, and it seems that the total control of the family over Bedouin social life did not allow its development until the '80s. (Sebba 1991, 233)

Now, what of socio-cultural transitions in non-nomadic settled societies? The global phenomenon of Third World urbanization is barely 45 years old: cities have grown from mere towns to sprawling megalopolises in less than 20% of the time taken for similar phenomena in Western Europe. Thus, the change from traditional rural life and its "ancient homes" to the "modern internationalized home" of the city has been revolutionary, not evolutionary: there has been no time, in other words, to evolve forms of living better suited to new environments, agglomerative sizes, and population densities. While the more ancient of these cities retain truly urban cores, their newer, peripheral, areas are simply giant "urban villages."

Impacts are relative to accustomed levels of population aggregation and conditions of existence. The trauma of rapid transition from small nomadic units to village living for the Bedouin is paralleled by the trauma of rapid transition from village living to city dwelling for rural Mexicans, neither has coping mechanisms appropriate to the change (Stea 1980, 1983).

Mexican towns, the ancient homesites world-renowned for their harmonious beauty, are organized at several levels: the nuclear family, the *familia* (the extended family), the *colonia* (roughly equivalent to neighborhood, or community, but more significant), and the municipality, or town government. The *colonia* is strongly organized around extraordinarily colorful *fiestas*, festive events that occur with great frequency around religious holidays and with less frequency around the visits of political dignitaries. A *cacique*, a powerful and wealthy local figure, is honored by being chosen as the *patron* of a fiesta. The fiesta serves as a focal point for community activity, reaffirming the community and the commitment of its residents. It is an occasion for painting and rehabilitating buildings and community infrastructure; it is, in short, the formal mechanism through which social responsibility is exercised at a level between the *familia* and the government. Thus, behavior associated with the "common good" is not informal and internalized; it is formal and externally controlled. In other words, because there has been little influence from the northern European bourgeois city, the idea of "citizen" (which preceded national citizenship, Rybczynski 1986), is still somewhat alien in a society that, until late in the last century, was largely feudal, ecclesiastical, and agricultural.

Sebba's (1991, 1992) Bedouin villages lack organization because no need for village organization, beyond the extended family, has previously existed; we hypothesize that the apparent chaos of the modern internationalized Mexican city is a reflection of the disappearance of a vital level of social organization, the community. There, while the *colonia* continues as a point of geographical reference, the social behaviors which reinforced its significance, and the responsibility of its residents to each other, have disappeared. Therefore, no meaningful *formal* intermediate level of social organization exists in middle-class urban *colonias* between the *familia* and the city. In a society highly dependent upon formal, traditional structures rather than informal social organization (other psychologists may wish to think in terms of locus of control), the absence of this level of social nesting is critical. The government has unsuccessfully tried to fill the gap by attempting (with much less success in middle-class than in peripheral lower-class areas) to structure the *colonia* government (Coreno and Stea, 1991).

The result of the above, at the level of the home, is what the Scandinavian residents of Mexico City who were interviewed in this study, commented upon: the contrast between the extraordinary neatness of the house interior and the street. Carried to another level, the chaos of the world outside the house is what impresses casual visitors to Mexican cities, not having experienced the tight structure of the *familia*, they often see only what appears to be near-total disorganization.

Several rays of hope have shone with the installation of a mutually-aided, government-supported self-help program called *Solidaridad*, or PRONASOL (Sweeney and Jimenez 1992) inaugurated several years ago and later expanded by Mexican President Carlos Salinas de Gortari, who wrote his doctoral dissertation on community participation (Wisner, Stea, and Kruks, 1991) in decision-making. However, it must be noted that PRONASOL has experienced more rural than urban success.

In the cities, the aforementioned chaos, compounded by urban alienation, is further reinforced by an alien physical environment: architecture in the ever-popular international style, and urban design, based upon turn-of-the-century European models, which physically breaks up colonias, and further reduces their social press. At this point, the visual chaos becomes compounded by an internationalized urban experience: fear. The traditional village mechanism for the broader exercise of social responsibility is absent; there is no basis for social organization intermediate between the *familia* and the municipal government. The architectural artifact called *home* still reinforces the *familia*, but nothing reinforces the community. Lacking an informal basis for neighboring or for the exercise of social responsibility, urban Mexicans naturally fall back on the *familia*, retreating even further from the larger social arena.

Conclusions

Over the years, presentations on the ancient home have progressed from visually entertaining but theoretically vacuous purely descriptive case studies (criticized by, e.g., Stea, 1990) to more insightful views of the vernacular which, while still case studies, attempted to relate ancient forms to social behavior (Fuchs and Meyer-Brodnitz 1989; Pavlides and Hesser 1989). Comparative studies have also begun to emerge, of two or more ancient or vernacular house forms (Kent 1990, 1991; Stea and Turan 1993), of vernacular and modern (Linzey 1987) or of the transition between the two (Cernea 1988; Cummings 1990) and of the role of external forces (Stea, Covarrubias, and Bossano 1990; Upton 1990). If socio-behavioral data is scarce on ancient domestic Scandinavia, such studies certainly exist on modern Scandinavia (Danermark and Ekstrom 1992, and Vestbro 1992, are two of the most recent). In addition, some valuable comparative studies have been performed by people completely outside the environmental design disciplines (Fathy and Yousef 1975). All of this has been further enlightened by a substantially expanded theoretical harvest (Abu-Lughod 1990; Kent 1990, 1991; Lawrence 1987; Rapoport 1985, 1990; Stea and Turan 1993).

Ancient and modern internationalized homes are connected through the values and behavior of the people who dwell in them. Social systems, like all large systems, are inherently conservative, they endeavor to maintain themselves in the face of change. It is this self-maintaining characteristic that bridges the contradiction represented by the ancient and modern institutionalized homes: while striving to adjust to social change, people also strive to maintain cultural continuity.

One should always conclude a presentation such as this by saying "more research is needed," but I suspect that a fair part of the needed research has already been done in many areas of the globe, it needs however, to be reinterpreted. The preceding analysis has been largely about Mexico, and Mexico is certainly not Scandinavia; in at least some respects, it may be as different as one can find. But, as all anthropologists know, one of the best ways to enlighten oneself about hidden dimensions of one's own culture is to study similar dimensions in markedly different cultures. That is the scholarly payoff, but there is a practical one as well: Scandinavian architectural involvement in the developing world is intense and widespread, and familiarity with the dimensions of domesticity in the Western hemisphere south of the U.S.A. can only be of future benefit. Representing Latin America – informally, at least – at this symposium, I hope that the insights shared on house and home in Mexico may yield greater understanding of relationships between societal self-maintenance and cultural change; and between traditional and contemporary environmental design, an understanding valuable not just to the developing world, but to Scandinavia as well.

Endnotes

1. The author would like to acknowledge the following who read and commented on earlier versions of this manuscript: Vivian Antaki, Noel Brissenden, Maggie Brunner, Silvia Elguea, Steven Matejovsky, Camilo Perez, and Palle Seiersen.

2. "Rootedness," or the attachment to a specific place is so strong, for example, among some rural Native Americans, that they choose to move in with relatives rather than to accept government housing in other areas of their Reservations.

3. In 1983, ex-U.S. President Ronald Reagan coined a new euphemism for the chronic recession-induced homelessness of the early 1980s by referring to the wandering of 3 million unemployed, displaced Americans, in search of jobs and homes, as "voting with their feet."

4. Rybczynski (1986) points out that rooms in which individuals can be alone, which did not come into being in Europe until the seventeenth century, were at first called "privacies." His detailed discussion of early indications of the importance of privacy, interestingly, center on a seventeenth century Oslo bookbinder and his family: "One can imagine Frederik and Marthe...sitting in the main room alone....

A simple scene, and yet a revolution in human relations is taking place. The husband and wife have begun to think of themselves – perhaps for the first time – as a *couple*...the importance of this event ...which was taking place all over Northern and Central Europe, cannot be exaggerated." (Rybczynski 1986, 47–48) Such events, and the values attached to them, are atypical of Latin America.

5. With regard to seventeenth-century Paris, (which influenced adjacent Spain, and, thus, Latin America), "Cooking was no longer done on the central hearth but in a separate room reserved for that purpose. Since cooking smells were considered unpleasant...the kitchen was usually located some distance away on the other side of the courtyard." (Rybczynski 1986, 38)

References

Abu-Lughod, J. 1990. The Disappearance and Despatialization of First World – Third World dichotomies. *Traditional Dwellings and Settlements Review* 13 (Fall).

Altman, I., and C.M. Werner, eds. 1985. *Home Environments*. Vol. 8 of *Human Behavior and Environment. Advances in Theory and Research*. N.Y.: Plenum Press.

Bonfil Batalla, G. 1990. *Mexico Profundo: Una Civilizacion Negada*. Mexico, D.F.: Grijalbo.

Buber, M.M. 1965. The nature of culture. In *Human face – Chapters in philosophical anthropology*. Jerusalem: Bialik Institute.

Cernea, M.M. 1988. *Involuntary Resettlement in Development Projects*. Washington, D.C.: World Bank..

Condon, J.C. 1980. ...So near the United States. *The bridge* 30 (Spring).

———. 1985. *Good Neighbors: Communicating with the Mexicans*. Yarmouth, Mass.: Intercultural Press.

Condon, J.C., and F. Yousef. 1975. Out of house and home. In *An Introduction to Intercultural Communication*. Indianapolis, Indiana: Bobbs-Merrill.

Coreno, V., and D. Stea. Using the Government: Community Organization and Environmental Design in a Mexican Colonia. Forthcoming.

Cummings, B.J. 1990. *Dam the Rivers, Damn the People*. London: Earthscan Publications.

Danermark, B., and M. Ekström. 1992. The Elderly and Housing Relocation in Sweden: A Comparative Methodology. In *The Meaning and Use of*

Housing: Methodologies and their Applications to Policy, Planning, and Design, ed. E.G. Arias. Aldershot, U.K.: Gower/Avebury.

Diaz-Plaja, F. 1975. *El espanol y los siete pecados capitales.* Madrid: Alianza Editorial.

Dovey, K. 1985. Home and Homelessness. In *Home Environments.* Vol. 8 of *Human Behavior and Environment. Advances in Theory and Research,* ed. I. Atlman and C. Werner. N.Y.: Plenum Press.

Fried, M. 1963. Grieving for a Lost Home. In *The Urban Condition,* ed. L.J. Duhl. N.Y.: Basic Books.

Fuchs, A.R. and M. Meyer-Brodnitz. 1989. The Emergence of the Central Hall House-Type in the Context of Nineteenth Century Palestine. In *Dwellings, Settlements, and Tradition: Cross-Cultural Perspectives.* eds. Bourdier, J-P., and N. Alsayyad. N.Y.: University Press of America.

Goffman, E. 1974. *Living in Latin America: a Case study in Cross-Cultural Communication.* Lincolnwood, Illinois: National Textbook Company.

Hall, E.T., and M.R. Hall. 1987. *Hidden Differences.* N.Y.: Doubleday Anchor Books.

Kent, S. 1990. Activity Areas and Architecture: an Interdisciplinary View of the Relationship Between Use and Space and Domestic Built Environments. In *Domestic Architecture and the Use of Space,* ed. S. Kent. Cambridge: Cambridge University Press.

―――. 1990. A Cross-Cultural Study of Segmentation, Architecture, and the Use of Space. In *Domestic Architecture and the Use of Space,* ed. S. Kent. Cambridge: Cambridge University Press.

―――. 1991. Partitioning Space: Cross-Cultural Factors Influencing Domestic Spatial Segmentation. *Environment and Behavior* 23 (4).

Lawrence, R. 1987. *Housing, Dwellings, and Homes.* N.Y.: Wiley.

Lawrence, M.P.T. 1987. Speaking to and Talking about Maori and European Educated Comportments Towards Architecture. University of Auckland School of Architecture Study Papers. Aukland, New Zealand.

Pavlides, E., and J. E. Hesser. 1989. Vernacular Architecture as an Expression of its Social Context in Eressos, Greece. In *Housing, Culture, and Design: A Comparative Perspective,* ed. S.M. Low and E. Chambers. Philadelphia: University of Pennsylvania Press.

Paz, O. 1950. *El laberinto de la soledad.* Mexico, D.F.: Cuadernos Americanos.

Perin, C. 1977. *Everything in its Place: Social Order and Land Use in America.* Princeton, N.J.: Princeton University Press.

Rapoport, A. 1969. *House Form and Culture.* Englewood Cliffs, N.J.: Prentice-Hall.

———. 1985. Thinking about Home Environments: A Conceptual Framework. In *Home Environments*. Vol. 8 of *Human Behavior and Environment. Advances in Theory and Research,* ed. I. Altman, and C.M. Werner. N.Y.: Plenum Press.

———. 1987. On the Cultural Responsiveness of Architecture. *Journal of Architectural Education* 42(1).

———. 1990. Systems of Activities and Systems of Settings. In *Domestic Architecture and the Use of Space,* ed. S. Kent. Cambridge: Cambridge University Press.

Relph, E. 1984. *Place and Placelessness.* London: Routledge, Chapman, and Hall.

Riding, A. 1989. *Distant Neighbors: A Portrait of the Mexicans.* N.Y.: Vintage Books.

Rybczynski, W. 1986. *Home: A Short History of an Idea.* N.Y.: Penguin.

Sebba, R. 1991. The Role of the Home Environment in Cultural Transmission. *Architecture et Comportment* 7(3).

———. 1992. The Three Faces of Cultural Change. Mimeo.

Sebba, R., and A. Churchman. 1983. Territories and Territoriality in the Home. *Environment and Behavior* 15(2).

Seiersen Frost, P. Personal communications, 1992.

Sennett, R. 1987. *The Fall of Public Man: The Social Psychology of Capitalism.* N.Y.: Random House.

Snyder, P.Z., E.K. Sadalla, and D. Stea. 1976. Socio-Cultural Modifications and User Needs in Navajo Housing. *Journal of Architectural Research* 5(3).

Stea, D. 1980. Psychosocial Studies of Nomads and Squatters: Two Applications of Cross-Cultural Environmental Psychology. *Revista Interamericana de Psicologia* 14.

———. 1983. Critical Elements in Culturally-Adaptive Housing and Settlement. In *Environment and population: Problems of Adaptation,* ed. J.B. Calhoun. N.Y.: Praeger.

———. 1990 The Twelve 'Smudge Pots' of Vernacular Building: Notes on Explorations into Architectural Mythology. In *On Vernacular Architecture: Paradigms of Environmental Response,* ed. M. Turan. Aldershot, U.K.: Gower/Avebury.

———. 1991. La Cultura de la Pobreza y Diseno Ambiental. *Gutemberg Dos* 5.1.

Stea, D., J. Covarrubias, and L. Bossano. 1990. Complexity, Tradition, and Modernity. *Traditional Dwellings and Settlements Review* 39 (Fall).

Stea, D., and M. Turan, eds. 1993 *Placemaking.* Aldershot, U.K.: Avebury.

Stea, D., and D. Wood. 1971. *A Cognitive Atlas: Explorations into the Psychological Geography of Four Mexican Cities*. Clark University Place Perception Research Reports. Worcester, Mass.

Steward, J. 1955. *Theory of Culture Change*. Urbana, Ill.: University of Illinois Press.

Studer, R.G. 1990. The Scientification of Design: Alternative Platforms. *Triglyph* 10 (Summer).

Suttles, G. 1972. *The Social Construction of Communities*. Chicago: University of Chicago Press.

Sweeney, A., and M.T. Jimenez. 1992. *El Programa Nacional de Solidaridad: A Promise for the Future of Mexico*. Mimeo.

Upton, D. 1990. The Tradition of Change. *Traditional Dwellings and Settlements Review* 14 (Fall).

Vestbro, D.U. 1992. A Study of Collective Housing: Experience from a Swedish Perspective. In *The Meaning and Use of Housing: Methodologies and their Applicacations to Policy, Planning, and Design*, ed. E.G. Arias. Aldershot, U.K.: Gower/Avebury.

Wisner, B., D. Stea, S. Kruks. 1991. Participatory and Action Research Methods. In *Advances in Environment, Behavior and Design*, ed. E.H. Zube and G.T. Moore. N.Y.: Plenum Press.

11
The Origin of the Hall in Southern Scandinavia

Frands Herschend

Introduction

In the late 1980s the course followed by archaeology took a decisive turn in as much as reconstructions of the past became uninteresting in themselves. Prehistory lost some of its artless charm when understanding the present instead of the past became the final product of archaeology. Although around 1970 there were theoretical arguments to put an end to traditional archaeology (e. g., Johansen 1974) seminar papers and contributions to archaeological congresses on themes well within the traditional boundaries of the discipline stood out as instructive examples of why this archaeology was running short of its justification as a research discipline.

No sooner was the feminist perspective developed (Bertelsen *et al.*, 1986) than it was made obvious that archaeological prehistory was a one gender male phenomenon and that archaeologists, male and female, had been taken in by believing the material propaganda of prehistory (some of which was once considered neutral, Malmer 1963), to be a fair description of how it *was*, rather than an adequate mirror of how it *is*.

The same mocking attitude towards the so called past could also be inferred from studies of the history of archaeology. Such studies, of which Eggers (1951, 23 ff.) was an early attempt, showed that essential ingredients in the interpretation of prehistoric problems reflected the common opinions in the age of the interpretative archaeologist himself rather than problems of prehistory, (cf. Kristiansen 1985; Herschend 1980, 33 ff.). The reconstructions of prehistoric techniques, such as understanding how the Iron Age house was constructed, immediately disclosed not only that the reconstructions themselves cannot in any formal way be shown to be correct (Coles 1973), but also that the mere fact that they were produced in our day made them look ridiculous. There were several non-intuitive lessons to learn.

One such group of lessons was tied to the fact that all reconstructors are to some degree fooled by modern technology (Edgren and Herschend 1979, 20). It thus turned out to be a fact that in house reconstructions where an electric drill was part of the armoury, dowel solutions (with rather slender dowels matching the capacity of the drill), were much more common than in reconstructions where only the auger was put into the tool-box. Although you may remedy one such mistake (or defend it as the ultimate truth) this endeavour turns out to be no solution. It simply opens up your eyes to the next and hopefully slightly more intricate problem. Eventually you end up trying to reconstruct the malnutrition or childhood experience of some average prehistoric carpenter before you start to think of forests and timber qualities long time lost. Then, if not before, you realize that reconstructing is a matter of hunting down an understanding that for theoretical reasons can never be gripped when once defined as being always somewhere ahead of you.

While proving the futility of any reconstruction, the way these attitudes towards gender, the history of archaeology, or house reconstructions produced knowledge seemed sound enough. With reference to the debate in philosophy and theory of science after the second world war – why not start with the late 1950s (e. g., Anscombe 1957; Toulmin 1957; Winch 1963) – it was relatively easy to argue that although lacking in complexity and objective truth, reconstructions of the past are nonetheless a necessary analytical step if you want to *understand* the present. It would seem that during the last decades understanding has become the research problem and archaeology a craft.

Instead of seeing all the shortcomings as blocking archaeological research you should consider them part of the conditions for creating knowledge out of the past. That is what archaeology is all about – bridging past and present, i. e., by creating a connection where the conceptual chain can no longer be followed. Take a concept such as *The view upon rationality in the food production in the Mälar Valley from 1000 BC and onwards*, and you will understand that so much of past knowledge has been lost that there is no point in aiming at a fruitful reconstruction or rethinking of it.

If this is a consequence of the theoretical development during later years, then what concepts are there left to be discussed in the final archaeological production of knowledge?

In my opinion concepts that we can already understand as social tension should be favoured among the many possible answers to this question, since material patterns pertaining to such concepts are of present day interest, and when recognized in a prehistoric context they gain a possible prehistoric ground. If so they may become intricate in as much as they help us to point out social problems that are inherent to our society.

For that reason, this article is about the tension between the individual and the collective. Such a concept can never be treated exhaustively, nor can it be adequately discussed, since the very discussion of it changes the concept.

To begin with, an individual could in the ideal case be a member of a collective in such a way that he or she was indispensable, while at the same time the individuality of the person was defined solely in relation to the collective. Figuratively speaking, we may refer to the unity of hand and fingers, arguing that the individual finger is defined by its being a part of the hand while the hand in itself can be the ideal hand only with five fingers. Now and then we like to think of the nuclear family in this balanced way.

If this delicate balance exists, then it can also be distorted. Today we know of a lot of more or less artificial collectives in which differently defined individuals take part as more or less anonymous elements, elements that can to a certain degree be dispersed without affecting our notion of the qualities of the collective. Labour force in industrial production or the labour force use in warfare are classical examples of this very *individuated* type of human being, but *individuation* is a much wider phenomenon (c.f., Holter 1975; Beck 1987; Näsman 1992).

In contrast to the individual who has been reduced to a dispensable, almost set theoretical element of a set, we can also imagine the individual who is in fact protecting the collective by belonging to it and by defending it as well as by interpreting the ideals of it, often acting as judge, prosecutor, and shepherd in one person. In Western Europe, we seem to prefer this individual to be a *man,* and a mixture of a healthy stout brute and a slightly pathetic official moralist. Hartwig Frisch (1928, 280) pointed out the type by comparing the appearance and character of the likes of Charlemagne and Bismarck, and if we do not insist on the moustache we may add Churchill. Thus, there is not always a point in turning our heroes to ridicule. Having pointed this out, I feel free to find some suitable material patterns to prove my point, and that is where the *hall* enters the picture.

The ancient development of the hall

As a historical phenomenon, the hall is linked to king and feudal lord. It is the room or building in which he, as the head of his nuclear family, performs his rights and duties. He settles disputes and entertains his clients while organizing his economic and political system and space, keeping track of tenants and subjects. In southern Scandinavia, the hall itself is for archaeological reasons not a feudal invention, since if you follow the main development of the Iron Age *home*, you will soon detect that the branch to which the hall belongs was developed in the Late Roman Iron Age.

It is fair to say that in the beginning of the Iron Age the house defines the social space of home and household for a self sustaining nuclear family (Fig. 11.1). The separation of dwelling from byre at opposite ends of the house by means of an intervening entry area characterizes the typical house type of this and later eras. Both the dwelling area, and the economic area were of approximately the same size, and the buildings of the society seem mainly to be homes, (i.e., permanent residences). I take this as my rather arbitrary point of departure without bothering about how this came to be.

There is here an interdependence between the mode of subsistence, the simple building technology, and the general planning of the home. But the situation of the home seems to be stable only for a generation or two. Homes are seldom rebuilt on exactly the same spot, but often moved, the house torn down and the site tilled.

Time changed this pattern and the home – a single farm, or in other places, part of a planned or spontaneous village – became a relatively stable spatial phenomenon. Some of these stable settlements may have had demographic and economic causes, such as the "wandering villages,"

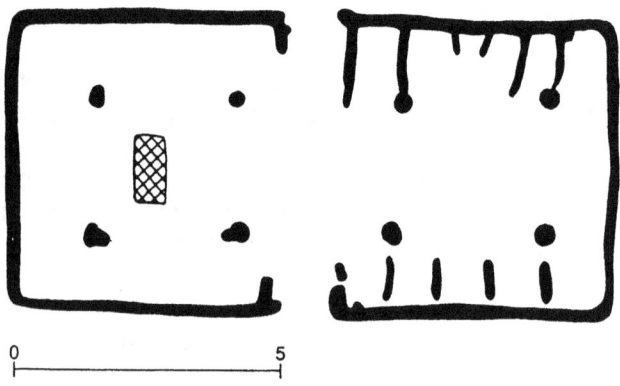

Fig. 11.1. The plan of the standard Pre Roman Iron Age farm house. (After Becker 1972.)

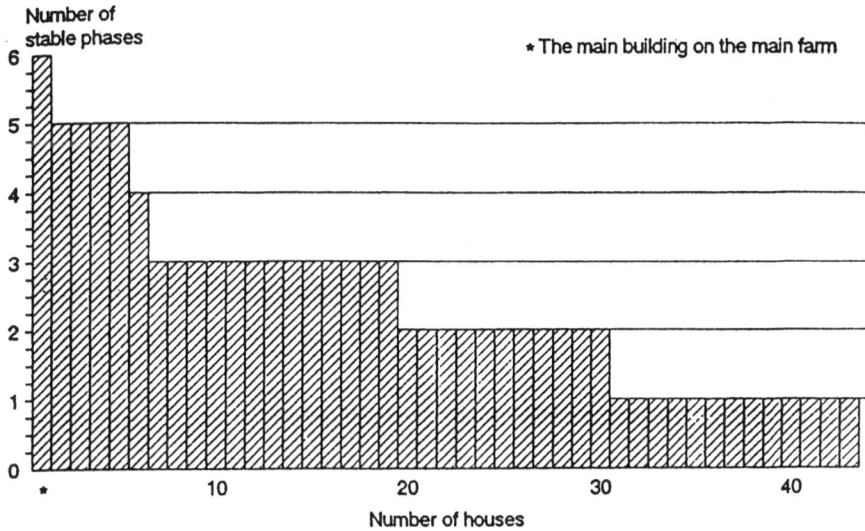

Fig. 11.2. The number of phases during which a house in Hodde is stable in its situation. The most stable house is the main farm. (Based on Hvass 1985.)

(stable within a geographic area), of Jutland (Lund 1988). Other causes may have been topographic, such as the farm mounds in northern Norway (e. g., Johansen 1982), but some are examples of places that for no obvious general reason have been favoured for centuries, e. g., some farm places in the Mälar Valley (Göthberg and Söderberg 1987). Recalling the phases of the Hodde village (Hvass 1985) stability and social status seem to have been interdependant (Fig. 11.2).

This growing stability is accompanied by a new room that becomes more and more frequent in the dwelling house. This room, I believe, was first noted in a systematic way by Björn Myhre (1980) as the dwelling room without a hearth. Some Danish archaeologists talk of the extra pair of posts introduced in the dwelling part of the main farm house (Fig. 11.3). Eventually two new postpairs are introduced creating first a room on each side of the original fire place room, and later two rooms in the short end of the main house (Hansen 1988; Hansen, Mikkelsen and Hvass 1991). The sequence is illustrated in by Hedeager (1988, 139).

The two room dwelling part became the standard interior design when farms reached a size which made it impossible for the nuclear family alone to maintain them, spatially difficult to organize the dwelling solely around the hearth, and when the number of people living on the farm increased

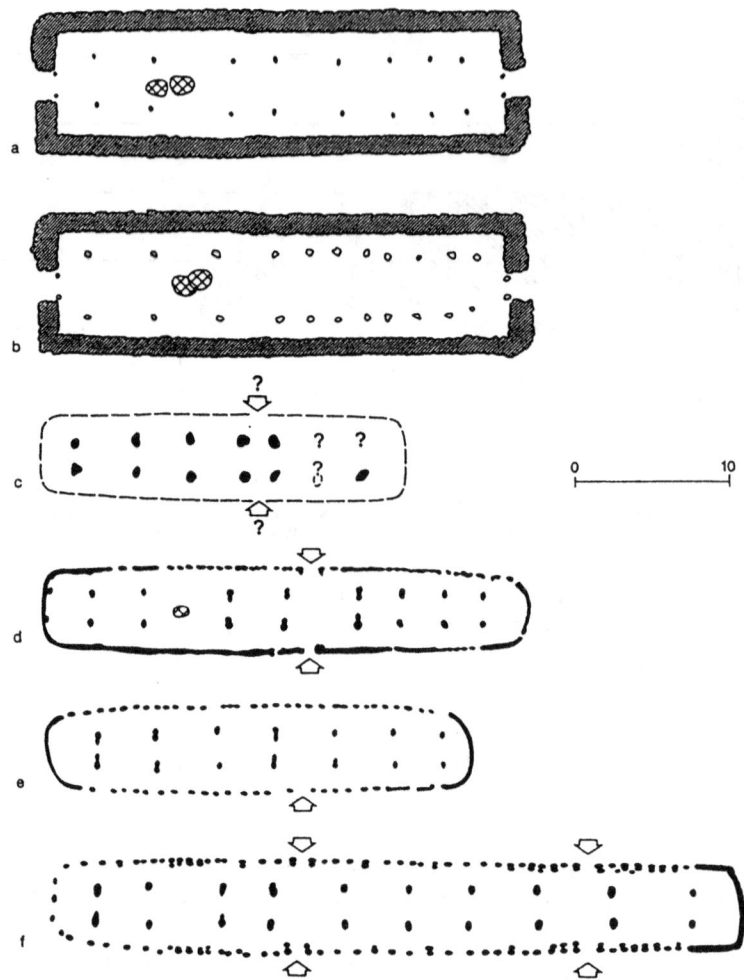

Fig. 11.3. The standard post setting in the dwelling part of larger long houses in south Scandinavia during the Late Roman Iron Age and Migration Period. (A and B after Stenberger 1940; C after Tesch 1992 fig. 18; D, E, and F after Hansen et al. 1991.)

(e. g., Onsten 1992). In that situation, the need for more space is obvious, but the fact that the farms grew instead of just multiplying, marks a social stratification in as much as several potentially self sustaining nuclear families never formed a home of their own.

Farms consisting of two houses, or in the case of big farms, one main house and some secondary ones, became more abundant in the second century A.D., and the second house or secondary houses seem mostly to have been reserved for storage and handicrafts (Mikkelsen 1990, 146 ff.) (Fig. 11.4). Later, some of the functions of the secondary house were probably added to the main building as a new room, for instance on Jutland, and for a while the number of farms with two houses was decreasing.

In the fourth century, a third house was introduced to the large farms. Such houses are not common in the record, but taken together they do form a pattern characterized by one or more of the following archaeological characteristics:

1. they belong to big farms

2. they consist of one room with a minimum of posts

3. they are singled out by their position on the farm

4. their hearths are *neither* used for cooking *nor* do they facilitate a handicraft

5. the artefacts found in the houses are different from those found in the dwelling part of the main house on the farm

The living rooms without a hearth and the other rooms, which later enlarged the dwelling part of the main house, were additions and to a certain extent a matter of growing farm size only, but the third house is an addition to the farm and a division of the dwelling. From the position of the entrances and their varying number, which seems very much to have been a matter of free choice, we may infer that its planning was not so strictly governed by spatial rules as that of the main house.

The state of preservation is obviously crucial if you want to find instances of this type of house, and one might therefore get the impression that it was always a very exclusive phenomenon and also a peripheral one, since in the central settlement areas all buildings are badly preserved.

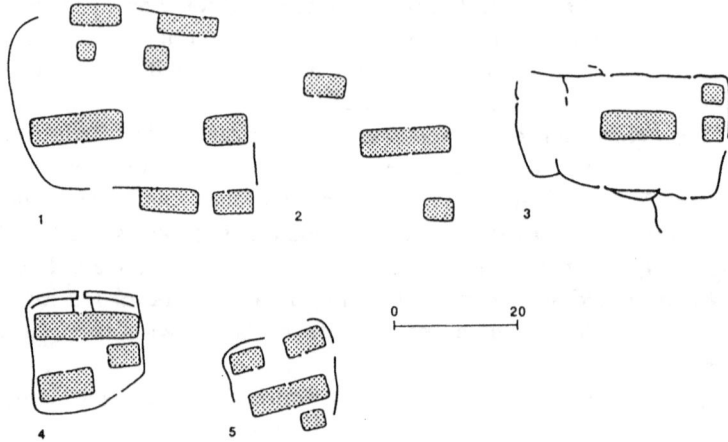

Fig. 11.4. A selection of farms from the Early Roman Iron Age, with one main house and one or more secondary houses. (A after Hvass 1985, the others after Mikkelsen 1990.)

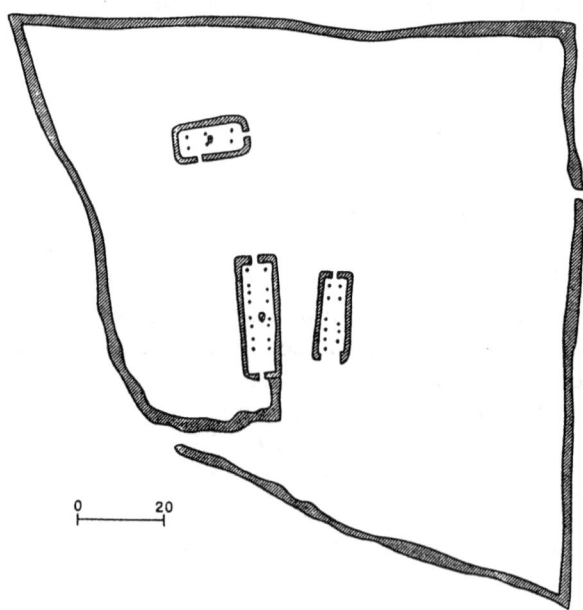

Fig. 11.5. A reconstruction of the spatial organization of the dominating farm in Vallhager on Gotland. (After Stenberger 1955, map 1.)

The Swedish material

Forced into the well preserved periphery, the fifth century example from Vallhagar in Gotland (Stenberger 1955) is probably the most instructive to begin with. Nearly all the houses in the settlement have been excavated, but judging from early maps, some farms in the southeast corner have disappeared. Nonetheless, the centre of the settlement is well preserved, so that an estimate of the original number of farms or households at 12 is not unreasonable. Several farms have been divided, but the southernmost of the two central ones seems to have escaped this fate almost entirely intact (Fig. 11.5).

It is probably significant that in Vallhagar the farm consisting of the houses 16, 18, and 19 (Lundström 1955; Gejvall 1955; Möllerop 1955) which escaped division, contains a hall, house 16 (Fig. 11.6). The roof supporting posts are markedly few and the mid-aisle relatively narrow. Both traits are modern in comparison with the main house and they indicate a thatched roof with a higher pitch than the main house. Even the plank lined benches are peculiar to the house, and so is the hearth. Although both houses, 16 (the hall), and 18 (the main house), were burnt down, only the hearth in the main house was surrounded by kitchenware. This indicates that the fire on the hearth in house 16 was meant to make the house light and warm, without being disturbed by those who cooked.

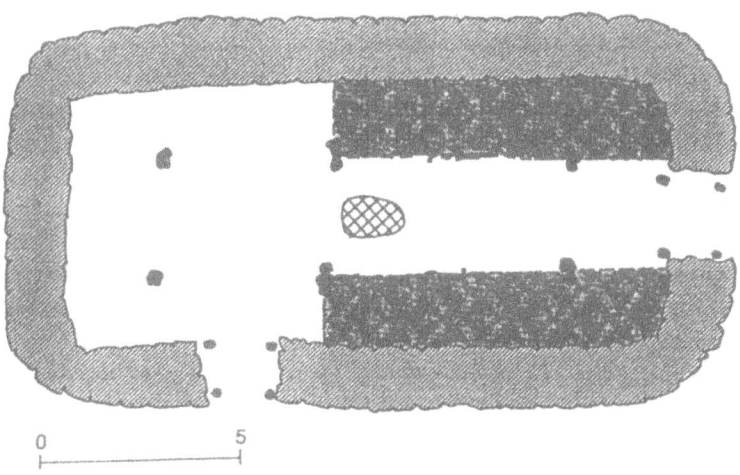

Fig. 11.6 The floor of the hall in Vallhagar, house 16. (After Lundström 1955.)

In the third house or the hall, luxury artefacts such as fragments of glass vessels, bronze jewellery, and ornamented ceramics predominate, together with artefacts for handicraft, such as small knives, wet stones and polishing stones. A spindle-whorl blank and some bone or antler waste supports the handicraft picture. In the main house, the overwhelming artefact category is household ceramics, and luxury and handicraft hardly exist. The artefact categories in house 16 could be found in other houses in Vallhagar as well, but the interesting thing is that on the big farm these categories are found only in the hall or third house. It is fair to conclude that the luxury part of the dwelling and activities that could easily have been housed in the main building were confined to a special house, heated in addition to the first.

House 16 is not a feudal hall in a political or economic sense, but it might well be the embryo of such a hall, in as much as it shows the will of the owner of a large farm to separate a part of his social life from the immediate contact with the main house collective, in which humans and animals make up the cardinal part of the subsistence economy. Obviously the third house or the embryonic hall represents some of the possibilities that the surplus production organized from the main house could result in.

The mixture of situation, spaciousness, luxury, and handicraft suggests that the house has had representative as well as leisure time functions for the family who owned the farm. It is essential that the third house is not a room for representation only, but also a way of actually separating the family from the immediate self-subsistence, putting them in a room where you could most conveniently engage in activities which are easily combined with listening, talking, and drinking.

When Mårten Stenberger in the early 1930s selected excavation objects on Öland, he chose two big farms, two of a medium size, and a small and insignificant one (Stenberger 1933, 1935). In Rönnerum, he first mapped what was left of a large settlement area, and saw that the big farm had at a late stage in its history been divided into two by a wall. Originally the farm consisted of the same sort of houses as the Vallhagar farm discussed above (Fig. 11.7). In Rönnerum Stenberger (1933, 125 ff.) excavated only house VII, finding the main house too big, and knowing that house V was probably a pure farm building.

House VII (Fig. 11.8) is characterized by the stone lined bench, the narrow mid-aisle, the long space between the postpairs, and the big hearth not used for cooking. The house was not burnt down and the excavation was a very rapid one, thus not offering up a great many artefacts, but sherds from a glass vessel and a rivet from a shield boss were found on the floor, while the lack of household ceramics was conspicuous.

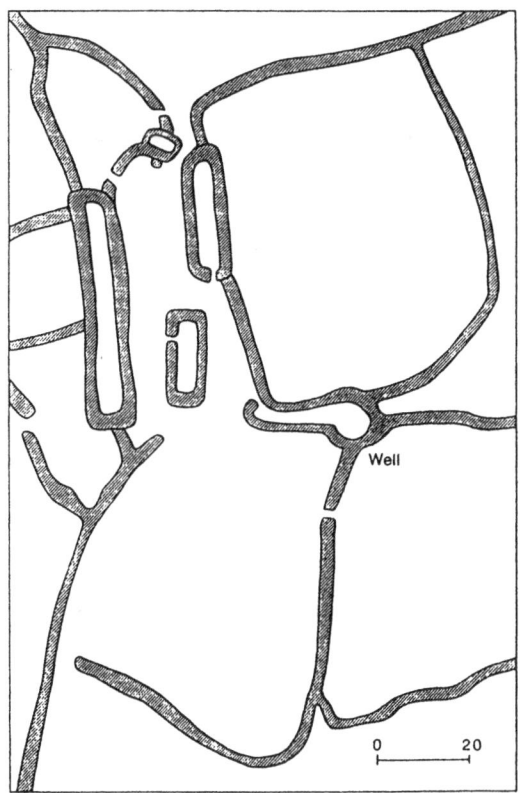

Fig. 11.7. A reconstruction of the spatial organization of the dominating farm in Rönnerum on Öland. (After Stenberger 1933, fig. 56.)

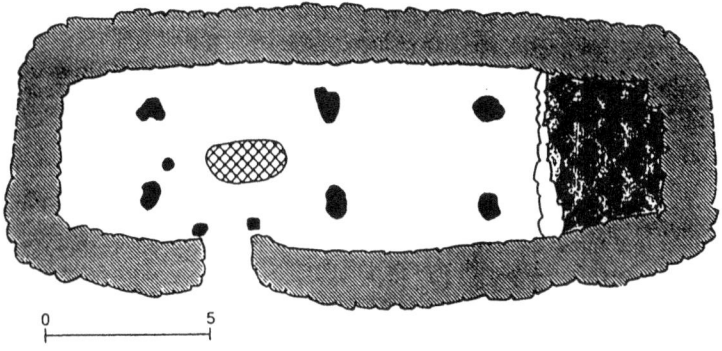

Fig. 11.8. The floor of the hall in Rönnerum on Öland, house VII. (After Stenberger 1933, fig. 86.)

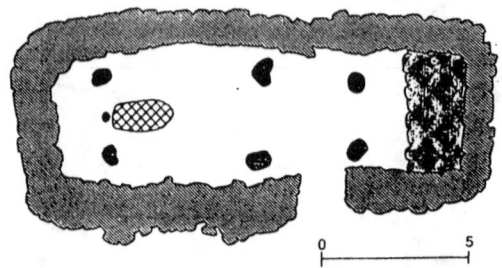

Fig. 11.9. The floor of the hall in Övetorp on Öland, house II. (After Stenberger 1933, fig. 87.)

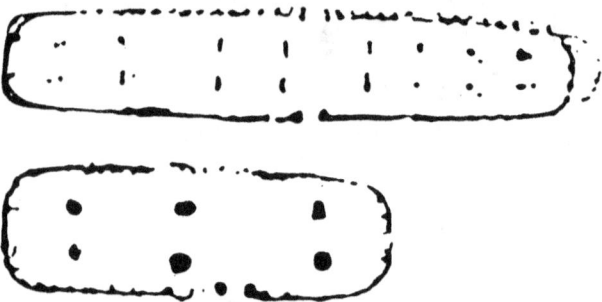

Fig. 11.10. a) A typical 4th century main house on a large farm in Southern Jutland. (After Hansen 1988) b) The third phase of the Hall in Dankirke. (Based on Hansen 1990)

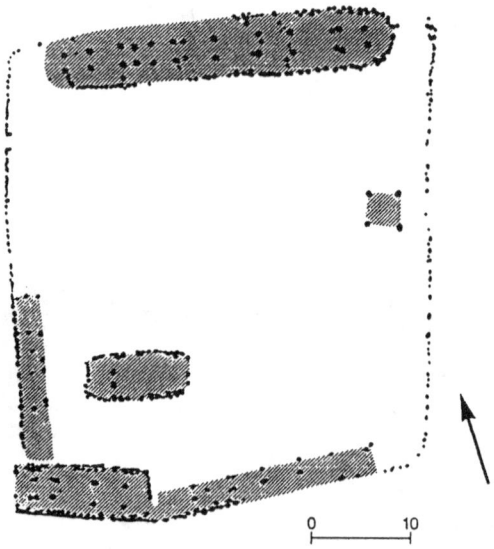

Fig. 11.11. A reconstruction of the spatial organization of the dominating farm in the third phase of the Nørre Snede village. (After Hansen 1988)

Övetorp, once a large farm, (Stenberger 1933, 131 ff.) is a parallel to the farm in Rönnerum and house II (Fig. 11.9), the equivalent of house VII. Although the excavation plan gives the impression that the farm has been totally excavated this is not the case. Only parts of the upper floor, created after a thorough rebuilding of the farm, were cleared, and in House II the floor was not more than touched upon. What we see is thus the end phase of the farm, when it was divided into two households. This division even affected the hall building where the construction of a partition wall called for a second bench, doorway, and hearth. The very small scale of these rooms in the hall underlines the symbolic value or status attached to this, the extra dwelling house separated from the main building.

The Danish material

Turning to the Danish material, it is hard to point out a hall before they become apparent architectural monuments, such as the one in Lejre (Christensen 1987, 1991). The difficulty is due to the state of preservation characterizing most Iron Age houses, but it does seem reasonable to consider house V in Dankirke (Hansen 1990) to be a hall and not the main house of the farm, since in these parts of Jutland and northern Germany the main house is a long house of a distinct and different planning (Fig. 11.10). Compared to a contemporary long house from the area, the differences are striking – huge posts and side beams spanning seven meters in a narrow mid-aisle must have been awe inspiring in this sparsely forested area. The imposing building is matched by the very rich artefact material found in connection with the house area.

In the excavated villages in southern Jutland there are no obvious halls to be seen, but examining the main phases of, for example, Nørre Snede (Hansen 1988), many farms lack a second and third house, although these houses can from time to time be seen, as in phase 3 on the dominating farm closing the village street in the east. No detailed plan has been published of the farm that signifies Main Phase 3, but the farm plan and the second and the third house on this farm (Fig. 11.11) belonged to the dominating farm and phase 3. Like several parallels in Vorbasse (Hansen et al. 1991) this house is situated in the middle of the yard, and constructed with only one pair of internal posts. This means that the house walls are high and stout enough to conveniently support a cross beam with queen posts that in their turn support the side beams. The wish to create a column-free floor is characteristic of the third house on big farms. In Vorbasse, where on the whole the farms are large, there are several examples. In the very large, somewhat later, and solitary farm Mørup (Mikkelsen

1988), we meet the same characteristics in plan of the farm with three houses (Fig. 11.12).

Although it must be considered a tentative hypothesis, there is much to suggest that the third house is indeed the hall of the very large farms in southern Jutland, and thus the very origin of the Anglo-Saxon hall (Fig. 11.13).

A Norwegian example

The hall is most often a house, but in some special cases, for example at Borg on Västvågöy in Lofoten (Stamsö Munch et al. 1989), it is a room. At Borg, Tromsö Museum excavated parts of a large farm some years ago. The floor layers were to a certain extent preserved and it was possible to connect artefacts and rooms with each other. This example (Fig. 11.14) is late, Viking Age in fact, but the long house with an entrance room and the rooms in a row is an echo of the classical southern Scandinavian Iron Age house. The order of the rooms is somewhat different since here at Borg the entrance room separates two dwelling rooms – the standard dwelling and the hall respectively. In the hall room, at the summit of the hill where the long house is situated, the posts are relatively far apart. The mid-aisle has been lowered to create benches in the side-aisles and in the upper part of the room, and although there is a big fire place, very few household ceramics and soap stone sherds were found in the room. On the contrary, the artefacts are dominated by an exclusive collection of glass vessels and imported ceramics. In comparison with the more kitchen-like dwelling, the mixture of luxury and handicrafts once again stands out as characteristic of the hall in its embryonic, or in this case, peripheral form. The hall at Borg is a curious echo of the rural Late Roman Iron Age hall in a period when in more southerly regions, the phenomenon had developed into the central room of royal buildings filled with housecarls. The hall room at Borg would seem to indicate that people were conscious of the roots of the hall.

In the examples so far, the connection between economic strength and the embryonic hall has been obvious, but turning to the last example, the ideological and military connections seem to take over.

The Swedish fort example

For several reasons, Öland in the Baltic became the region where settlement planning took an experimental turn in the Migration Period. A growing population, the unrest in southern Scandinavia, the development of a metal economy, and close contacts with the Roman army in the

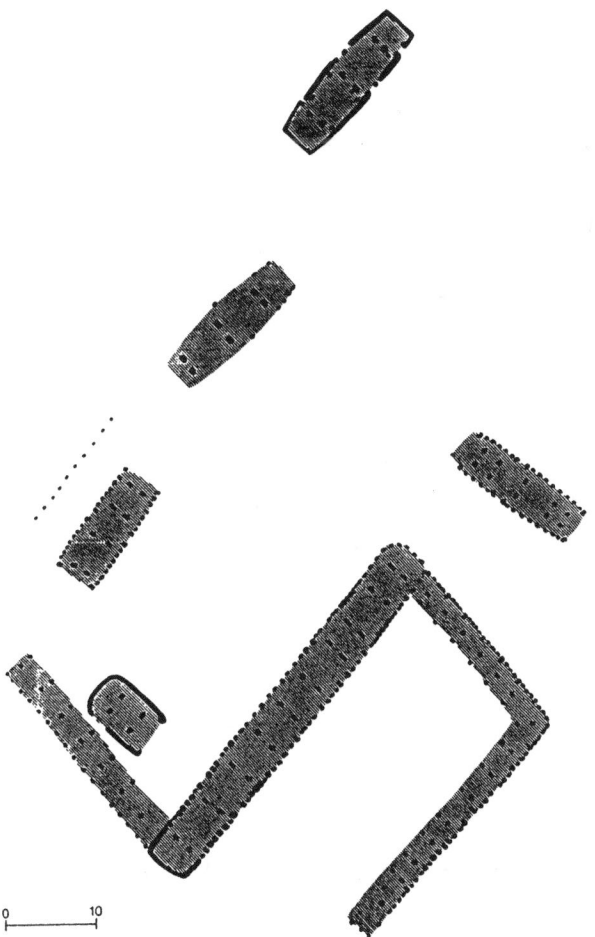

Fig. 11.12. A reconstruction of the spatial organization of a presumed second phase of the farm Mørup in Southern Jutland. (Based on Mikkelsen 1988.)

eastern part of the Empire in the 5th century all lay behind the creation of ideal settlements in the form of fortified villages (Herschend 1991).

The Eketorp ring fort is the only one excavated, and here the planning fulfilled several aims. The point of the defence works was to create a fortification for the civilians both inside and outside the fort. This was accomplished by the stout wall and the portcullis gate which would have

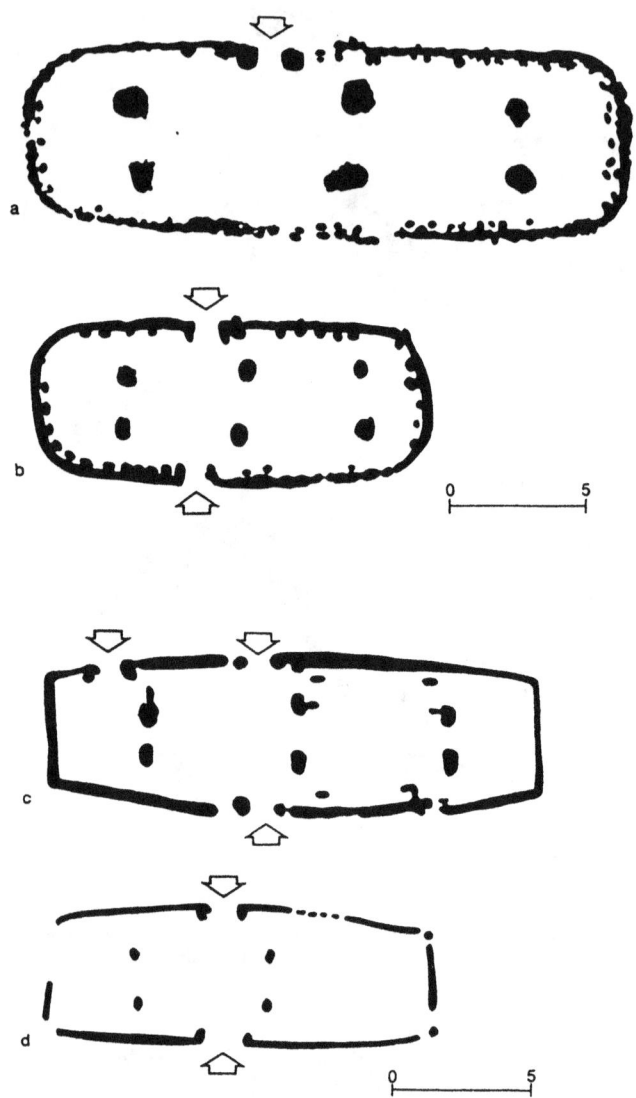

Fig. 11.13. Halls from southern Jutland. A and B from the 4th century. C and D from the 6th century. (A after Hansen 1988, fig. 11; B after Hansen 1990, fig. 7; C after Hansen et al. 1991; D after Mikkelsen 1988.)

Fig. 11.14. The main house at the Borg farm. (After Mikkelsen and Herschend 1992.)

been open even during a siege, allowing peasants from the surroundings to reach the security of the fort. From the beginning, the defence system had several traits adopted from Roman fortifications, but they were abandoned and the system was changed to a Germanic and probably more suitable one, given the attacks that could be expected.

The planning of the settlement gives a very egalitarian impression, as it seems to have regulated the breadth of the facades along the streets and squares. Eketorp is a permanent settlement and a colony, but not a way to compress the surrounding population into a fortified village. On the contrary, people are given homes of their own in the new fort. They breed live stock and manages the byres, but their one-sided economy is dependant on that of the farms around the fort. As a social experiment the ideal, densely populated ring fort settlement did not last long (Herschend 1985, 1991).

Some of the inhabitants must have belonged to a military organization defending the fort, and others to an organization that was more egalitarian. Therefore it seems that the two organizations were mixed in the fort, one managing the population surplus and the other the defence in the area.

A settlement study shows that among the seemingly equal houses, house 03 is nonetheless outstanding (Fig. 11.15). It occupied the best position in the south-western facade, facing the largest square in the fort, and was located at the centre in the most regular planned part of the settlement, equipped with a canopy entrance, and thus co-opted and blocked several of the few public spaces in the fort. Through the canopied entrance, there was a small foyer, and after that, the hall room through which one could reach the standard dwelling room. This was the only house in the settlement with two dwelling rooms, and in the outer one we find the only hearth that was not used for cooking. Here, we find no benches in the side-aisles in this room, but the contrast between the artefacts in the two rooms strikes you when you map the distribution of household ceramics and weapons. Normally, these groups cannot be set off to mark different aspects of everyday life, but in a fortification it is possible. Therefore it seems significant that it is in the central house of the fortified settlement, separated from the food-preparing women, in the room with the hearth that supplied the light and the heat, that we find the weapons (Fig. 11.15).

This means that the central hall room was planned into the ideal settlement in order to mirror a society that was in principle egalitarian, but nonetheless in need of a *primus inter pares,* in this case for protection. Concentrating the military organisation to a room in one of the households is a way of pointing out the individual leader, and connect leadership with the room.

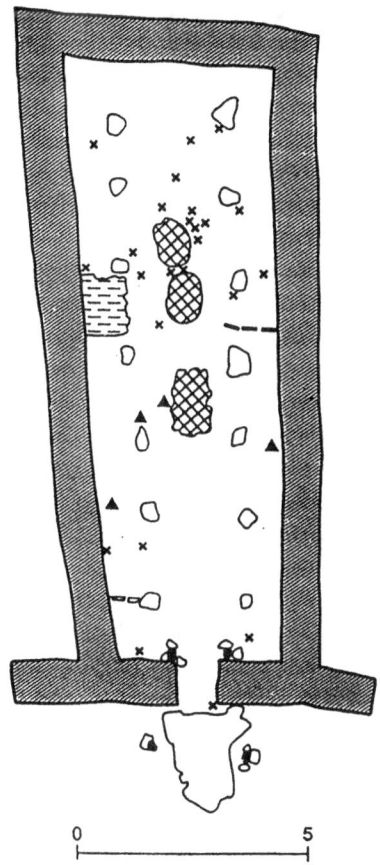

Fig. 11.15. The hall in Migration Period Eketorp on Öland, house 03. (After Herschend 1988.)

Frands Herschend

The space of power

Although the examples are few, they suffice to show that the hall is the room of leadership in an economic as well as a military sense already in the fifth century. The point is that a part of the social power proceeds from the home, i.e., from one of the socio-psychological platforms later to be found in developed feudalism namely: the unity of home, nuclear family, responsibility, power, and the individual acting for the collective. The interesting thing is that, centuries before we can talk of feudalism, the hall constitutes the room as a social space for the individual who in that room is the head of a nuclear family – a positive notion common to rich and poor – and not just one of a team that ran an estate. It is in the fusion between the military power which could be temporarily bestowed upon any strategically gifted murderer, and the economic power inherited by the sons of the best farms, that individuality became a public, social concept invested with a room, the embryonic hall. Thus created, it could not be rooted out, and came to be a natural counterpoint of different collectives such as the *thing* (public assembly) the village-assembly, or later, the tenants. Some time during the Late Roman Iron Age, it became possible within the nuclear family to breed an individual which acted for the collective and to make it a publicly accepted, social norm.

When the upper levels of the hierarchy managed to create a house for this individuality – a room separated from the subsistence economy – they also created a place for an oral tradition in which the individual of a certain stratum of society became the hero. What can be done in the hall other than eat, drink, talk, and entertain neighbouring hall owners, while developing an oral fiction? The hall gives a man the possibility to gossip with selected members of a certain social stratum, and this is quite a new political possibility in a society where otherwise everybody on the farm would be sitting around the hearth in the main building listening him.

One of the earliest sagas commenting upon southern Scandinavian society, the first part of the *Beowulf* poem, is the final product of a long oral tradition, reflecting the cultural history of the middle and the later part of the first millenium. Bearing in mind the archaeological record of the third house of the large farms, it is not surprising that the saga is about the hall and the individual, symbolizing the good and orderly society, a society threatened by monsters whose sole purpose was that of destroying the hall functions, and thus the whole society, frustrating its leading members.

In this poem, the tension between the individual and the collective is shown in many ways and at least in one very instructive and gruesome variation. Beowulf, who is morally and physically fit to kill the monster

Grendel, is temporarily allowed to take charge of the hall and use it as a trap for the monster whose pleasure it is to eat and kill all those who sleep there (Herschend 1992, 154). Instead of just waiting for the monster inside the door, Beowulf puts one of his men next to the entrance as a sleeping decoy, having realized that Grendel, encouraged by killing the man, will continue into the interior of the hall where he will be trapped in Beowulf's grip (verse 720 ff.). In a way, the plan does work, since, as expected, the anonymous Geat inside the door is killed and Grendel is probably death marked when he, rather unexpectedly, manages to escape.

This is the extreme tension in a nut shell, either you are the good individual in charge of the hall, indispensable to the collective and a member of it, like Beowulf, or you are an element of it, in this case one of the 14 men chosen by Beowulf to represent the Geatish nation, and reduced to a decoy, necessary perhaps but no doubt dispensable, an anonymous element to be added or subtracted, and valued as a decoy only.

This says a good deal about the unpredictable dynamics of the home and the family. Thus, it must have been within this notion of the home of the early Iron Age, that it appeared to be legitimate to create a relatively private room to surround, bring up, and sustain individuality as a public social norm.

Today, there are many rooms for individuality, as there should be, but it is nevertheless comforting that when individuality is nowadays put forward as a socio-political public norm, it most often happens in rooms which are at least relatively public. In a period when decision makers on the political and economic level are brought forward to us as individuals and members of a nuclear family, there is no doubt a danger in the semi-private room, for example, a study turned into a television studio. Here, the owner of the room chooses either privately to build up his individuality and interpretations of society with his like-minded peers, or he may decide to address the public as their loyal hero. He uses the privacy of the room to make his individuality a public norm.

Although we may recognize the problem of individuality and collectivity in its modern varieties, the point must surely be to not forget that the tension between the individual and the collective is a never ending problem that is still present in the home.

Those who built the first embryonic halls as the third house on their farms did not foresee feudalism, but it so happened that they invented a new check in the play with the tension between the individual and the collective, and that turned out to be no easy matter to handle, although handling it is absolutely necessary.

References

Anscombe, G. E. M. 1957. *Intention*. Oxford: Oxford University Press.
Beck, U. 1987. Beyond Status and Class. In *Modern German Sociology*, ed. V. Meja. N.Y.: Columbia University Press.
Becker, C. J. 1972. Eisenzeitliche Dörfer bei Gröntoft, Westjütland, 3. Vorbericht: Die Ausgrabungen 1967-68. *Acta Archaeologica* 1971 (Copenhagen).
Bertelsen, R., et al., ed. 1986. Were They All Men? *AMS-varia* 17 (Stavanger).
Christensen, T. 1987. Lejrehallen. *Skalk* 5 (Højbjerg).
———. 1991. Lejre's Possible Maritime Connection. In *Aspects of maritime Scandinavia AD 200-1200*, ed. O. Crumlin-Petersen. Roskilde: Vikingeskibsmuseet.
Coles, J. 1973. *Archaeology by Experiment*. London: Academic Press.
Edgren, B., and F. Herschend. 1979. *Nya gamla hus*. Riksantikvarieämbetet & Statens Historiska Museum. *Rapport* 1979:3. Stockholm.
Eggers, H. J. 1951. *Der römische Import im Freien Germanien*. Vol. 1 of *Atlas der Urgeschichte*. Hamburg: Hamburgisches Museum für Vokerkunde und Vorgeschichte.
Frisch, H. 1928. *Europas kulturhistorie*. Copenhagen: Gyldendal
Gejvall, Nils-Gustaf. 1955. Building 18. In *Vallhagar. A Migration Period Settlement on Gotland/Sweden*, ed. Marten Stenberger. Copenhagen: Munksgaard.
Göthberg, H., and S. Söderberg. 1987. E18-projektet. Skäggesta. *Tor* 21 (Uppsala).
Hansen, H. J. 1990. Dankirke. Jernalder boplads og rigdomscenter. *Kuml* 1988-89 (Århus).
Hansen, T. E. 1988. Die eisenzeitliche Siedlung bei Nørre Snede, Mitteljütland. Vorläufiger Bericht. *Acta Archaeologica* 58 (Copenhagen).
Hansen, T. E., D. K. Mikkelsen, and S. Hvass. 1991. Landbebyggelserne i 7. århundrede. In *Fra stamme til stat 2. Høvdingesamfund og kongemagt*, ed. P. Mortensen and B. M. Rasmussen. Århus: Aarhus University Press.
Hedeager, L. 1988. Oldtid o. 4000 f.Kr.–1000 e.Kr. In *Det danske landbrugs historie 4000 f.Kr.–1536*, ed. C. Bjørn. Odense.
Herschend, F. 1980. Två studier i öländska guldfynd. I Det myntade guldet. II Det omyntade guldet. *Tor* 18 (Uppsala).
———. 1985. Fällgallerporten i Eketorp-II, Öland. *Tor* 20 (Uppsala).
———. 1988. Bebyggelse og folkevandringstid på Öland. In *Folkevandringstiden i Norden. En krisetid mellem ældre og yngre jernalder*, ed. U. Näsman and J. Lund. Århus: Aarhus University Press.

———. 1991. Om öländsk metallekonomi i första hälften av första årtusented e.Kr. In *Samfundsorganisation og regional variation,* ed. C. Fabech and J. Ringtved. Århus: Aarhus University Press.

———. 1992. Beowulf and Sabas: The Tension between the Individual and the Collective in the Germanic Society around 500 A.D. *Tor* 24 (Uppsala).

Herschend, F., and D. K. Mikkelsen. 1992. *The main house at Borg.* Mimeo.

Holter, H. et al. 1975. *Familien i klassesamfunnet.* Oslo: Universitetsforlaget.

Hvass, S. 1985. *Hodde. Et vestjysk landsbysamfund fra ældre jernalder.* Copenhagen: Akademisk Forlag.

———. 1988. Jernalderens bebyggelse. In *Fra Stamme til stat i Danmark.* Vol 1. *Jernalderens stammesamfund,* ed. P. Mortensen and B. Rasmussen. Århus: Aarhus University Press.

Johansen, A. B. 1974. *Forholdet mellom teori og data i arkeologi og andre erfaringsvitenskaper.* Bergen.

Johansen, O. S. 1982. Viking Age Farms: Estimating the Number and Population Size. A Case Study from Vestvågöy, North Norway. *Norwegian Archaeological Review* 15 (Oslo).

Klaeber, F., ed. 1950. *Beowulf and the Fight at Finnsburg.* London: D. C. Heath and Company.

Kristiansen, K., ed. 1985. *Archaeological Formation Processes. The Representativity of Archaeological Remains from Danish Prehistory.* Copenhagen: Arnold Busck.

Lund, J., 1988. Jernalderens bebyggelse i Jylland. In *Folkevandringstiden i Norden. En krisetid mellem ældre og yngre jernalder,* ed. U. Näsman & J. Lund Århus: Aarhus University Press.

Lundstrøm, Per. 1955. Building 16. In *Vallhagar. A Migration Period Settlement on Gotland/Sweden,* ed. M. Stenberger. Copenhagen: Munksgaard.

Malmer, M. P. 1963. *Metodproblemen inom järnålderns konsthistoria.* Lund: Gleerup.

Mikkelsen, D. 1988. Enkeltgård eller landsby. En Arkæologisk undersøgelse med udgangspunkt i et gårdanlæg ved Mørup, Jylland. Paper from the Department of Archaeology, University of Århus.

———. 1990. To ryttergrave fra ældre romersk jernalder – den ene med tilhørende bebyggelse. *Kuml* 1988-89 (Århus).

Munch, G. S., et al. 1989. Borg i Lofoten. *Norwegian Archaeological Review* 22 (Oslo).

Myhre, B. 1980. *Gårdsanlegget på Ullandhaug I.* Stavanger: Stavanger Arkeologisk Museum.

Möllerop, O., 1955. Building 19. In *Vallhagar. A Migration Period Settlement on Gotland/Sweden,* ed. M. Stenberger. Copenhagen: Munksgaard

Näsman, E. 1992. Individualization and Institutionalization of Childhood in Present-Day Europe. In *Childhood in Europe,* ed. J. Quortrup. Forthcoming.

Onsten, A. 1992. *Eldstad och bostad.* Department of archaeology, Uppsala University. Mimeo.

Stenberger, M. 1933 *Öland under äldre järnåldern.* Stockholm: Almqvist & Wiksell International.

Stenberger, M. 1935. En järnåldersgård på Norra Öland. *Fornvännen* (Stockholm).

Stenberger, M. 1940. Der eisenzeitliche Hof bei Dune in Dalhem auf Gotland. *Mannus* 32 (Leipzig).

Stenberger, M., ed. 1955. *Vallhagar. A Migration Period Settlement on Gotland/Sweden.* Copenhagen: Munksgaard.

Toulmin. S. 1957. *Forsight and Understanding.* Bloomington, Indiana: Indiana University Press.

Winch, P. 1963. *The Idea of Social Science.* London: Routledge and Kegan Paul.

12
Sustaining a Sense of Home and Personal Identity

Marjorie Bulos
Waheed Chaker

Introduction

Secondary data suggests that the numbers of people who work at or from home in Britain are likely to increase significantly, making homeworking a pervasive and enduring element of an economically restructured post industrial society.

It is argued that people who carry out their employment mainly in their homes place themselves willingly or unwillingly in a situation where they are viewed as exceptional or abnormal, in some cases deviant. A brief review of historical meanings of home stresses the importance of the separation between home and work and the creation of an ideal notion of home as an entity which people seek to achieve and display as a place of security, relaxation, and domesticity. Women are central to the social work which has to be done to create and sustain both the ideal and the actuality of these desired characteristics.

Home working constitutes a physical, interactional, and personal disruption to homefullness. How this disruption can and is dealt with to retain for themselves and others an enduring senses of home and their personal identity within it is demonstrated by the use of case studies of homeworkers. It is shown that the processes invoked to create and sustain notions of home provide the meeting point of personal interactions, the design and use of space, and emotion. The visual materials are explained through what people say about their work at home and what they choose to show us of their homes and work places.

The employment context

In 1979 the British Department of Employment initiated a programme of research on homeworking. This programme produced a significant body of published material (Hakim 1987, 1-5) which constitutes a unique record of homeworking in the UK. The final report from the programme provides the most complete account of the nature and extent of homebased work in Britain currently available (Hakim 1987). This report showed that 1.7 million people either worked in their home, had their homes as their workplace, or worked from home.[1]

There has been no subsequent research into homeworking of a similar scope and authority. There have however been a number of significant statements made by organizations representing employees and by academic analysts which suggest that in the decade subsequent to the national official research programme, homeworking has become pervasive throughout all areas of employment and self-employment (Henley Centre 1988; TUC 1987, 1991).

Looking forward over the next decade, it is likely that homeworking will become prevalent for increasing numbers of people across a broad spectrum of income and types of work. The pressure for change towards more use of homeworking comes from a variety of sources:

1. employers seeking to sustain production within increasingly competitive international markets in manufacturing industries which traditionally relied on homeworkers will continue to use homeworkers as a source of cheap unregulated labour (TUC 1991)

2. employers who have labour intensive processes will try to re-base much of their workforce at home through relocating existing employees and through subcontracting or franchising out parts of their operations to self employed ex-employees (Felix 1989, TUC 1991)

3. employers who want to retain or involve women workers with children or other domestic responsibilities (Dennisons 1991)

4. an increase in the number of self-employed people who work in or from their homes to establish small businesses or through the scarcity of employment (Brown and Scase 1991)

5. an increase in homeworking amongst minority ethnic groups as a consequence of a weak labour market position and as a mechanism for avoiding the experience of overt racial discrimination in broader institutional contexts.

Recognition that these processes are already at work and support for them has recently been expressed by the Department of Employment. Ursula Huws, co-author of the book *Teleworking Towards the Elusive Office* (1987) has been commissioned by them to explore teleworking in a number of different occupational contexts. The expected reports will give an overview of teleworking in the UK, describe a series of case studies of teleworkers, and provide advice and guidance for employers in the use of telework (Denbign 1992).

These changes will create an increasingly fragmented, scattered, and isolated working population for whom paid work is carried out: in their homes, partly at home, and partly in more centralized workplaces, or more nomadically from home. It is not too difficult to envisage a time within the next two decades when the numbers of people who work in specialized and centralized work places such as factories and offices are a minority of employees and the self-employed.

These trends are not confined to Britain. In Australia 25% of the workforce are reported to work at home (Denbign 1992), while in America homeworking is sufficiently well recognized for housing schemes to reflect the needs of homeworkers (Ahrentzen 1990). In European countries such as Portugal and Spain, traditional areas of home working have expanded in hand embroidery, footwear, and garment manufacture. In Scandinavian countries traditional crafts continue to be carried out at home and new technologies are serving to bring homework and tele-cottages into communities as a means of sustaining employment, education, and social services in remote and sparsely populated areas (BT & ACRE 1991; Tate 1991).

Activities in the wrong place!?

Just as a weed can be described as a plant in the wrong place, so paid work can become a deviant or subversive activity when undertaken in what has come to be regarded as private domestic space – the home. People who carry out their employment mainly in their homes or use their homes as a work base place themselves willingly or unwillingly in a situation where they are viewed as exceptional or abnormal, in some cases even deviant (Randall 1991). This same author in a subsequent paper analyzes data from homebased workers to conclude:

> Their meanings (i.e., home and work), have been constructed by a majority for whom the separation of home and work has become a norm. Consequently, the respective images or representations of home and work are a problem for those who work from home. (Randall 1992, 6).

Homes as separate, private arenas pre-date the industrial revolution in western Europe. A recent commentary on the Dutch painter Pietre de Hooch identifies the centrality of home as "the private:"

> *The Courtyard of a House in Delft* (Figure 12.1) is a testament to the Dutch seventeenth century preoccupation with the home as both the seat of private virtue and the microcosm of the well run commonwealth. The painting stands at the opposite pole from those other, livelier scenes of drunkenness and affray also common in Dutch art of the time: an image not of the tavern with its sensual and moral temptations, but of a place where stillness and security are charged with an ethical value. Its theme, emphasized by the painter's tight, narrow framing of his image, is enclosure – which is presented here as a state of grace. (Graham-Dixon 1992, 12)

Fig. 12.1. By courtesy of The National Gallery, London

The industrial revolution brought changes expressed at different times and in different ways across western Europe which by the mid to late nineteenth century created a split between home and work. The house/home became regarded as a sphere of life separate and different from the public places and in particular people's place of work. Women became the creators and guardians of homes in which activities were domestic and private, woven around the ideal of home as haven and respite from the demands and travails of "real" work. Homes also became the site of gendered power relations in which ownership, control, and domination of women by men and children by their parents were safeguarded from the interference of others through the notion of privacy. In Britain, these aspects of home were well noted by social observers such as the novelist Dickens, and evoked by Angela Holdsworth (1988, 9) as the opening for her story of women in the twentieth century:

"I want", said Bella Rokesmith, "to be something much worthier than the doll in the doll's house." When Charles Dickens wrote those words in *Our Mutual Friend* in 1864, women had little chance of being anything else. As many manual and most professional jobs were closed to them, it was a struggle for women to support themselves. All they could hope for was a marriage to a good man and a lifetime of keeping his house and raising his children. Once married, women's property and income became their husband's by law. Circumstances forced them to depend on the goodwill of father, husband, or brother. Independence, a fulfilling career, even a decent job were not for them. Women were not allowed to vote, nor stand for Parliament, nor hold any kind of public office. By necessity, their horizons were limited to their own private world at home.

In the time since the mid-nineteenth century most of these constraints on women's lives have been removed but the home as a private and secret domain remains central to British society and to other once industrial societies. Studies of working class life in the 1950s emphasized the extent to which women were in and around the home while men went from the home to factories, mines, and to public places. Slaughter (1956) was able to conclude from his study of a Yorkshire mining community that:

> Women provided a haven for a tired man when he returns from work; here he expects to find a meal prepared, a room clean and tidy, a seat comfortable and warm, and a wife ready to give him what he wants.

For middle class women, the experience of the private domain of the home was no less confining, as the founder of the National Housewives Register reflected on her experience of the early 1960s:

> We were reasonably well educated. We all had reasonably satisfying jobs. We never even considered...leaving the children and going back to work until they were at least at school. But we needed more stimulation. We needed to talk about more things in the world than just the confines of the home. (Holdsworth 1988, 33)

During the next decades as women moved out of the home into full and part time employment the home, children, and domestic commitments continued to dominate their pattern of planning and set their priorities. Their lives continued to be woven around assumptions about the continued stability of men's work as full time outside the home, and to see themselves as first and foremost homeworkers and creators of family stability (Martin et al 1988).

The function of home in various settings and groups in a post war British context has given a further impetus in maintaining other cultural norms and practices, such as being a site of self-help and economic activity or shelter from a hostile world in which a cultural identity can be maintained.

It is not surprising therefore to find contemporary writers emphasizing certain aspects of the meaning of home in a consistent manner as constituting the core meaning of home as it is perceived in the British context. A number of recent studies have examined the meaning of home for individuals in different circumstances of gender, class, and age, all of which show a degree of consistency in the way people talk about and describe their homes. Factors that are often identified and repeated as constituting the essence of home are: privacy, comfort, happiness, calm, family, and possessions.

There is considerable evidence that these terms conjure up images which are more ideal than real and that tenure, age, gender, employment status, and ethnicity severely effect the individual's ability to reach this ideal state. Recent studies identify the significance of these dimensions of difference in people's experience.

Sixsmith and Sixsmith (1990) have shown the subtle ways in which change brought about by age and unemployment impact on the way people experience their homes. They argue that the experiences of age and unemployment can increase the significance of the privacy afforded by the home, while the role of home as a place for family life can fail or become eroded through marital dissent or death, and potentially lose its capacity to satisfy the desire for comfort and ease.

Saunders (1990) uses data on tenure and the relation to meanings of home to show that the increased control over one's immediate environment which comes with owner occupation leads to greater ontological security.

Madigan and Munro (1990) examine the gender difference in Britain to show that women's experience is differentiated from that of men, arguing that they have significantly lower levels of control and enjoyment of their homes, differences which are increased by current trends of co-modification in the housing market.

Finally Bell Hooks (1991, 41-42) forcibly identifies the cultural significance of "homespace" for her and others as the "site of resistance" for black women in all those societies where white culture is dominant:

> This task of making homeplace was not simply a matter of black women providing services; it was about the construction of a safe place where black people can affirm one another and by so doing heal many of the wounds inflicted by racist domination. We could not learn to love or respect ourselves in the culture of white supremacy, on the outside; it was inside, in that "homeplace," most often created and kept by black women, that we had the opportunity to grow and develop, to nurture our spirits. This task of making a homeplace, of making home a community of resistance, has been shared by black women globally, especially black women in white supremacist societies.

What is centrally accepted is what home ought to be like and the nature of what is to be created and maintained, and who should be responsible for creating and sustaining a sense of home.

It is women's work in a social sense to create and sustain a home which provides ontological security for all the members of the household and achieve a private and secure domain within which the affairs of the family can be conducted without interference from outsiders. The home also constitutes the site for the establishment of a constellation of supportive and interdependent relationships through which activities for getting by and surviving both economically and socially can be accomplished (Pahl 1987, 1990).

Making their space and sustaining a sense of home

The authors' experience of research into homeworkers' use of space within the home has yielded data from interviews, observation, and questionnaires which shows that the experience of becoming a homeworker addresses this ideal and creatively seeks to sustain and enhance a sense of home when paid employment becomes part of the "home." The photographs and commentary show how this is accomplished in the specific circumstances of different types of homework. However, to make sense of this, some points about the homework experience need to be made.

Those homeworkers who make a personal and positive decision to become homeworkers often identify the desire to be a more integral part of home and family life as the most important factor shaping their decision to work at home or as the outcome of that experience which is most valued (Bulos 1992). For these people, enhancing and sustaining certain aspects of the home experience are central to their ability to work at home. The desired and actual aspects of home life positively identified as important in this aspect are: emotional warmth, family involvement, closeness of familial relationships, and peace.

Ambiguities and potential conflicts arise from the contradictory feelings that homeworkers express about the way their work at home is perceived and treated by other members of the household and non-household members, both those associated with their work and friends and neighbours. They may be regarded as "not really working," on call for chores and to take messages, a novice or "pretender" in their work activities, or being at home only until "real" work in a "proper" work place can be achieved.

Homeworking thus constitutes a physical, interactional, and personal disruption to homefullness in a context where it is the very ideal of the home which is being sought through homework activities.

As a result, those working at home have to create interpretations and meanings about both the nature of work and home which in a sense are innovative to them and their immediate and surrounding significant others (Mead 1934). Being able to successfully establish a feeling of stability and a valued identity for themselves as homeworkers is arguably a necessary condition for their continuing to work at or from home, and to retain the very family and personal qualities that they value and seek. This work of turning the abnormal into the normal, the weed into the "natural" and conserved wild flower requires the invoking of processes to create and sustain a new notion of home and the role of working activities within it. The way people organize, use, explain, and describe the space they construct and furnish for their use as homeworkers provides the meeting point of personal interactions, and the design and use of space and emotion.

In a previous paper we concluded that:

Two clear and extreme models of how homework can and should be accommodated in the home environment emerge (from the data analysis). The first of these seeks to replicate in the home the separateness of the conventional work experiences. The second emphasizes the need to achieve a new configuration in which the notion of the home becomes altered to accommodate work as a regular "normal activity." (Bulos and Chaker 1991).

Photographs of people at work within their homes, the way they explain what they are trying to achieve through the organization of space, and our observations of their work activities enable the identification and description of the strategies adopted to preserve and enhance a sense of home. These materials also enable insight into how meanings are negotiated and ambiguities resolved. Social order becomes established through these activities. Specific gender issues are also identified which relate to the centrality of women's role in the creation of homes.

The single most important way in which people seek to establish employment activities in the home in a manner that preserves and acknowledges home as a private and domestic place is through the construction of work places which are characterized by physical and social closure. These most often take the form of a separate work area; this is most likely to be an existing room, but sometimes may be a purpose built extension, a converted garage or loft, garden shed, caravan, or purpose built hut of some kind. Although people with single dwellings, especially those with a garden, yard or out buildings, can more easily achieve extra space through such additions and conversions, most homeworkers are unlikely to have such easy opportunities. Ingenuity and variety characterize this process. Some of these options are shown in Figures 12.2 and 12.3.

Figure 12.2 (Personal services): here a chiropodist treats a patient in a surgery built on the sideway of a semi-detached house replacing a walkway and side entrance to the house. The room measures 16 by 7 meters and contains all equipment, records, and instrumentation necessary for practice as well as space for those accompanying patients.

Fig. 12.2

Fig. 12.3

Figure 12.3 (Subcontracted professional services): here a carpet designer works in an upstairs front room which was formally a bedroom.

These illustrations show a number of features which require emphasis: the extremely economical use of space and the incorporation and use of normal domestic furniture and decorations. Indeed, at the same time as the domestic environment is invaded and changed by employment, so the individuals employment surroundings are domesticated.

Fig. 12.4    Fig. 12.5

In other circumstances, people share space which is in dining and living rooms, or in kitchens and bedrooms. Mostly people set out their work in an enduring and formal fashion. For Total Re-Think, a graphic design firm, this means allocating half a room which is at the centre of a two bedroom flat. One half is furnished for work and the other for living, (Figure 12.4). The partners in the firm both live and work in the flat.

Typical of women using typewriters, word processors, and computers is using a corner of an existing room, (Figure 12.5). Furniture and position are used to create physical and social distance.

For many, almost all their living space has to double up for employment purposes. Here, other devices have to be used to set off the employment sphere from the private domestic one. The hairdresser shown in Figure 12.6 is caught between the moment work finishes and the evening meal begins. When her clients leave, all the equipment she uses is stored until the next day.

As illustrated here, we can see that homeworkers share a number of consistent and enduring desires which are expressed in a variety of ways.

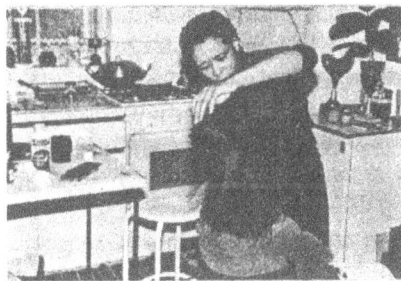

Fig. 12.6

The visible settings are solutions to the problems of fulfilling the functional requirements of working in the homeplace. Thus, even these quite simple occupations require specialist machinery, equipment, and furniture, and at the same time keeping an environment which is domestic in scale and preserves the private elements of household life.

To conclude

The disruption of home by paid work activities creates a situation in which people have a heightened awareness of the importance of home and the ideals which this represents as a private domestic domain. Creating work space requires and compels addressing overtly these meanings and using the reorganization of space, machinery, furniture, and other artifacts to sustain and reinforce positive meanings of home. In many cases, homework is chosen as a means of drawing the individual nearer to home in an ontological, interactional, and physical way. The individuals ability to alter and re-fashion their homespace is clearly an integral part of this process.

As homework becomes more prevalent within advanced societies, architects, builders, interior designers, and furniture manufacturers will be compelled to recognize and address these changes. The materials presented here show that this may not be a mechanistic or easy task, given the importance of diverse and complex functional, emotional, and social factors which are embodied in the final outward expression of enduring physical arrangements generated by people for their own use. These are shown to be personal, idiosyncratic, and domestic in scale. As a result, they have little to do with the conventionally perceived executive home office or high-tech fantasy dwellings displayed in popular literature, television, and design catalogues.

Serious questions also arise in respect of employment conditions: health and safety, personal and accident insurance, access and rights of collective organization, and representation. Evidence from Britain suggests that for most homeworkers, not only are incomes low relative to those in similar occupations which are organizationally based, but that they also are less likely to be members of unions or to have any other kind of representation (Bulos 1991, 1992; TUC 1991).

Urban regeneration and the viability of remote settlements should perhaps take into account the potential for homeworking and the neighbourhood networks which could be generated around particular types of homeworking, which could be harnessed to the process of community formation. In this respect, certain kinds of homework may assume particular significance: childminding, personal and professional services, or repair and maintenance services developed on a low-tech basis to serve local populations. Thus, urban planners need to incorporate considerations of homework in plans at local and regional levels.

Endnote

1. The differences here can best be illustrated by examples. A person works at home when all paid work activities occur there: for example a sewing machine operator, partly at home, where most work is in the home but visits are made to offices elsewhere or clients e.g., domiciliary chiropodists. Home is base for many types of jobs such as jobbing builders and sales people.

References

Ahrentzen, S.B. 1990. Managing Conflict by Managing Boundaries. *Environment and Behaviour* 22(6).

Brown, P. and R. Scase. 1991. *Poor Work: Disadvantage and the Division of Labour.* Oxford: Oxford University Press.

B.T. & ACRE. 1991. *Telecottage Today.* Chichester: ACRE.

Bulos, M. 1992. *Place, Space and Identity: A Study of Homeworkers.* London: South Bank University.

Bulos, M. and W. Chaker, 1991. Homebased Workers: Studies in the Adaptation of Space. *Housing: Design, Research, Education,* ed. M. Bulos and N. Teymur. Aldershot: Avebury

Denbrigh, A. 1992. Telework Gathers Official Momentum. *Ownbase* (May/June).

Dennison, S. 1991. Home Sweet Home. *Public Finance and Accountancy* (February 2) CIPFA.
Felix, G. 1989. *Evaluation of Remote Working.* Sheffield: Department of Employment.
Graham-Dixon, A. 1992. A Bricklayer's View of the World. *The Independent Newspaper* (July 28).
Hakim, C. 1987. *Home-based Work in Britain: A Report on the 1981 National Homeworking Survey and DE Research Programme on Homework.* Department of Employment. Research paper No.60. London: HMSO.
Henley Centre for Forecasting. 1988. *A Cost/Benefit Analysis of Teleworking.* London: HCF.
Huws, H. 1989. *Towards the Elusive Office.* London: Longmans.
Holdsworth, A. 1988. *Out of the Doll's House.* Milton Keynes: BBC Books.
Hooks, Bell. 1992. *Yearning: Race, Gender, and Cultural Politics.* London: Turnaround.
Madigan, R. & M. Munro. 1990. Ideal Homes: Gender and Domestic Architecture. In *Household Choices,* ed. T. Putnam and C. Newton. London: Futures Publications.
Martin, R. et al. 1988. *Women and Employment.* London: H.M.S.O.
Mead, G.H. 1934. *Mind, Self and Society.* Chicago: University of Chicago Press.
Pahl, R. 1987. *Divisions of Labour.* London: Longmans
———.1990. *On Work.* London: Longmans
Randall, J.M. 1991. "At Home", "At Work:" A boundary crossed. In *Housing: Design, Research, Education,* ed. M. Bulos and N. Teymur. Aldershot: Avebury.
———. 1992. Contradictory Images of "Home". Paper presented at the annual IAPS Conference, July, Thessalonika, Greece.
Saunders, P. 1990. *A Nation of Home Owners.* London: Unwin Hyman.
Sixsmith, J. & Sixsmith, A. 1990. Places in Transition: The Impact of Life Experiences on the Experience of Home. In *Household Choice,* ed. T. Putnam and C. Newton. London: Futures Publications.
Slaughter, M. 1956. *Coal is our Life: An Analysis of a Yorkshire Mining Community.* London: Golance.
Tate, J. 1990. Homework in Europe. Mimeo.
Trades Union Council. 1987. *Homeworking: A TUC Statement.* London: TUC.
———. 1991. *Homeworking and Homeworkers: A TUC Seminar for Trade Unionists.* London: TUC.

Part Four
Home and House: Lessons from the Past for the Present

13
Denmark's Living Housing Tradition

Jørn Ørum-Nielsen

To disregard tradition means losing the advantages of a broad perspective and forfeiting the most valuable support available, which is the accumulated knowledge gained by many centuries of human experience. Difficulties that we, as architects, encounter today are not looked at for the first time. Solutions have invariably been found in the past.

– Kaare Klint.

Introduction

In order to design houses and homes that fulfill people's needs, it is necessary to begin by identifying these needs. They are not easily defined, as they relate to intangible aspects of housing such as providing a balance of community and privacy, a sense of security, a sense of belonging, which are all crucial to providing a sense of *home*.

Future tenants, provided they can be identified, are at best only able to provide a limited assessment of their needs and they are certainly unable to answer for coming generations, most of whom have not yet been born! The only possible alternative is to look back at the choices and decisions that past generations have made.

Official housing standards are concerned with functional needs and structural quality control, but by their very nature provide little or no help beyond the purely physical requirements. More in-depth understanding is needed to achieve well designed living environments, where houses and neighbourhoods fulfill the needs of successive generations of people of all age groups. This gulf between designer and the successive generations of users presents the unavoidable dilemma of housing planning. Architects are left to find their own solutions, and often their very limited personal experience is the only basis for their decisions in designing housing environments for others.

I believe that only equipped with a thorough knowledge of traditional housing patterns developed by generations of users will the designer be able to bridge this gulf and gain a real understanding of the basic issues of housing.

Learning from the past

The widespread failings and criticism of modern housing design indicates the need for designers and planners to take a closer look at the decisions that people made when building their own homes in the past, before these decisions were taken over by professionals. Obviously, housing should be designed primarily to ensure the needs of the inhabitants rather than the needs of the professionals involved in the financing, design, and production of housing. In Denmark's post-war years there was a misguided belief that it was possible to plan workable housing for the future without knowledge of past housing models. These schemes reveal the attitude of many designers who evidently believed that their personal solutions would be of a standard high enough to ensure generations of users a workable living environment.

Traditional housing patterns provide us with pre-tested solutions from which we can learn important lessons. The domestic building tradition is rooted in product-development controlled primarily by the user. As a result, a set of values and norms have evolved that are still applicable to the most crucial aspects of dwelling. Our vernacular tradition considers all elements of housing (both tangible and intangible), in a coherent manner. It counterbalances values that are rooted in the natural environment with customs of social behaviour and cultural heritage.

If we are ignorant of these previous models that have been tested and tried and have proven their worth through generations of use, we deny ourselves the opportunity of using them as points of departure for new developments in housing. However, with a sound knowledge of these models, we gain the option of using and being inspired by them. It is a fallacy to believe that freedom exists in a vacuum; without restraints complete freedom becomes meaningless and will tend toward anarchy.

Planners too often attempt to find new housing solutions based primarily on invention and fantasy, where there is little understanding or consideration of the daily activities and the socio-psychological requirements of family living. Of the various fields of work in which designers and planners are involved, housing has the greatest direct effect on the quality of people's lives. Among those who are subjected to failed designs, the effects are most damaging for the elderly and small children, as both groups are especially vulnerable due to their limited mobility and high dependency on the quality of their immediate surroundings.

Continuity of growth is the essential characteristic of the responsible development of a domestic building culture, where the testing of old concepts leads to new adapted ones. To ignore the past and attempt to invent new concepts, which have no precedent, is irresponsible. It is unfortunate that so many housing schemes fail as a result of this attitude.

User design – a democratic influence

An examination of old Danish housing types is particularly relevant as plans and patterns of housing have evolved from models that were developed and tested by the inhabitants themselves. This evolution represents 6000 years of uninterrupted product development. These highly evolved and well-tested models express our need for protection, security, comfort, and our need for a strong relationship with our surroundings; crucial issues, which must be dealt with if a meaningful sense of home and belonging is to be achieved.

For this reason alone, traditional dwelling patterns are democratic in spirit, in the sense that their development and organization are the result of user-initiatives, made independently of specialists and professionals, who are often influenced by considerations other than those directly related to the daily use and function of the dwelling. Traditional buildings demonstrate a range of practical solutions, which respond to many of the technical and functional requirements at the core of housing planning, for instance: being able to adapt to climate and environment as well as to changing needs, and being able to create comfortable and secure indoor and outdoor spaces. Our main concern has always been, and remains, the need to economize natural resources. These priorities remain unchanged; they are timeless and therefore cannot be outdated.

By constantly fusing old concepts with new ideas, building traditions can be seen as a safeguard to superficial "pop" influence in the development of new housing. These concepts challenge political and commercial influences and pressures, as well as the aesthetic formalism of much recently built housing.

Jørn Ørum-Nielsen

Adapting to an unpredictable future

Længeboligen (Ørum-Nielsen 1988) is a summary of my study of Denmark's old houses and housing patterns. One of the essential themes of the book is the idea of flexibility and adaptability to changing circumstances of generations of users that is characteristic of traditional plan types and technologies. Such an adaptability criterium is crucial in determining the development of house types and housing patterns. By contrast, modern housing planning and construction is specifically adapted to a unique technology and family organization which epitomizes this particular period. As a consequence, contemporary housing developments do not have the same adaptability to changing conditions that is ingrained in centuries of housing built before the beginning of industrialization.

Change and variability are part of the basic conditions of life; our existence is dynamic. Nevertheless, by far the largest percentage of housing construction that has been built in the twentieth century is bound to static planning paradigms and construction technologies that are not tolerant of change. As a result, housing structures have to a great extent become rigidly defined by the particular ideas that were current at the time of planning. Many of these ideas have become rapidly outdated and inadequate with regard to the layout of the dwellings themselves and particularly to their grouping and interaction.

The conclusion we can draw from this is that it is insufficient to let the perceived needs and economic framework of the time be the sole determinants of what we build, as these trends will quickly change. Design decisions made purely on the basis of an analysis of functional needs current at the time will soon prove faulty. One means of avoiding this pitfall is to include a substantial content of ideas related to traditional housing patterns in our design process.

Responsible housing design is based on a much wider range of considerations than is currently applied. If we in Western Europe continue to practice housing design with regard for only the most basic economic and functional requirements of the time, contemporary designs will continue to become dysfunctional within a single generation, as is the case with many Euro-American schemes built in the 1960s and '70s which are already obsolete. These kinds of schemes, which obviously have failed to stand the test of time, did not foresee the steady growth of single-parent and divorcee families as well as the extended families of Second, Third, and Fourth World immigrants, who have different cultures and lifestyles, in addition to the internal cultural varriance within Western society. The designers of these schemes ignored the fact that family structures are dynamic and continually expand and diminish in response to socio-economic changes. If we are to create enduring housing developments we have to accept that there will always be unpredictable changes and we have to allow these to positively influence our choice of house types and building technologies. We have to look to traditional housing, which has been enduringly successful due to the fact that it anticipates the future being unpredictable.

Greater flexibility

The interests of society reach much further than a mere adjustment within the framework of the individual tenancy. The concept of flexibility must therefore be developed to encompass far more than simply the ability to change and adapt the layout and size of individual dwellings. If buildings and developments are not to be outdated, an extended structural flexibility is required. This broadened sphere of flexibility is perhaps the most important factor in our building and housing tradition, which for centuries has been decisive in the development of housing types and building technology. In the context of changing family structures, adaptability is of critical importance; the framework of a family's existence should be adaptable to changing circumstances and be capable of adjusting to varying household sizes and composition.

The integration of functions and client interests based on flexibility, which every old Danish provincial town displays, is part of our heritage, a heritage however, that specialized and professional planners of the last fifty years have largely ignored. Housing, business, and institutional construction have been dealt with as isolated entities which bear little relationship to one another. This has resulted in the zoning of specific land uses to separate areas in the community. However, precisely by separating and isolating categorized groups from one another, the city's greatest asset and its salient feature, namely the variety that emerges through mingling functions, has been lost. Those who have visited modern western urban areas are all too familiar with the results of this kind of planning which has created deserted bedroom communities, uninspired industrial parks, sterile commercial and shopping centres, and dreary institutional districts. The most unfortunate consequence of this is that the home and its surroundings have become devoid of life and interest. The many social activities of everyday urban life in all its aspects that are integral and important parts of a living home environment have become suppressed.

It is of little help that there are well designed and well functioning buildings presently being built. Their dislocated influence is hardly felt. Even the best of our new housing developments do not function ideally as little activity happens in and around the dwellings. All too often these buildings are mere shells deprived of content.

Variability and integration

Mingling, variability, and integration were all key concepts in urban construction of earlier ages. Each *individual* structure may perhaps not have been equally attractive or successfully designed, but they were normally part of a totality that promoted, and ensured a rich living environment. The choice of building techniques ensured an almost limitless functional integration, allowing changing uses of buildings and their re-adjustment from one purpose to another e.g., transitions from dwelling to production or from dwellings to institutions. The key was a total modular co-ordination ensured by the highly developed, well tested, and refined timber frame technology. The layout of each house was easily altered, the house itself could be dismantled into pieces and rebuilt in new contexts; this we know occurred frequently.

Traditional building technology was the aspect of the building that made changing uses possible, encouraging continual adaptation and regeneration, unlike most current building technologies which are intolerant of change. This failing is most obvious in residential construction, which in its rigidity creates an insurmountable obstacle to change, prohibiting forms of community living other than the traditional nuclear family for which the buildings were originally designed.

Historic models – tested and proven prototypes

A review of the development of planned housing in Denmark, including Nyboder, the housing for the Medical Association, the workers co-operatives, and the most recent low rise, high density developments, reveals their dominant common feature to be the adaptation of traditional housing patterns.

Time and again, this successive order of buildings demonstrates that truly significant developments in housing concepts, historically and presently, use traditional patterns as their point of departure. This line of succession is clearly evident and illustrates that adaptation, cultivation, and repetitive use of basic models over time have established a limited selection of well-tested prototypes.

Thus, there are two main conclusions to be drawn from this analysis of traditional building and housing types. The first demonstrates that only a limited selection of basic plan types is used over a time span of several thousand years. These similar plans have been continuously reused with only minor adjustments .

The second conclusion concerns the resiliency of these basic house and plan types. The more simplified a plan appears, the greater its adaptability and flexibility. These requirements of adaptability and flexibility have evidently been decisive in the selection and evolution of basic house types over time, resulting in types which are without exception tightly structured and generally uncomplicated.

Elements of housing design

The elements that are dealt with so successfully in traditional housing are the same elements we have the most difficulty in coping with in residential planning – perhaps because solutions are never specific but rather tend to encompass inbuilt checks and balances.

The main elements are:

1. a balance between privacy and community

2. standardized repetitive production techniques in creating personalized environments with a human scale

3. randomness in a controlled environment

4. adaption of static building structures to the dynamic of people's lives, thereby allowing for changing use of buildings over time

5. most importantly, quality solutions being achieved by economy in the broadest sense of the word: economy of scale, economy of use, economy of resources

Many of these elements are ambiguous and contradictory, which is why housing has proven to be an extremely difficult area to control. However, over time solutions have been found that are both simple and effective.

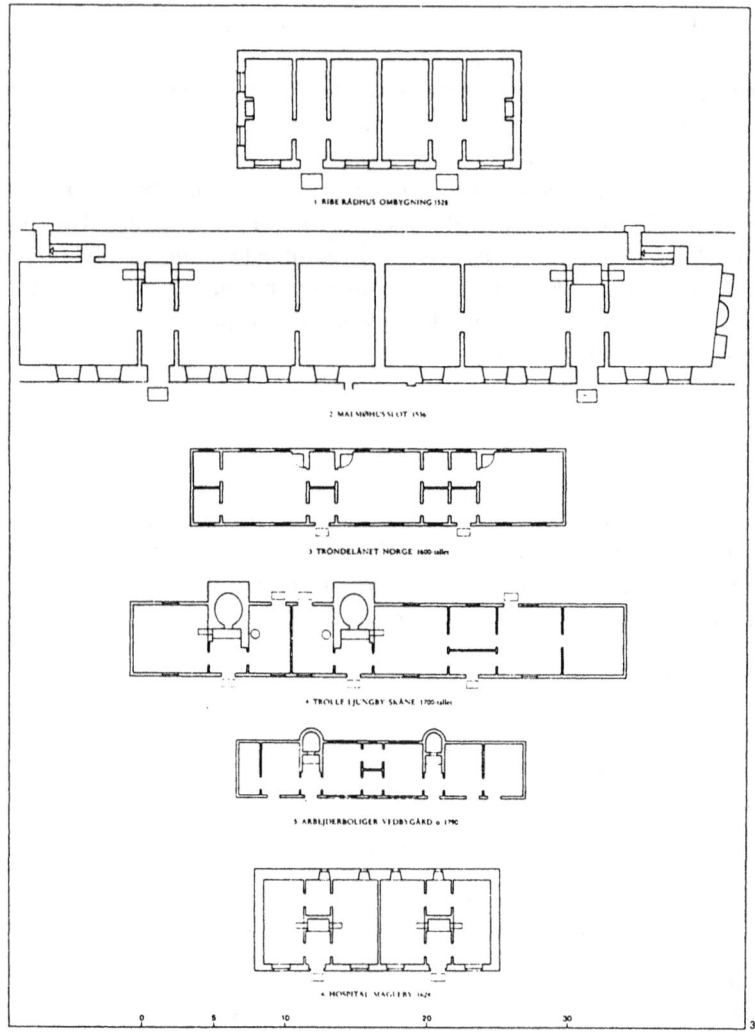

Fig 13.1. (From Ørum-Neilson 1988, p.142)

Figure 13.1 illustrates a wide range of applications of the typical Danish traditional *længe* (wing or longhouse, one of the basic planning elements of northern European Medieval buildings). Malmøhus Slot (plan 2, Fig. 13.1) is the King's residence and is essentially identical in plan, (except for size and wall thickness), to the workers' housing from Vedbygaard (plan 5, Fig. 13.1). For centuries the bilateral længe plan was viewed throughout Scandinavia as a prototype building model, especially in rural settings. Whether for wealthy aristocrats or impoverished peasants, for expanded households, combinations of individuals, or small families, the Scandinavian people had a deep familiarity and understanding of this building type. For many, its use was simply taken for granted.

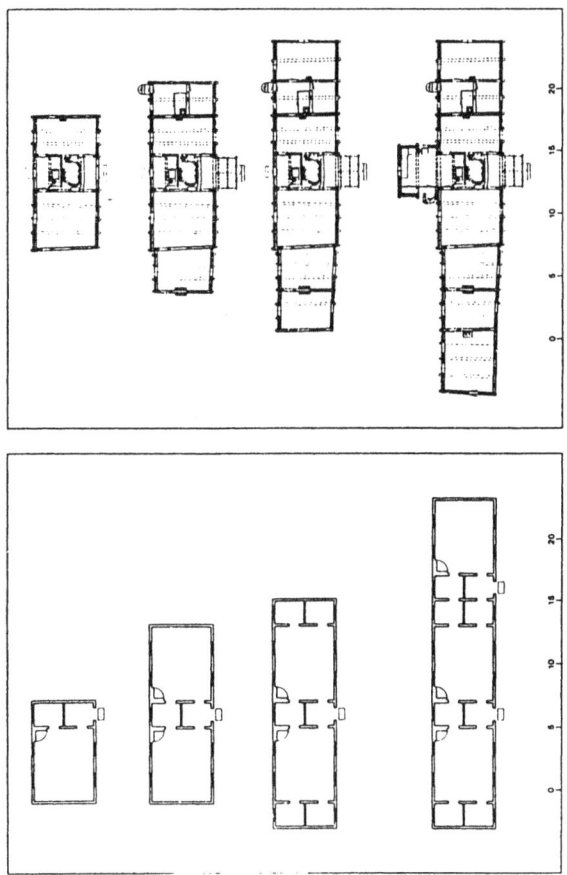

Fig 13.2. (From Ørum-Neilson 1988, p144)

Figure 13.2 illustrates a sequence which develops from a simple, three-bay dwelling, enlarges to a bilateral dwelling, then to an extended bilateral dwelling, and further to a double bilateral, in which the intermediate spaces are accessible from either side (based on the development history of an existing dwelling). The method of changing the size of one's dwelling, either by buying part of a neighbour's adjacent house, or selling part of one's own was, for some time, a common occurrence. The use of bilateral plans in a row-house configuration is a logical anticipation of inevitable demands for such changes in buildings that were expected to endure not only for a few years, nor only for the lifetime of an individual, but for many successive generations.

Initially, these vernacular forms and patterns might appear characteristically spare and over simplified. However, when studied more closely, the deceptively simple concepts reveal many inbuilt layers and a high degree of sophistication. Clearly evident is the adaptation of static building structures to the dynamics of human habitation, and an understanding of the need for flexibility and for accommodating future requirements that are unforeseeable.

Fig. 13.3

Ærøskøbing (Fig. 13.3) is typical of the provincial urban building tradition. The rows of connected houses and shops that today line the streets of most eighteenth and nineteenth century Danish towns are evidence of a method of town-building that may have been practised in Denmark from the end of the Middle Ages. The walls of these buildings not only designate the boundary between public and private, they physically and perceptually define the public streets and squares, which are outdoor "rooms" in which the community lives its collective life. These "rooms" include the yards, gardens, and outbuildings hidden from the public eye. These spaces give the town's residents the opportunity to grow a garden, enjoy the sun, listen to birds, or simply to escape from the pressures of urban or domestic life. Buildings and homes are links between the town's private and public spheres, and have direct access to, and become integral parts of both.

The buildings, constructed by their owners or local craftsmen, are different versions of the traditional *længe*. They are long and narrow, one or two story buildings, with a loft under a steeply pitched roof, comprised of varying numbers of transverse structural bays. Town dwellers built the only house types they were accustomed to, transplanting them (sometimes physically) from their former use as farm buildings to the new town setting.

Initially, buildings were free-standing, but as towns became more heavily used, the spaces between were in-filled, and the detached farm version of the *længe* became a row house. Land within the town became scarcer and scarcer, and the resulting pressure for compact development created the densely clustered, highly defined urban forms we now associate with Medieval towns and cities.

The building block for Danish towns like Ærøskøbing is always the *længe*. This may seem to be coincidental, but in fact the form of such towns is directly related to the form of the *længe,* and so is the fact that these towns continue to be seen as wonderful places to live, after hundreds of years of use. Consider the hypothetical list below of design requirements for a building that would work effectively in a town like Ærøskøbing. In addition to being structurally sound, and appropriately designed for the specifics of Denmark's climate, such a building must:

1. be able to connect with buildings on either side to help form the division between public and private outdoor spaces

2. be variable in length, within the modular and incrementally consistent rhythmic pattern of doors and windows in adjacent buildings

3. be low on the street frontage, one or two stories, with a roof sloping away from the street to allow light into the street, with the same configuration on the garden side

4. be adaptable to streets running in all directions, both straight and curved, and flexible enough to form part of the boundaries of other public spaces where those are needed

5. allow light to enter the rooms from either street or garden side (preferably both)

6. have an interior layout which allows access to both street and garden

7. have a basic structure that is permanent and capable of being used for many generations; it must also be flexible, allowing many different users to adapt it to their own living patterns and tastes

8. be easily constructed at a reasonable cost, by local builders, and with readily available materials

In effect, the building type defined by these criteria is the *længe*. In other cultures, of course, there are other kinds of towns, and other building types that best fit the local urban structure. The thrust here is not that the *længe* is the only workable urban dwelling type in the world, but that in Denmark, as in other cultures, where workable towns and cities have developed over long periods of time, the town and the town's buildings are essentially and inextricably interconnected. If one changes the context of a house, one changes the house. More importantly even, houses and homes are integral parts of the neighbourhood and the urban environment; thus home is more than simply the house, it also encompasses the neighbourhood.

Our experience of towns like Ærøskøbing, their flowing streets, clearly organized in hierarchies of importance, their squares of various sizes, for market or church or other important communal gatherings, their richly textured, yet consistent buildings, punctuated by church spire or town hall, all demonstrate a logical beauty in the town's arrangement. We can perceive the centuries of development and refinement that have shaped these towns, how they seem rooted in the land and as much a part of the larger landscape as are trees and fields. Life in such towns offers community and allows privacy, it combines excitement with tranquility, is caring and neighbourly and rich in form, safe and dependable, and is the prerequisite for a home within a community in the best sense of the word.

Dragør's (Fig. 13.4) old town is a community of about 400 buildings, mostly single-family homes, built during the eighteenth and nineteenth centuries. Initially, the town seems like other towns from the same period, developed more or less haphazardly over many years, yet the town's structure and appearance are the outcome of a particularly interesting planning concept that is unique among traditional Danish towns. In fact, each house, far from being haphazard in shape, plan, and orientation, is shaped and located by a consistent, logical set of rules.

Although the original houses were always one room deep, the length of houses varied. Each house is either "one-sided" or "two-sided," that is with the kitchen-entry bay located at the end of the unit, or located between sets of rooms on either side. This latter "two-sided" or bilateral plan is common, allowing the house to be used by either a single household or two

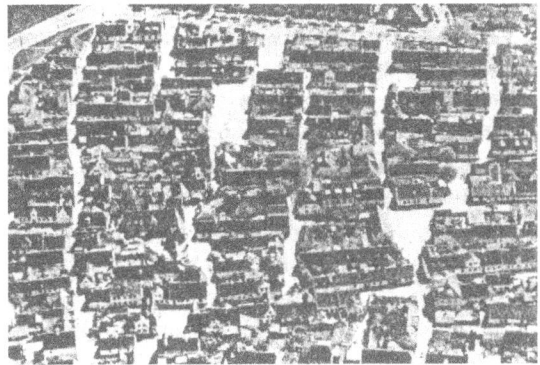

Fig. 13.4

separate households. In both plans, rooms vary in size; there were either one or two rooms beyond the kitchen-entry, extended in either direction. Direct garden access is thereby ensured.

Notable attributes are:

1. long, narrow building shapes providing well lit interior spaces and overall accessibility; dwelling units easily sub-divided or combined
2. rational technology in simple and user-friendly buildings
3. user participation in forming the environment ensures that repetitive building procedures are not monotonous
4. human scale and direct access between indoor and outdoor living spaces
5. clear definition of spaces for community and privacy
6. resilient patterns adaptable to change, small dwellings combining into large units and larger dwellings with built-in subdivisions

The town of Dragør combines the best features of planned communities with the best features of randomly built communities: commonly understood and respected rules ensure efficient and economical use of the town's site, whilst ample light and fresh air is assured for every home. Nevertheless, every street posesses its own unique character, each block is different from every other block, and since homeowners are free (within the broad limits set by the basic rules), to build their own houses as they wish, no two houses are exactly alike. One's visual impression of the town as a whole is dominated by a sense of variety and improvisation. Everywhere, there are departures from the norm, reflecting both changing circumstance and the varying personal tastes of many generations of citizens. These variations on the town's basic themes are contained by, and have become an integral part of, the original scheme. There is a clear sense of underlying order, which is not too rigorously enforced, so that Dragør's physical structure remains consistent, whilst avoiding monotony.

Dragør as it appears today is an exemplary model of all the positive aspects that a flexible and adaptable low-rise, high-density urban residential structure should contain. It is no coincidence that this small town has been an inspiration to generations of architects in their attempts to develop new housing, which responds to contemporary ideals. The combination of urban regulation and individual freedom as found in Dragør, has in recent years been a stimulus in the revival of low rise, high density residential planning in Denmark.

Fig. 13.5

Nyboder (Fig. 13.5.), built in 1631 to house the families of naval personnel, was Denmark's first large scale residential development, and it revealed a new vision, both in site planning and building design. The long, narrow, one-story housing blocks lay parallel to each other, far enough apart so there was sure to be plenty of light and air to the relatively shallow dwellings. Between the rows of buildings (forty of them, containing 600 dwellings in all), were alternating streets and garden areas, so that each dwelling was given both service and amenity access. This concept is similar to the above-mentioned traditional "Ærøskøbing-pattern." The garden areas, intended for growing food, and to "benefit and cheer" the inhabitants, were originally unfenced, though they were later subdivided into smaller plots to provide each dwelling with its own defined yard. Each of the dwellings in Nyboder enjoyed fresh air and good light and each was given access to space for growing vegetables. These were unusual attributes for housing of that time and, with a guarantee of permanent use upon retirement, it was clearly meant to tempt men serving in the navy to make a permanent commitment to that service.

It is in the bringing together of well designed dwellings and a well planned neighbourhood that the Nyboder project achieves its brilliance; it remains one of Denmark's best examples of the relationship between good planning and good building design in urban housing.

The original planners produced with Nyboder an entirely new design for an urban dwelling, based on the tradition of Danish rural housing. In each of the dwellings in the original Nyboder there is a transverse bay which serves as both hall and kitchen, with doors to both street and garden, these dwellings are one story in height, without longitudinal partitions, thus providing daylight from two sides, a familiar pattern in traditional rural *længer* but in this instance it is used for the first time in a large scale urban development.

Dwelling by dwelling, row by row, the buildings were identical, housing shipyard workers, ordinary seamen, and officers; all were provided with equal conditions. This was an unusual policy for the time, perhaps reflecting the pattern for sharing close quarters onboard ship. These are the first known examples of standardized and mass-produced dwellings with gardens, based on an overall plan, and the first use of the traditional *længe* in a planned urban context. The project is unique for its time, and a model for the renaissance of Danish row-house development three centuries later. In the course of the intervening centuries, Nyboder has undergone many changes, but the basic urban design principles from the original development survive in today's Nyboder: the clear, orderly layout of streets and buildings, the simplicity of building form, and the uniformity of individual family dwellings.

These planning and design principles were unique to Nyboder at the time of its construction. It was the first use of the row-dwelling as the basic unit of a planned urban housing scheme,and represented the first in a long sequence of row-housing schemes in succeeding centuries, which eventually included factory worker's housing and co-operative housing. Nyboder also has provided the foundation for the most recent developments in low-rise, high-density housing.

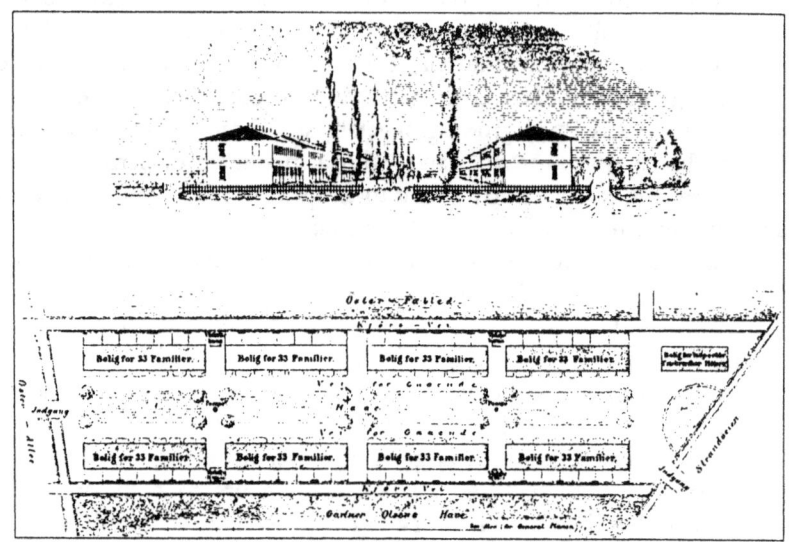

Fig 13.6. (From Ørum-Neilson 1988, p.201)

Figure 13.6 illustrates sanitary housing for workers families, built 1865 on the outskirts of Copenhagen, following the great cholera epidemic. The new development was officially called The Medical Association Housing, but it was commonly known as Brumleby.

The design was given to Denmark's leading architect at the time, Michael Gottlieb Bindesbøll, who responded to the challenge, producing in just a few weeks a design that would eventually be seen as one of Denmark's most influential housing developments. In many respects this design reflects important aspects of Denmark's traditional urban residential patterns, primarily the two-sidedness of dwelling units. Bindesbøll's plan provides a remarkably complex and stimulating public setting for the inhabitants, within an uncomplicated and economic framework.

To a large extent the richness and complexity is accomplished by the careful juxtaposing of opposing and complementary site characteristics related to one another, yet clearly separate. For example, Bindesbøll has carefully zoned the quiet and noisy areas of the site: the street side is allocated to the noisy activities, whilst the side with small gardens and the large, green common, is allocated to quiet activities. Regarding these two sides in another way; the garden side is primarily for pedestrians, whilst the other side is for vehicles, one side is expressed by nature, the other by services; one side is "soft," the other "hard;" one side is "recreational," the other "businesslike;" one side is "rural," the other "urban." There is nothing complicated in the way this is achieved, in fact, the buildings are simply aligned in rows with generous spaces between them. Each space between building rows alternates between service and recreation so that each building faces a different character on either side.

To allow these dualities to co-exist required an awareness that such characteristics could be built into the scheme, an understanding of how certain characteristics might reinforce or detract from each other, and an attention to small details of planning and design. The primary entrances to the dwellings might have been situated on either side of the building, but are instead located on the street side, where the busy, social aspects of coming and going, meeting neighbours, gossiping are integrated with the urban, noisy side of the site.

Further, there are small, private gardens connected to each block and belonging to lower floor residents (upper floor residents also had access to private garden plots, located at the ends of the greens). These gardens could have been located on the street side, where they would have buffered the street entry from the noise and activity on that side; instead, they are on the side where the common is located and where their presence reinforces, and is reinforced by, the quiet, natural, "soft" aspects of the greater space. In this position, the gardens provide both a social and a physical transition between the "hardness" and the privateness of the buildings and the "softness" and openness of the green. Over time, this narrow transitional band has become the area where the most creativity has been expressed by residents, a place where differing needs and lifestyles extend beyond the privacy of dwelling interiors into public visibility.

The experience of the alternating worlds on either side of the buildings is nowadays more striking than ever, as each tenant has had the opportunity to add informal structures on the garden side of the buildings. This has resulted in a more or less haphazard construction of small sheds and outhouse structures, which serve as informal extensions to the living space. These structures give the communal space an atmosphere of informality and create a collage-like effect. The contrast between this area and the street side has therefore become even more marked.

This results in an overridingly positive experience of the scheme, where the inhabitants have been encouraged to create a community by virtue of their involvement in the actual physical development of the scheme. This is due partly to the two-faceted nature of the buildings that places people in contact with two different sets of neighbours, each of whom has, in turn, another set of neighbours on the other side of the building, thereby consistently providing opportunities for the residents to congregate for collective activity. The linear "village green" provides perhaps the most dramatic of these opportunities. However, of equal importance is the provision in the plan of a narrow central zone, running the full length of the site, which is at present reserved for shared facilities, and which provides ample space for future expansion (there still remains space for new facilities). In the original construction, a small portion of this zone was used for laundry facilities and toilets. Later inclusions were Copenhagen's first workers' cooperative store, a bathhouse, meeting hall, children's nursery, library, woodshop, and even a fire station. Each of these activity centers was constructed as the result of initiatives taken by Brumleby's residents, who also founded their own medical benefit association, local chapters of workers' political parties, and choir.

We will never know whether this was the result of the architect's foresight and good intentions, as he left no personal notes, but it is clear that the organization and the details of this development have encouraged social activities and generated community participation. There remain residents of Brumleby whose grandparents were among the first occupants; many children who were born and grew up in this small community, who have subsequently moved away, and have found that other housing environments do not offer the same quality of life.

Over the years, the original apartments in Brumleby have shown great adaptability and have been significantly transformed. There are many ways these dwellings can be altered, by joining the rooms in new combinations, most often on one level, but also by creating connections between floors. Though Bindesbøll could not have predicted the specific transformations that have occurred in these buildings, he would certainly have been aware of the basic adaptability inherent in the building-type he chose in Brumleby, and he may well have understood that the dwellings were the most forgiving part of the system. If so, it was clearly an accurate judgement; while the dwellings have changed to a large extent, the site plan functions as it was projected by Bindesbøll in 1853.

Brumleby is one of the earliest examples of a designer having intentionally traded public amenity for private amenity, perhaps in this case because providing richness and variety for collective consumption was far cheaper than providing it privately, dwelling by dwelling, but also perhaps because it was a trade-off that would be most beneficial in the long term. This was a revolutionary concept in its time, when workable and enjoyable public spaces usually developed by accident, if at all. The design of Brumleby effectively balances built form and open space, vehicles and pedestrians, privacy and community, in achieving a wonderful living environment for Copenhagen's least affluent citizens.

Unfortunately, architects were slow to recognize the degree to which Bindesbøll's careful and far-sighted ideals underlay Brumleby's success, and its influence on other projects remained minimal in ensuing decades. It was not until the renaissance of row-house garden dwellings in the 1920s and 30s that the importance of the planning and design ideas used in this project began to be recognised by the architectural profession. Today Brumleby remains a success and continues to invite the creative adaptations of new generations. Its prolonged successful existence is an ongoing inspiration to those who live in it, and to those who visit it, for its critical lessons in the discipline of urban design.

Fig. 13.7

The residential community Jystrup Savværk (Fig. 13.7), planned by the Vandkunsten design team and built in 1984 is a co-operative housing community built on a traditional street concept and based on community living as an integrated part of everyday life. It is an extraordinarily compact building, one large single structure containing 21 family dwellings with shared guest facilities, and common recreational and dining spaces, which are all linked by a glass-covered public space and connecting inner walkways.

There are strong references to the small traditional village clustered on either side of its main thoroughfare. Jystrup Savvœrk has a communal shared area that is large in relation to the number of dwellings and inhabitants. It is interesting to note that the residents of this cooperative have surrendered a considerable 40 per cent share of their private dwelling space to the community. Private space is clearly defined and provided with minimal kitchens and limited living areas. The residential community's central area includes a common kitchen and dining hall, laundry room, workshops, hobby and music rooms, as well as guest rooms for visitors.

A consequence of this conscious distribution of space is the small size of each dwelling unit, as the total project is built within the space limitation imposed by subsidized housing regulations. The glass-covered street linking the dwellings is unheated, but is suitable for play and active recreation for a large part of the year. The inner streets help to blur the transition between the private and common areas of the residential community. At the same time, the street can be viewed as a climatic zone, an "overcoat" that retains radiant heat. This project helps to expand our perceptions of the interface between private and communal dwelling space.

Conclusion

Substantial renewal in housing is dependent on the understanding of precedents, and durable innovations are, most often, rooted in ideas from the past. I maintain that it is not possible to introduce meaningful and workable new concepts in housing that have no precedent.

It would be inconceivable for us to abandon our cultural heritage, our customs of social behaviour, language or manner of dress as we identify ourselves by these factors. In the 1950s and '60s, however, under influence of the modern movement, that is precisely what occurred in housing. The cost has been great, and the people who are subjected to these environments will continue to pay in consequence of bad decisions that were made.

I do not suggest that we replicate our traditional housing models. In architecture, nostalgia is useless, even destructive. We cannot, nor should we, attempt to replicate the past. I am convinced that we should study closely the traditional housing models that still survive to understand their meaning and content, and their pragmatic and their responsible approach to housing. I am convinced that we should be sensitive to their lessons concerning human scale, community sense, respect for individual privacy, order and variety, adaptability to change, ingrained sense of involvement, and of belonging and of feeling at home. All these factors are impossible to legislate, but are nevertheless more important than the easily defined factors that housing codes and regulations usually respond to. The sum of these latter well-intentioned building restrictions makes it impossible for future towns like Ærøskøbing or Dragør to be built.

This unhappy state of affairs becomes even more absurd when one realizes that if today's building codes were to be enforced, most, if not all, of the few surviving old residential areas would have to be demolished. Many of the qualities that we admire and see as inspirational to our work are no longer seen as acceptable, nor do they comply with current building regulations that are intended to ensure the quality of new housing! This, in spite of the fact that these old residential areas combine beauty and proven usability; crucial factors that are missing in much of the "law-abiding" housing that we build today.

Building codes are continually being revised and updated. To avoid being forced even further away from the in-built sensitivity that is characteristic of vernacular building patterns, we must understand the importance of preserving the few examples of traditional housing that still exist. Meaningful housing debate is generated by comparisons. To be able to evaluate and adjust new housing concepts in comparison to traditional models and ideals, it is crucially important in keeping this debate alive. By doing so we will hopefully avoid repeating some of the mistakes and large scale excesses in housing seen in recent years in Denmark as well as in many other countries.

Tradition can be perceived as inbuilt wisdom, an advanced and comprehensive accumulation of knowledge that, if made accessible, will provide us with the necessary insights into the ecological, social, and technological fundamentals of housing and urban planning.

The development of traditional housing types and patterns in Denmark demonstrates an ongoing fusion of the permanent with the temporary. Accumulated knowledge and experience provided by our collective memory interacts with new developments in a changing society. Without exception, traditional building types have economy as their primary driving force. An economy of resources, which leads to functional and flexible plan solutions and a maximum utilization of all available opportunities.

Today, the greatest challenge in housing is to define the balance between the individual and the community, in the realm of management and organization, and within the framework of the daily lives of individuals and families. The role of architecture is to establish a framework that allows people to participate in developing and building their home and its neighbourhood within a structure that allows and encourages social activities, unlike most contemporary housing. I believe there is no way of moving towards this goal other than by constantly ensuring that elements of past design be incorporated into contemporary housing design.

Uninterrupted continuity of development is vital if a tradition is to be kept alive; conversely, continuity without change is stagnation. To respect tradition is not an attempt to cling to the past, neither should it be seen as an attempt to recreate social values that have been lost.

A thriving tradition has nothing to do with nostalgia for the past. It has a vital role to play in contemporary housing developments. Tradition is dynamic in the sense that elements are continually being reassessed and discarded, whilst other elements are introduced. It is a forward looking process.

A tradition that is kept in use promotes constant progress and renewal, which are imperatives to the well-being of our communities.

References

Abrahamsen, P. 1987. *Bevaring - set fra Dragør*. Copenhagen: Ejlers Forlag.
Alexander, C. and S. Chermayeff. 1963. *Community and Privacy*. N. Y.: Doubleday.
Alexander, C., et al. 1977. *A Pattern Language*. N. Y.: Oxford University Press
Alexander, C. 1979. *The Timeless Way of Building*. N. Y.: Oxford University Press.
Aren, H. 1980. *Radhuset som Folkbostad*. PhD diss., Chalmers Institute of Technology, Göteborg.
Bredsdorff, P. 1945. *Huset i Byen*. Copenhagen: Akademisk Arkitektforening.
Cronberg, T. and E. Jantzen, 1982. *Building for People*. SBI Report 299, Copenhagen.
Erixon S. 1982. *Svensk byggnadskultur*. Malmø: Walter Ekstrand Bokförlag.
Fischer, E. 1949. *Dragør*. Copenhagen: Foreningen til Gamle Bygningers Bevarelse.
Gehl, J. 1987. *Life Between Buildings*. N.Y.: Van Nostrand Reinhold.
Hansen, E. and M. Pihler. 1971. *Lægeforeningens boliger på Østerbro*. Copenhagen: Kunstadademiet/Arkitektens Forlag.
von Jessen, C. and M. Pihler. 1980. *Byhuset. Byggeskik i købstaden*. Copenhagen: Gyldendal.
Lundberg, E. 1935. *Herremannens bostad*. Stokholm: Akademiens Förlag.

Marcus, C. 1986. *Housing as if People Mattered*. Berkeley: University of California Press.
Minnhagen, M. 1973. *Bondens bostad*. Lund: CWK Gleerup.
Nationalmuseet 1979. *Historiske huse i Dragør*. Copenhagen: Nationalmuseet.
Rasmussen, S.E. 1941. Ærøskøbing købstad. *Arkitekten* 6.
———. 1949. *Byer og bygninger*. Copenhagen: Forlaget Fremad.
Stadsingeniørens Direktorat 1947. *København. Fra bispetid til borgertid*. Copenhagen: J.H. Schultz Forlag.
Torgny, O. 1984. *Skånelängor*. Stockholm: Liber Förlag.
Vasstrøm, M. 1985. *Holmens by*. Copenhagen: Orlogsmuseets skriftrække 1
Ørum-Nielsen, J. 1988. *Længeboligen*. Copenhagen: Arkitektens Forlag.
———. *Om flexibilitet i boligbyggeriet*. Forthcoming.
———. 1995. *Dwelling – At Home – In Community – On Earth*. (English translation of *Længeboligen*). Forthcoming.

14

The Home and Housing Modernization

Tomas Wikström

In this paper some expressions of the spatial dimension of *home* will be discussed. This will be done on the basis of experiences from research on housing modernization. Taking part in evaluations of renewal projects in three Swedish housing areas built in the forties and fifties has made me aware of the home as something very central and at the same time overlooked.[1] I have come to see home as an expression of people's continuous creation of space around themselves. Viewing home as a process intrinsically related to place underlines its vulnerability to drastic changes, like those of housing modernization. The inspiration to intepret home in terms of human space-making originates most of all from reading *Mensch und Raum* (Man and Space) by German phenomenologist Otto Friedrich Bollnow. However, I am not going to discuss Bollnow's work as such. Instead I will make use of his ample treatment of inhabited space to shed some light on my own observations.

The threatened home

The housing areas of my study are results of the Swedish neighbourhood planning of the forties and fifties. Generally, the buildings are three or four storeys, where the flats, mostly with two or three rooms and a kitchen, were considered large enough for families. When my study was carried out, they were occupied by couples and single persons. Many of the inhabitants now were middle-aged or elderly people, who moved in when the areas were new, and whose children had long since left home. Young people moved in when flats were available, but normally moved on afterwards to larger dwellings as soon as they had children.

Although the flats had "modern" equipment and were well maintained, in some respects they were worn and out of date. Kitchens, bathrooms, and accessibility for the handicapped, among other things, did not fulfill the current building regulations. The owners, *allmännyttiga* (public) housing companies, foresaw problems with attracting new tenants. Thus, even though the inhabitants themselves were relatively satisfied, renewal projects, aimed at modernization of the flats and upgrading the grounds, were initiated. The negative response from many of the tenants was a shock for the planners and the employees of the housing companies.

The spontaneous reaction from many inhabitants, especially those who had been living in the areas since the early days, was that modernization was a threat to the calm and safe life in well-known surroundings. The promised improvements were not enough to balance the negative response of these people. Their reaction revealed emotional ties to home, neighbours, and neighbourhood that appeared strange and out of fashion. I initially found these reactions difficult to relate to the housing areas, as the buidings were products of modern neigbourhood planning. In some cases these bonds seemed to be so strong, that breaking them by moving would lead to disaster. Others, however, had weaker ties to home and neighbourhood. For some young people, the flat was just a place where they slept and stored their belongings.

The people that I interviewed were only in exceptional cases forced to move permanently. Among those who were, some experienced a great and definite loss. Most of the inhabitants, however, were vacated only for a few weeks. Their stories about how they handled the worries, disturbances, and changes of the modernization process gave an abundance of information concerning their relations to home.

Our attempt to spread this knowledge to politicians, property-managers, planners, and architects turned out to be very instructive for research. When we told them about old people's strong ties to their homes, about social networks being concentrated around staircases, and informal care among neighbours, many of them were provoked. Why these negative and sometimes aggressive reactions?

In my opinion, it was the fact that people were attached to certain places – instead of moving freely on the housing-market – which was awkward to those working with renewal of housing areas. This irritation is understandable. Nobody likes to see her- or himself as responsible for cutting off the bonds between fellow-beings and their homes. It was our pointing out the importance of the spatial dimensions of people's everyday lives, that was new and provocative to planners and others. A concept of home, which is strongly related to place, demands as a prerequisite a completely new way of planning for renewal and modernization.

Fig. 14.1. The three housing areas represent the height of Swedish neighbourhood planning. For many of the inhabitants, plans of modernization were a threat to their homes. Norra Göta, Borås, 1943–47. (Photo from Tomas Wikström.)

Fig. 14.2. For the individual or family home means rest, refuge, independence, and a place for everyday domestic routines. Less obvious, and often forgotten by planners, is home as a part of a neighbourhood. Bollnow's concept *lived space* makes visible the interdependence of home and local context.

It became evident that home was something complicated, "irrational" and at the same time very important. *Home,* in the sense people in the housing areas used the term, obviously did not exist in the minds of planners and builders. This lack of understanding of the meaning of home explains to a certain degree why the renewal processes in two of the areas led to conflicts. I hope that deeper knowledge about what home is for people will benefit the practice of planning and building in inhabited environments.

Bollnow on space, dwelling, and home

In *Mensch und Raum* (1990)[2] the concept of space, as it evolved around the human habitat, is considered to be primary. Thus home becomes something essential and central for human life. In his account of space, Bollnow confronts *der erlebte Raum* (lived space)[3] with mathematical space. Mathematical space evolved historically as a reduction of inhabited space. The abstract, geometrical way of viewing reality was in many ways a conquest in the history of mankind, e.g., in the arts of warfare, navigation, and building. However, the success of this abstract concept of space continually threatens the original organic concept of space.

Bollnow represents a line of phenomenology called philosophical anthropology, which puts the emphasis on the complexity and manifoldness of empirical reality. Philosophical anthropology opposes all kinds of reductionism in the view of man, e.g., man as a machine, a social being, etc. The essence of man is seen as a meaningful, coherent formation, and understood in relation to all perceptible features of man, all sentiments, feelings and drives. But even this complex being is not taken for granted. To Bollnow this is a working hypothesis, which never can be finally confirmed. In the broad field of philosophical anthropology, Bollnow's own work is dedicated to phenomena like safety, anxiety, happiness, togetherness, body, and home (Lübcke 1987, 156–159).

What is meant by lived space? To Bollnow, space is created through human action. His starting point is people's concrete relations to, and the creation of space within the guise of philosophical anthropology. To decide the essence of space one must act on detailed empirical observations. Thus, the spaces intended by Bollnow are inhabited. Originally the creation of space is the result of common human labour, and is therefore in itself common (Bollnow 1990, 269). *Wohnen* (to dwell) becomes a central concept, to which Bollnow constantly returns. Dwelling is not just man's way of living in a house, it is expanded to man's way of being in space.

In this "be-dwelled" space the exterior relation between subject and object is dissolved, its spatiality is characterized by the unity of space and man. As I interpret Bollnow, the essence of (inhabited) space lies in this absence of distinction between subject and object. Approaches, for which man is seen as an object in a container (an apple in a basket) or a perceiving subject in an objective, geometrical space, are merely useful as instruments for certain purposes. However, Bollnow makes us aware of the immense reduction implied by such concepts of space, currently prevalant in the fields of planning and design. To understand home and dwelling, one must try to conquer this reductionism.

Homes and dwelling in three housing areas

Mensch und Raum discusses a number of aspects of inhabited space. Some of these will applied on the homes I have come to know through my studies. Thus, I have chosen to distinguish between six aspects of home, namely:

1. safety, shelter

2. going out and coming back

3. autonomy

4. domestic routines

5. neighbours

6. to be rooted

The place of safety and shelter

...and then we came back home and felt the cosy warmth...
— Anonymous tenant.

When asked about what home and *hemkänsla* (sense of home) meant to them, most people, as expected, started talking about their dwellings. That was where they found warmth, safety and comfort. "When my husband was still alive," an old lady told me, "we went for walks, and then we came back home and felt the cosy warmth. 'Thank God we have a home,' I used to say." Some of the people interviewed described the sense of home as the satisfaction of having a safe place to return to. To provide shelter and protection is one of the most original purposes of home. "It is always nice to unlock the door, enter into your own, and lock the door behind yourself." Against the exterior space, Bollnow says, where man is active and has to struggle, where danger prevails, stands the safe space of home. Here man no longer has to be on guard, but can relax (Bollnow 1990, 129-130).

The contentment of home was preferred to the dangerous temptations of the world outside by one man interviewed: "We are not restless people, but home-bodies." Adapting to the simple everyday life was his attitude, and served as a guide for his strivings. To Bollnow, people's struggle to create a safe spot in the world is very important. For him the life of the existentialist is homelessness in the extreme. It is that of "the eternal stranger, without bonds to any place, always on his way, but never reaching his destination" (ibid., 125). According to Heidegger we are all "thrown" (*geworfen*) into this world. However, there is a possibility to overcome this predicament. To dwell is "to be at home at a certain place, to be rooted and belong there" (ibid., 125).

When they heard about the forthcoming modernization, many of my interviewees felt that their whole existence was threatened. To cope with this, initially rather vague threat, a mental strength was demanded. An old couple, who really wanted to stay on, could not bear the tension and stress. They decided to move before the modernization started.

The place of goings and comings

...Everything is close...
– Anonymous tenant

Most of the people that were interviewed had a very good knowledge of the surroundings. As they spoke about the housing area, they constantly – and spontaneously – pointed towards the places they talked about. Starting out from where we were sitting, they showed me directions with different meaning. There was the town center, the wood, the shop, the playground etc. Their homes appeared to be centers, from which their picture of the surroundings was built up.

Here, home stands out as the point of departure for movements and trips in a surrounding world, revealed because home is situated just there. Journeys to and from work, shopping in the center of town and idle walks, make home the "zero-point" of space which according to Bollnow should not be confused with another zero, the perceiving subject of perception psychology (ibid., 55-56). The spot Bollnow refers to is characterized by going out and coming back. It can be a temporary center, like the chair in the café or the hotel room in a foreign city. The most important point in space, however, is the space where one permanently rests and dwells. The double movement of going away and coming back is reflected in the division into a closer, interior world and a more remote exterior world, on one hand home and neighbourhood, and on the other the wide outer world (Bollnow 1990, 81). Around the dwelling the world is built up concentrically, of places nearby and far away, of streets and buildings that are well-known and others that disappear in an obscure background (ibid., 59). Moving to another place means to create this surrounding world once again, and become acquainted to it.

The importance of this well-known and close world becomes clear from people's stories about their experiences during the building period. They complained about the grounds turning into a dusty desert, a muddy field or a storage yard for building materials. Some of them missed their neighbours during this time, when everyday patterns of meetings and chats were interrupted. In an opposite way the importance of the close world shows up in the interest many of the inhabitants took in the ongoing building work. An old man, who constantly complained about disturbances, admitted when the modernization was completed, that he missed all the exciting events of the building period.

The home as the centre of space must not be taken as something definite (ibid., 55, 123). Children grow up and leave home. The original home will probably always be very special to them. But most of them will create new homes and new worlds around them. Some of the people I have interviewed, have chosen or been forced to move several times. To build a new home and a new surrounding world was always a great effort for them. One of the few tenants who had to move because of the modernization, managed to bear her loss by cultivating new acquaintances.

Thus, the dwelling appears as the centre of space and of existence. However, it's importance weakens, almost to disappear completely, when other important centers occur. From one young male informant, the place where one only goes to sleep, has lost most of the qualities of home. Still, for him it definitely was home. The importance of the dwelling can also grow, to become the place where almost all important events of life occur. For the old person, who has lost his or her mobility and vitality, home becomes synonymous with the dwelling or even the bedroom. So home is nothing static, it's meaning and importance varies between individuals, age-groups, lifestyles, classes, and cultures.

Tomas Wikström

The place of autonomy

...Feeling at home is when you're the one who decides
the strength of your coffee...
— Anonymous tenant.

In your own flat, you are the one to make the rules, to develop routines and an order of your own. To many of the people interviewed, self-determination was the most valuable feature of home. "This is ours, here we have decorated the way we like it," was an elderly woman's way of expressing the meaning of home. Another woman often visited her sister, but was always very pleased to come home. To her, home meant small but important things in life, like being the one to decide the strength of her coffee.

This aspect of home has many names: autonomy, control, self-determination, ease, freedom. It seems to be connected to might, in the sense of power to accomplish, but also to the absence of the powers of the exterior world, to which one must always submit. For most people, home is the only place where they are in power to make decisions. The professionals of the modernization process have to face the problem of dealing with this autonomy of home. In the projects studied, it couldn't be avoided that the building process restricted this important quality of home. However, flagrant trespasses in most cases could be avoided. My experience is that restrictions of dwelling that are agreed upon between tenants and owners are bearable even in cases when living conditions for the tenants become difficult during a shorter period.

The interviews gave several examples of people's strong emotional reactions to what they regarded as trespassing or violating. To the outsider, the harm done sometimes seemed to be rather small. Narratives about for example craftsmen, who, after having done adjustment work, left without bringing out the litter, were frequent. It was very clear, that the walls of home for the interviewees constituted a boundary, which they expected to be respected.

That the autonomy of home is acknowledged by society, appears for example from the Swedish expression *hemmets helgd* (the sanctity of home) and from the existence since the Middle Ages of legislation against *hemfridsbrott* (violation of the privacy of the home).[4] The way people responded even to very limited violations, makes the home stand out as "animated." Bollnow uses the example of the farmer's reaction, when his field is trodden on, a reaction which the material harm in itself doesn't explain. Conceptions of the sanctity of home can be understood only through an analysis of the sacred character of space (Bollnow 1990, 129–131, 148).

In many interviews people stressed the word "we." To them home was a common, mutual creation of space. Bollnow opposes a notion of interpersonal use of space that is based upon rivalry; the original creation of space was common (Bollnow 1990, 269). The dwelling of the small group (household, family) becomes unbearable when rivalry prevails, yet the creation of space in the modernization process is characterized by rivalry. Due to division of labour in society, the activity of building is separated from dwelling. Not only do these activities represent radically different ways of handling space and matter, they also differ concerning their relations to power in society. Producers of buildings are separated from consumers, and the modernization process brings out conflicts of interest between them. These conflicts, however, do not occur between parties of equal strength. To people with limited social, financial, and personal resources, modernization represents the outer world threatening their only sanctuary.

In this context, words like rivalry and territory can be misleading. It is true that people's reactions to trespassing can be seen as territorial behaviour. Bollnow also makes comparisons with the territoriality of animals (ibid., 296). In using this as the only model of explanation, however, one overlooks essential conditions of the situations in question here. The concept of territoriality does not explain conflicts and contradictions on the level of society. Neither does it shed light upon *what* it is that people try to protect.

Self-determination may be an important feature of home, but it is not unrestricted. The renewal projects provide many examples of the vulnerability of people's homes. The house owner has the power to break up the close worlds people during many years have built around themselves. People's appropriation of space carries no weight compared to ownership. Tenancy is an obvious restriction of the autonomy of home. To people who rent their dwellings, Bollnow's warning against total trust in the safety of home is especially important (ibid., 138).

The place for everyday domestic routines

...The smell of mum's meat balls...
— Anonymous tenant

In one of the housing areas, a number of flats were to be vacated to allow for their merging into larger units. An old man was tempted by the housing company's offer of a new flat in another neighbourhood, and accepted to move. He moved although he felt at home and got on well in his old place. Very soon he started to regret that he had moved. He realized that he had been part of a community of nice and considerate fellow humans.

The women who were his close neighbours, his sister-in-law and another woman, were fully aware of the loss that his moving out would cause. While the man was not aware of what everyday life was all about, the women were conscious of the daily routines of dwelling.

The modernizing process makes apparent some of the routines or rituals that distinguish the home appear clearly. In one of the projects, tenants stayed in their flats while these were being repaired. They told me about their constant vacuum-cleaning and scrubbing, to keep the dirt out. Others, having vacated their homes for a short period of time, made daily visits to their flats to check that everything was all right and to move boxes and furniture around as building work went on. Under normal circumstances – but for some of them even surrounded by the dust of building activities – this cleaning, arranging, and caring behavior was connected to a feeling of satisfaction. Taking back lost space, e.g., putting things back into drawers and cupboards or rolling out clean carpets, was what brought some of the tenants most satisfaction. Thus the home appears as something that is continually recreated by everyday praxis, by daily routines which to a large extent are not reflected on but become clear in a situation of change. In this way the home can be seen as a process.

The Bollnow term *Handlungsraum* (space of action) reflects this perpetual re-creation of space. On the other hand, the view of the dwelling as a communication system, or interconnected activity stations (which played an important role in the development of my own discipline, building functions analysis), belong to an abstract analysis and have little to do with the space where one lives and dwells. The spaces where people work and rest are arranged in another manner. Here the things one needs are *Zur-Hande* (ready to hand, within reach) in a well known, self-evident space and not only *Vorhanden* (at hand, existant) (Bollnow 1990, 205–207). Here, as in many other cases, Bollnow refers to Heidegger. The arrangement of active human beings, utilitarian goods and places, Bollnow calls space of action. Arranging, furnishing, and cleaning can be seen as a perpetual *einräumen* (making room for, arranging) that create inhabitable space (ibid., 207–209). But there is more to everyday living than that.

"To feel at home? Well, it's the woman...," was the spontaneous answer I got from an elderly gentleman. To a young woman, the notion of home was connected to her mother's care and attention. She talked about the smell of meatballs and the feeling of safety, knowing mother was at home. As a grown-up, she tried to re-establish this wonderful sense of home for her child. But being a professional woman, with a lack of free time, and with the child at the day-nursery, the gingerbread cookies for Christmas had to be made of store-bought dough. However, it cannot be overlooked that home traditionally was, and to a large degree still is, the domain of women.

The notion of home as female is supported by the experiences of my study. But this might give a biased conception of dwelling. Bollnow never explicitly discusses male and female creation of space, but in the spirit of philosophical anthropology, I would like to add a few empirical facts. There is another, male arranging of space, which can be exemplified with the carpenters messy workshop, where saws, drills and hammers are in reach, or the garage, where the wife refuses to go, but where the wrench has its special place. In the three housing areas under study, the male aspects of dwelling showed in the way men were fixing and pottering about. To mend a stiff lock, to change safety fuses, to furnish or to re-paper walls are examples of men's traditional duties in and around the home. This other side of domestic care is of course just as important for dwelling, as the duties traditionally connected with women.

Thus, male and female roles complement each other. To Bollnow, the complementary use of space of the family is inseparable from the home. Yet emphasis on the family must not be taken literally. What he says about the family seems to be applicable to any small group of people living together: a household, a group of friends going camping, or close neighbours. Bollnow thinks that it is not possible for a single person to establish a home (1990, 153–154). This is worth considering in times when more and more people, at least in Sweden, live alone. However, I would say that the single old lady, who expanded her home by caring for her neighbours, really had a home and knew how to dwell.

In these examples of the space-making of the couple, the family, or the friends, a quality of dwelling appears that is hard to grasp from a quantitative, scientific point of view. In the common creation of space – in friendly co-existence – people do not take space from each other but give each other space (ibid., 263). The space of actions is permeated by a space of feelings and atmospheres, which can be charaterized by love and friendship or rivalry and animosity. Love, affection and friendship multiply space, whereas hostility makes it narrow and cramped. In the affectionate, common creation of space there is a kind of miracle, which was expressed by an old man in this down to earth manner: "If you just have a good spirit, living in a small flat is never a problem!"

Tomas Wikström

The place of relations to friends and neighbours

...It's the old buddies and friends...
— Anonymous tenant

One of my interviewees, an old lady, was not upset about having had to move. When you consider all the distress and unhappiness of the world, and how well we are getting on here in Sweden, having to move is nothing to worry about was her opinion. To her, neighbourliness was the tight network of female everyday contacts evolving around domestic duties. This community she new from the inner-city neighbourhood, where she and her husband brought up their children. This was an everyday life of equality, common work, and mutual aid. Having moved to the outskirts of town many years ago, she hadn't found the same kind of relations to neighbours. To her, it made no difference to live in one part of the housing area or the other. It seemed as if this woman had emancipated herself from local bonds and that her home no longer was rooted in the neighbourhood, but rather was connected to a global world.

The life story of the woman described above might be seen as an expression of a transition from a local way of life, based upon interaction around home, to a more unfocused, global way of life. The local world still exists, as a vague expectation, and in the physical bond to the place where she lives. But her life is dominated by the modern, global world. Her present pattern of life differs from the old one by the absence of a solid, local world-view. Orienting herself in life and maintaining her identity is something she has to manage on her own. In doing this, she chooses a life-style, a global attitude, which helps her to survive the changes of life, among others, the modernization of her neighbourhood.

However, the vast majority of my interviews give evidence of relations to neighbours and local friends that are seen as important and sometimes vital. Some examples have already been mentioned, but I would like to mention a few more. We have the neighbours who help each other with little things like pushing in the daily newspaper (in the mailbox) when one of them is away; the ones that have time for a chat when running into each other in the stairs; the neighbours that react when somebody does not come and go as usual; the persons that always are well-informed about the plans of renovation, or even have connections into the administration of the housing company; the elderly people, who always introduce themselves to newcomers and give hints about what is expected from them as neighbours; and finally, the ones that take part in meetings of the local tenants organization and help organizing activities in the community center.

Yet this community is not boundless. Many of the people I spoke to, stressed the importance of keeping contacts and neighbouring on an appropriate level. When asked if she could ask neighbours for help with little things, one woman said: "That's no problem. We have a neighbour on the next floor who will help us. But that doesn't mean that we run up and down the stairs all day long!" The easy and unpretentious relations (shallow or deep) around the home are maintained by simple means. "It is so little one has to do to keep the good spirit. But we don't run to each other all the time." This informal way of defining private space from common – of defending the autonomy of home – seems to be vital for a good spirit among neighbours.

To live and dwell in Swedish housing areas from the forties and fifties often means to have manifold and diverse relations to other people in the close surroundings. It is important not to underestimate this friendly co-existence, even if its expressions sometimes are modest.

The place where one is rooted

...One plants one's own roots as well...
– Anonymous tenant

A young woman in one of the housing areas told me that she didn't feel rooted in her flat. It was when she went out in her small garden, that she experienced a strong feeling of being at home. Here she had spent many moments of happiness planting flowers and, as she said, her own roots as well. After modernization, for her it was a shock to find her lush garden devastated and replaced by cement tiles and a wooden fence. An old lady, who was forced to move due to the merging of her flat with another, first of all missed the comfort of getting on with her neighbours, the mutual trust and care, and the chats. The warm community she used to share with her old neighbours now was broken. An elderly gentleman was very upset, when he from his window saw that one of the japanese cherry-trees outside was harmed by a lorry.

The interviews gave many examples of people's sincere emotional bonds to the environment, where they lived, or – in a few tragic cases – from which they were forced to move. Their stories support the notion of a way of living and dwelling where people become emotionally involved and give of themselves to the spaces where they lead their lives. I have discussed how people dwell by protecting themselves from the outer world, by going out and coming back home, by defining a space of their own, by maintaining this place in the tasks of daily life, and by connecting home to the neighbourhood. The notion of rootedness reflects all these aspects of home.

Words like the comfort of home, the feeling of homeliness, and belonging express properties that people ascribe to their surrounding space, but which just as much are something they carry with them. They are atmospheres and sentiments, phenomena related to emotional life and primary to the division between subject and object (Bollnow 1990, 231). The people interviewed expressed in many ways the sense of home in the warm, close and free space of living together. It may be living happily with a beloved wife or husband, the smell of cooking or the feeling when one approaches one's house, the feeling of safety when passing the doors of good neighbours, or the satisfaction of returning home to make some coffee. The word home most of all expresses the "expansion" of space which is connected to affectionate community – from the "irrational" generosity of falling in love to the mutual enrichment of harmonic life (ibid., 258).

However, this strong and valuable rootedness is not shared by everyone. One of the old women that I interviewed differed from most of her neighbours by not worrying about the forthcoming modernization. On the contrary, she had great difficulties in understanding the anxiety of her neighbours, and found it hard to talk to them, having quite an opposite view. This woman had led a hard, poor, and rather mobile life with small possibilities of becoming rooted. But she had succeeded well in developing a way to live which made her existence bearable. Unlike her neighbours, who were vulnerable because of their dependance upon local ties, she was strong as an individual and in her connections to the outer world, to the library, the study circles and the shops downtown, and to the friends in other parts of town. To her, the modernization was just another confirmation of what she had learnt from life, never to trust the safety of home. Compared to her, the neighbours appeared as naïve and unconscious of the realities of life. Bollnow on one hand warns against taking the safety of home for granted. Man must keep an inner freedom that makes him strong enough to survive the loss of home. But, says Bollnow, he must on the other hand find a trust in the world, strong enough to continue to build homes (ibid., 138).

Conclusion

Bollnow (ibid., 123) writes that man needs a center, where he is rooted in space, and to which all her relations in space are connected. For "mythical" man dwelling was never a problem. To him the world was objectively centered in the middle of space. However, in the modern world, this is problematic. With the loss of this objective center, there is a risk of loosing one's roots, of homelessness. That is why, according to Bollnow, modern man has to consciously create this middle in his space, by dwelling (1990, 125). To dwell, man needs more than a house or a flat. It is, as Heidegger says, necessary to learn how to dwell. The people I have met in the three housing areas of my study, have given many examples of this ability to dwell, but also of the difficulties in attaining and maintaining "the true way of dwelling."

The modernizing process exposes the home as a place-related totality, as a complex local world. The breaking up of people's ties to home and neighbourhood, of local community, is a question that has received great attention. This has concealed the fact that home, as a special place, still seems to remain important to people. In the modern housing areas of my study, one finds homes that cannot just be moved without further notice. Today, it is important to deepen the discussion about the small, informal neighbourhood beyond the myths of local community.

It has often been said that research in the field of environment-behavoir studies should aim at supporting and helping the practitioners. However, as a researcher, I have taken the task to make life more complicated for planners and designers. Becoming aware of "invisible" qualities of the built environment – of all the intricate ties between people, homes, and neighbourhoods – certainly makes planning and design more difficult. I have seen some successful examples, though, of renewal planning that considers people's own creation of space. This kind of planning is a challenge for the future.

Endnotes

1. The researchers were sociologist Eva Öresjö, Ph.D, and Tomas Wikström, architect. The planning and building processes of renewal projects in Helsingborg, Borås, and Norrköping were evaluated (Öresjö 1988, Wikström 1988).

2. First published in 1963. For a short presentation, see Egenter (1992).

3. Dovey (1985) uses the translation lived space, referring to Bollnow's (1967) paper Lived-Space, published in *Readings in Existential Phenomenology,* ed. N. Lawrence and D. O'Connor. Englewood Cliffs, N.J.: Prentice-Hall.

4. The sanctity of the home was acknowledged by Swedish thirteenth century legislation that included a law against the violation of the privacy of the home.

References

Bollnow, O. F. 1990. *Mensch und Raum.* Stuttgart: Kohlhammer.

Dovey, K. 1985. Home and Homelessness. In *Home Environments.* Vol. 8 of *Human Behavior and Environments. Advances in Theory and Research,* ed. I. Altman and C. M. Werner. N.Y.: Plenum Press.

Egenter, N. 1992. O. F. Bollnow and the Ontology of Home and Movement Outside. Paper presented at symposium Dwelling in Scandinavia, 20–23 August, at The University of Trondheim, Norway.

Heidegger, M. 1954. Bauen, Wohnen, Denken. In *Vortrage und Aufsatze.* Pfullingen: Neske.

Lübcke, P. 1987. Bollnow: Stämningarnas väsen. In *Vår tids filosofi,* ed. P. Lübcke. Stockholm: Forum.

Öresjö, E. 1988. Urban Renewal and the Elderly. In *Buildings & People,* ed. The Departement of Building Function Analysis, School of Architecture, University of Lund. Lund: The University of Lund.

Wikström, T. 1988. This is Our Home! People, Sense of Community and Housing Renovation. In *Buildings & People,* ed. The Departement of Building Function Analysis, School of Architecture, University of Lund. Lund: The University of Lund.

15
What Can We Learn From the Reconstruction of Prehistoric Buildings?

Eje Arén

I will very shortly take you with me on a journey from the two-dimensional flatland into the three-dimensional reconstructed land of a physical house. My subject is: What can we learn from the reconstruction of prehistoric buildings?

I am an archaeologist, but since 1973 I have worked as an independent historical house-builder, thatcher, and carpenter, consulting to museums, municipalities, and private persons. In my team are also my wife, architect Eva Retzner and archaeologist Olle Andersson from the University of Lund.

When doing archaeological interpretations I make use of two methods: One is learning by doing, i.e., trying to reach a deeper understanding of prehistoric buildings by working as a craftsman myself. The other is learning by studying ancient but still living building traditions and their relationship to the surrounding nature in a global perspective.

The first house I want to show you is from an excavation placed in the surroundings of Lake Mälaren to the west of Stockholm, named Pollista. It is now reconstructed in Smedby Park in Upplands Väsby. The excavation report presented the remains of a house dated 1040 A.D. It consisted of 23 postholes (shown in Fig. 15.1 as numbered, solid figures). There was no fireplace and only few artifacts were found. The first thing to notice is the cigar-like shape of the two rows of postholes, which might place the house in the tradition of the Scandinavian three-aisled longhouses. Three observations indicate that we have another situation, though:

1. The surrounding cliffs and rocks restrict the possibilities for a wider building.

2. The findings are limited to the area between the two rows of postholes.

3. Indications of a fence are connected to the rows of postholes, which likely represent the outer wall rather than posts supporting a central nave.

These three observations make it possible to reconstruct the house as eleven meters long and three meters wide. It is necessary though to further reflect upon some significant features of the plan. How can we explain posthole A337? Shall we believe in the exactness of the excavation report? One thing is certain, the position of this posthole would create a problem higher up in the building construction if it belonged to a longhouse.

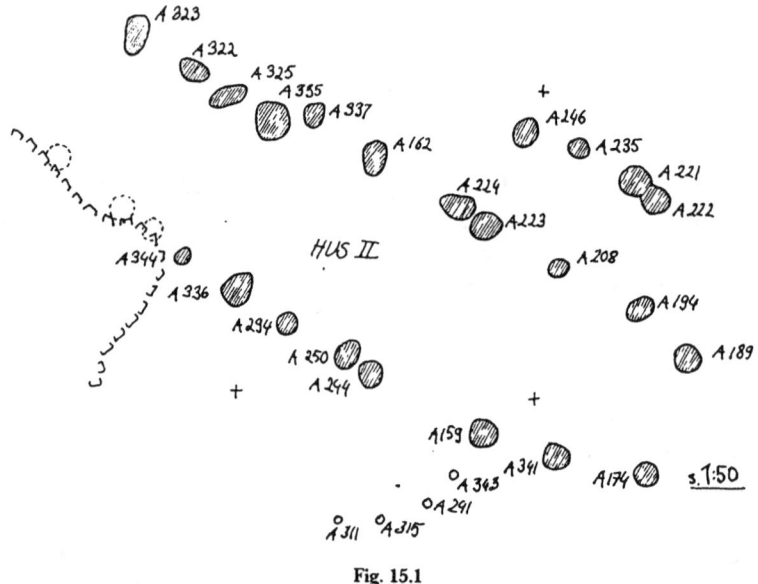

Fig. 15.1

Why are not the postholes placed in straight lines? Must every posthole belong to the actual house? What are A224, A223, A250 and A244? In the three-aisled longhouse, archaeologists interpret this doubling as an exchange of a rotten pair of posts. What does the postline A323 to A335 mean?

Our interpretation is as follows: Instead of a longhouse, we see three small houses, independent of each other. We imagine there to be three more posts standing on the rocks and therefore leaving no marks for the archaeologists.

The double-pair is simply the point where one house is added to another. We believe that A246, A235, A221 and A222 do not belong to the inner house construction. Rather they are marks of a fence for pigs or sheep. The posts A189 and A174 are interpreted as supporting a little shed roof. As a consequence, there would be three sheds, maybe for sheep, cattle, and horses, instead of one longhouse. The fence and the small passage between the houses have the obvious function to separate the sheep. No marks of thresholds were found. The best guess, however, is that the doors were placed towards the courtyard.

The aspect of landscape

Not only the buildings, but also the landscape must be a matter of reconstruction. Then I use a global model, a common rule used by people all over the world, and defined by the problems of transporting building materials.

Building materials are traditionally taken from an area within one square kilometer. The exceptions, of course, are the buildings of significant importance. This worldwide law can be illustrated by examples from observations made in Nepal.

As you walk in the landscape you can follow how the changes of nature influences the shape and construction of buildings. In all valleys at the level of 700 meters above sea level, you will see clay houses with straw. The lack of timber is obvious here. After two hours further climbing, you walk through a hillside forest of rhododendron. On the level of 1,400 meters the houses are constructed of wooden framework with horizontal planking. The foundations are made of limestone, but the roofs are still thatched.

In the evening of the same day, reaching the level of 2,000 meters, the houses are mainly built of limestone with only a few wooden details and rhododendron shingles as roof material.

In the case of Pollista in the Mälar valley, we note the same relationship between building materials and the surrounding nature. We believe that the main construction of the house must have been built of pine and oak. The Mälar landscape consists of an old sea-bottom interrupted by island-like moraine hills. Pine and oak are the dominant trees, with pine on the dry hills and oak in the wetter valleys. The postholes have no traces of wood, but just the fact that the house has been used for 90 years indicates that the posts were made of oak. The characteristic of the framework is a consequence of the qualities of the oak. Oak resists rotting and is easy to cleave. Its crooked growth is not a drawback since the framework technique admits utilization even of the shortest of planks. The longest part, at about 2-1/2 meters, is used for the standing posts. The longhouse has a different quality, constructed of the much straighter and longer pine timber.

Fig. 15.2

The finding of a ploughbill leads us to presume that there must have been cultivated fields, and fields mean grain, which could have supplied the roof with straw. The agriculture of the early Middle Ages was dependent upon the availability of manure, which was collected in dunghills. The dunghill is a consequence of the Scandinavian need to keep the cattle indoors during the wintertime. Cultivated brushwoods and meadows were necessary to feed the cattle. Two cows need ten hectare of meadow and ten hectare of brushwood. Besides, the brushwood gives firewood, timber, roof rafters, and osiers for the houses. To be brief, the presence of the cattle indicate the whole landscape.

Therefore, you can say that this house and its former household influenced the landscape, but the landscape is also readable in the remaining of the house. There is an evident and perceptible relation between the building and its surroundings. This relationship occurred on two levels:

1. The literal affinity between the built form and the elements of the landscape in terms of their visual and material identities.

2. The interdependence of three aspects of the cultural landscape to make a settlement tradition:

    a) The socio-economic system of grain-cow-dung-grass agriculture

    b) the use of materials and planning in an architectural tradition to accommodate this socio-economic system,

    c) and the landscape itself which provided the basic material and aesthetic premises for settlement.

A possible term to use that would indicate this sort of settlement system is the old Scandinavian *hem* (home). Because it indicated not just the house, but also the territory of the farm or hamlet (Brink 1987, this volume; KLNM 1956) it would seem to cover the activities and spaces of the Pollista dwelling.

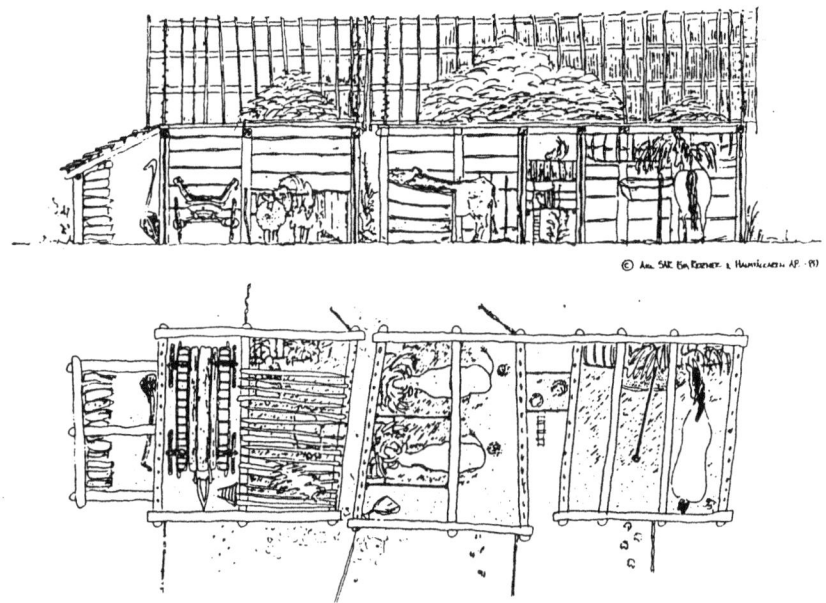

Fig. 15.3. House II, barn

The inner aspect

On the same site, there are living quarters as well. The plan from the archaeologists show marks of a ten meter long and four meter wide house, placed at an open angle to the stable (Fig. 15.4).

Traces from a fireplace tell us it is a dwelling. In the southern part of the house, the lack of postholes and the line of stones indicate another type of wall construction – the posts stood on a horizontal beam which lay on the stone foundation almost like a half-timbered house. The area around the fireplace has been constructed as a chimney-room surrounded by a wall made of organic material, cow dung.

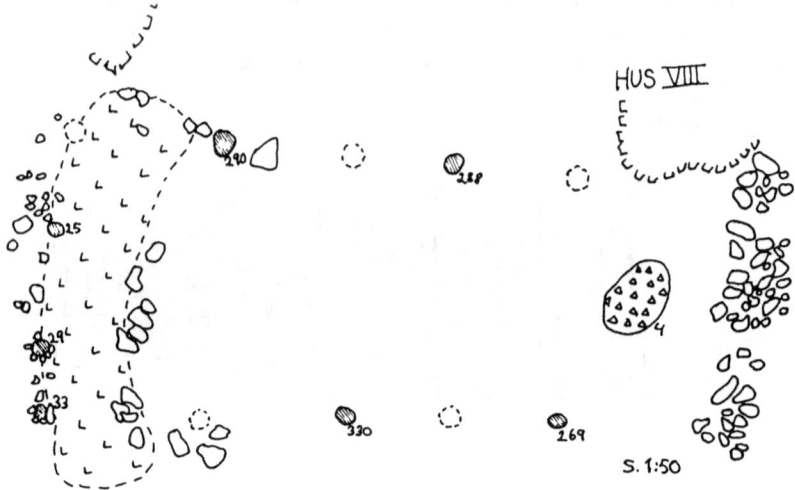

Fig. 15.4. House VIII

The reconstructed house (Fig. 15.5) is divided into different spaces responding to the different needs of the people living there: The barn part of the house is divided into a threshing area and a storage area. The dwelling part is divided into the chimney-room and the area for other indoor activities. From here a flight of stairs leads up to the sleeping loft.

Fig. 15.5

An analysis like this can give us an idea of the inhabitant's daily life, but we know nothing about the inner landscape of the inhabitants. Nothing about their personal fortunes, their beliefs, their fears, dreams, disgraces or taboos – which must have affected the physical form of their buildings. The reconstructors obviously recreate based on the contents of their own inner landscapes. That is why there is no such thing as a historically true reconstruction. So what can we learn from reconstructions?

The bored and distracted people of today, filled with sectorial thinking and surrounded by prefabricated high-tech materials, might get an experience of deep understanding and empowerment from visiting such houses: "If they could build this – I must be able to too!"

I don't believe that the idea of reconstruction is to entertain. It should make people step aside, reflect, see, feel, and finally understand. The natural materials of a building in a true relationship with the surrounding landscape may show us an extra dimension which is lost in the building industry of today. Craftsmen are now trying to imitate machines. They leave no traces of their hands and give no hints of the connection between man and nature. Nature is consistently being denied. But with the growing insights of the importance of a balanced ecology, this attitude is out-of-date. "Modern" today, is not to rule and suppress nature, but to reconcile with it and to cooperate. This cyclical attitude can perhaps be physically exemplified by reconstructions of prehistoric buildings.

These building reconstructions present us with a tradition where the attitude of integration between cultural exploits and the original premises of the land were likely much more important than in the present. Today, we can with impunity utilize the worldwide mercantile system to distribute all the "necessary" goods of our own settlement tradition. Yet pollution, landscape and place destruction (see Porteous, this volume), and general existential malaise about the state of our living situation make us stop up and think that all is not right.

Such reconstructions are thus not necessarily solutions to modern-day problems, but something yet more exciting: provocative guides to the new solutions that we and future generations will have to come up with to deal with the dwelling of several billion people on the planet without destroying its ecology, or the human spirit. In this sense, the concept of home, an all-inclusive term to mean the locally interpreted space of settlement, will be useful in developing these future strategies. Finally, by the process of exploring and understanding that is generated by practical building, a deeper and more balanced connection to nature – inner as well as outer – is possible.

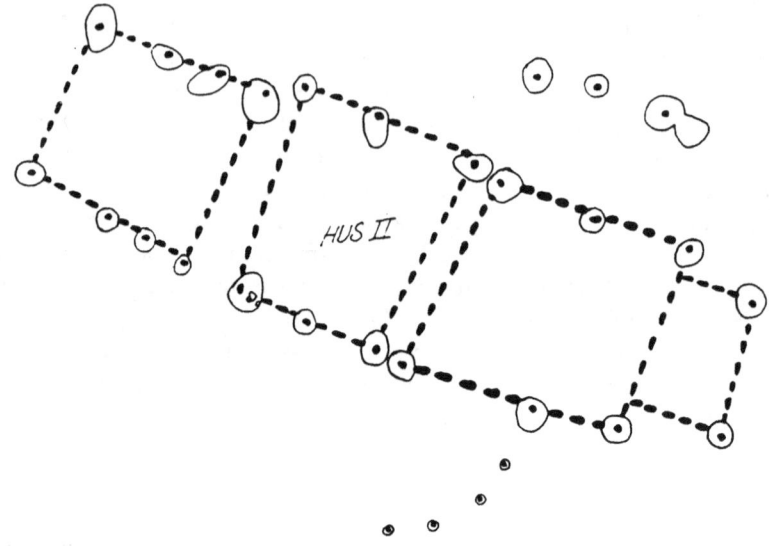

Fig. 15.6 House II reconstruction plan of barn.

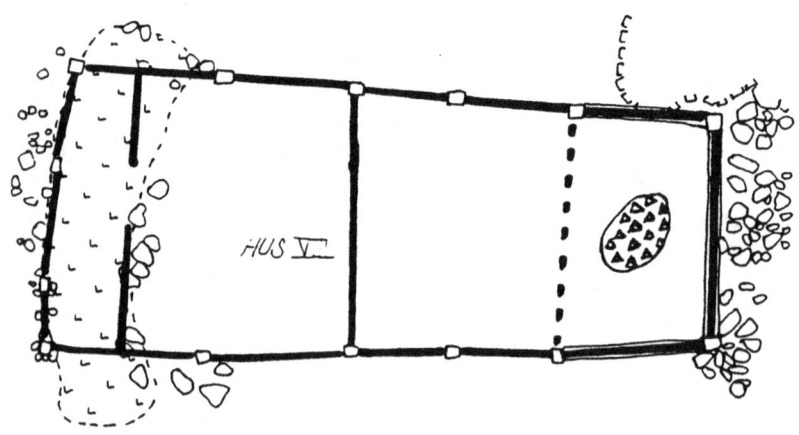

Fig. 15.7 House VIII reconstruction plan of dwelling.

Part Five

Afterword, or Further Research Issues in Confronting the Home Concept

David N. Benjamin

Notes toward the definition of the *home*

Exactly because of the diversity of the articles in this volume, it seems prudent to include a short overview of the work already done, and some indicators of what the concept may mean in specific cultural situations and across cultural boundaries.

The modern era of scientific literature on the home probably begins 1678 with J. Hofer's thesis on *nostalgie* (nostalgia), or *nosomonia, philopatridalgia,* and homesickness (McCann 1941, 165). Otherwise, ancient literature such as sagas, lyric peoms, folk songs, and church records or biographies mention home:

1. From northern Europe, examples are *Beowulf* (Wrenn 1954), *Gretti's Saga* (Hight 1914), the song of *Veraldur* (Koefoed 1989), and *Eric the Red's Saga* (Erik den Rødes Saga 1961).

2. From other regions, one example is the Greek lyric peom *The Wanderer* by Theognis (Barnstone 1967).

Thus, the concept having to do with the positive, affectionate association of humans to a domestic residence location that we apply to the term *home,* was known and used by writers and bards atleast as far back as the Middle Ages, and perhaps all the way to the time of Christ's birth. (I have however not been able to find any etymological histories of non-western homelike concepts – this is a neglected but vast and fruitful area for research.)

In the scholarly context, the home concept is also prevalent, even being used in compound constructions in the *International Encyclopedia of the Social Sciences:* "Homelessness," "Home Economics," "Home Ownership," "Home

Rule," "Homestead," "Homework," etc. (Sills 1968). Indeed, a cursory review of research oriented reference literature shows that *home* used alone, or as an element in compound constructions, is used in many sources: "Heimat," in *Wörterbuch der Soziologie* (Hartfiel 1972) and in *Soziologie Lexikon* (Reinhold 1991), "homestead movement," in *International Dictionary of Regional European Ethnology and Folklore* (Hultkrantz 1960), "homestead," in *Dictionary of Human Geography* (Goodal 1987), and in *Dictionary of Anthropology* (Winick 1956), "home," in *Dictionary of Mythology, Folklore and Symbols* (Jobes 1961), and used to describe dwellings in the article on the Burusho in *Encyclopedia of World Cultures* (Page 1992).

This is not to say that there is comprehensive agreement about the meaning of the term among scholars, only that it is already widely used in the literature and therefore needs to be confronted. The term cannot simply be deemed inappropiate and then forgotten – what shall be done with all previous writing that used the term as a key element for its meaning? Further, alternatives to *home* may be no more "objective" or precise than the original, the alternatives must be tested in the service of research and the literature. Finally, scholars have apparently used the term because it is a user-defined category in the environment (for example, Gullestad 1984, 1993), and thus the empirical imperative of EBS methodology should lead us to study the term, in spite of its drawbacks (cf., Rapoport in this volume).

Indeed, the very breadth of meaning of the term taken together with its prevalence should inspire us to try to understand the essence of the concept, not to "improve" the term like some new dishwashing soap or throw it out like last-year's automobile, but rather to deepen our understanding of it.

The home is often identified in the scholarly literature with the house (Madge 1968). This is not false, but it only reveals one small level of the meaning of the term, rejecting its abstract connotations and its spatial extension to include a surrounding territory. Indeed, in the same volume of the *International Encyclopedia of the Social Sciences*, the article "Homelessness" suggests that the home is also a subjective, affective phenomenon. Even though the term includes connotations of warmth, safety, emotional dependence, and a fixed place of residence, the authors claim that it currently does not necessarily connote a family, household, or exclusivity. Rather, its essence extends beyond residential arrangements (Caplow et al. 1968, 495). Thus, the opposite of home suggests ways to get at its essence.

Caplow et al. (ibid., 494) claim that, "Homelessness is a condition of detachment from society characterized by the absence or attenuation of the affiliative bonds that link settled persons to a network of interconnected social structures." Thus, the home can be seen as some phenomenon that assists in manifesting these affiliative bonds to social structures, either through the demarcation of a spatio-temporal place where these bonds occur, and/or as the label for a place or state of mind where these social structures are experienced. (In this connection, it is interesting that there exists no direct opposite for *homelessness* in English as found in other Germanic languages: In Danish *Hjemløs* (homeless) vs. *hjemmeværende* (he/she who is at home), thus Caplow et al. use "the settled" to oppose "the homeless.")

The authors of "Homelessness" accept the popular term *homelessness* as an informant defined category; they attempt to define it and understand its role, however ambigious and difficult that may be. Here, we see that contemplation of both terms together inspires thought in the humanities and social sciences about issues of the day, extending to politics, (cf. the fierce battles for who has the right to live in contemporary homelands) and warfare (the definition of strategic being a military effort "directed against an enemy's homeland rather than used on a battlefield," *Collins English Dictionary* 1991). Indeed, the twentieth century has been called the "century of the homeless man" (Caplow et al. 1968, 497).

The five aspects of meaning

To get at the meaning of the term, and the roles it plays in the popular and scholarly contexts, *home* can be considered from the following five viewpoints: as a word, a descriptive term in the social scientific, humanistic, and architectural literatures, as a juridical term, as a condition in psychiatric research, and as a cultural phenomenon in the individual and collective life of diverse human groups.

The word. The lexical symbol *home* has evolved from a joint origin in both the Germanic *Heim* (dwelling, world, one's farm, village district), and the Greek or Proto-Germanic verb *Keimai* (to lie down) (Brink 1987, 24–25; Brink this volume; KLNM 1956). The early connotations of this term are thus not limited to the exclusively physical habitation itself, but include concepts of dwelling and affection. These essential components of the meaning have continued right up until today, although the connotation of the physical house seems to have begun to take precedence since the nineteenth century (Rapoport in this volume; Kent in this volume; Mejborg 1888; Kunstler 1993, 102 ff.)

The descriptive use of the word. Scholarly literature from ethology to theology has used the term to describe a place of either regular residency or an origin for the ritual of return, either in the literal physical sense (Porteous

1982; Rapoport 1990a, 238; Rapoport 1990b, 14; Rapoport 1980, 1977, 1970; Spradley 1975), or psychically, covering the mythological and therapeutic uses of the concept. Thus, after the long journey through childhood and early manhood, Nouwen (1992, 5) writes, "The son-come-home was all I was," referring to his subjective realization of return. In a related way, Bradshaw (1990, 56) defines the return to home for therapists: "Homecoming is a restoration of the natural." It involves, "going back through your developmental stages and finishing your unfinished business."

The juridical meaning of the word. Birkeli (1932) and Carlsson (1935) mention several important documents from the era of early Nordic law that define the home and the role it played in medieval society. Thus, the home as the domestic territory of a dweller started at the boundaries of the farm and became more sacrosanct as one came to the house, until one reached the high seat itself, the seat of honor and the ritualistic place of passing down the rights to the farm. Within this territory, sanctions came into force concerning violence or murder commited against the owner, much stricter than those in force outside the home (see Brink this volume).

Today, the home is defined as a term in modern law dictionaries, and although it has lost some of its sanctions against violent intrusion by strangers, the territory of the home is still a legally binding definition to this day (Black 1979). Members of the elite in Western society take these boundaries very seriously, as sociologist David Halle found out when he was threatened with arrestation by the architect I.M. Pei and the U.N. Secretary-General Boutros Ghali, merely for knocking on their front doors (Halle 1993, xv, 1-2).

The word in psychiatric research. The psychic aspects of the home concept mentioned above are related to the study of homesickness, a condition with symptoms characteristic of emergency emotional behavior, the prerequisite for its existence being the absence from home (McCann 1941, 179-180). This response to not being at home has been reported among a highly diverse group of people, including various non-literate peoples showing that atleast the experience of home and its loss, if not actual knowledge of the term, is worldwide (ibid., 170).

The empirically derived cultural phenomenon. This category of the term is a more complex issue than simply defining a unique word. Several different cultural groups from all over the world that may or may not have had lexical cognates, or the same concept, use the English *home* to communicate in the global media. This is apparently not merely a matter of faulty translation, but when scrutinized, many non-western society's use of the term seems to be very similiar to the Germanic meaning. In addition, there very likely exist conceptions of home native to non-western cultures that are for all intents and purposes equivalent to the western one. This complicated tangle of definitions is hard to conceptualize, but provides ample incentive and a large body of study for the field of EBS (see Table 1).

Table 1: The term *home*		
native western speaker's $home_1$	non-western use of $home_1$	non-western native $home_2$
use relatively similiar homes $home_1$ now being used to identify and calculate the design of non-western $homes_2$ or settlements (Mills et al. 1993)	unsure whether concept is fully understood, prevalent because of global media	$home_2$ as analogy to $home_1$ or a concept not yet acknowledged by scholarly research.
use of above $homes_{x...n}$ dependent upon sub-culture membership of actor and listener, and context of communication		

Because non-western native speakers may have their own conception of the home, examining these other conceptions may inspire the western re-thinking of the concept, or by the use of analogy, an aid in the explication of how societies from the present or ancient past interpreted their relation to positive and familiar spaces or states of mind.

All this is *an addition to* the challenge that the western home presents to scholars who wish to define it. We can take as a starting point the empirical research on the home of Norwegian families performed by Gullestad in the 70's and 80's (Gullestad 1984, 1993). She recognizes its basic duality in that, *"hjem* (home) brings together in one notion both the idea of a place and the idea of a social togetherness associated with this place." The term thus describes a phenomenon as having both material and intangible social, emotional, moral, and spiritual connotations (Gullestad 1993, 131).

The home is an important setting for domestic life, and in turn it symbolizes this setting. For Norwegians, it is essentially, "the frame of family life together," since it is the "domain or activity field for selected social occasions," which contribute to an elaboration of essential family values: the unity of the family, common work, togetherness, identity, self-realization, good motherhood, and the validation of the individual (mostly the female, motherly), personality (Gullestad 1984, 18).

As a framework, the home is a physical and abstract structure within which we conceive of and interpret both domestic life, and activities outside the home. It is thus a nearly total frame for our early development and later life that members of distinct cultural groups create.

Sack (1986, 74) has posited that people, especially those in slowly changing peasant societies, become emotionally attatched to such frameworks as the home because they reify the world it helps to manifest. They are at home because things are as they should be, and after all, they have always been that way.

The home is thus the result of the human being's propensity to reconstruct what is perceived into an understandable and meaningful system (Levi-Strauss 1972, 15–16). This construction normally has both a physical and psychic component. The first is a physical systematization of the environment at successive spatio-temporal scales, while the second is a culturally learned frame within which interpretation about life occurs within a more or less autonomous, and emotionally charged meaning system, binding the familial, social, and cultural aspects of life to a particular place.

The home is an interpretation of the domestic territory as meaningful (cf. Hodder 1990, 38, 45–46), since it is a physical and abstract framework for tasks and ideas significant to a society. Thus, the home conceptually and spatially frames the interpretation of domestic daily life, while at the same time it provides the significant objects of interpretation: the residential buildings and spaces along with the various domestic rituals and economic tasks of the group (Benjamin Forthcoming; Douglas 1991, 289; Saile 1985, 85 ff.).

It may be that the term *home* should be split into two, one for scholars to use in description, and the other would be the several different *homes* of individual cultural groups, these latter defined for scholarly use based on in-depth empirical studies. Nonethless, it seems wothwhile to provide here a definition that brings together many aspects of what scholars have identified about the home's meaning, if only as another beginning point of the ongoing discussion of the term. I have chosen here to regard the home-as-state-of-mind as being a metaphor, and not part of the actual definition.

AFTERWORD

The home is that spatially localized, temporally defined, significant, and autonomous physical frame and conceptual system for the ordering, transformation, and interpretation of the physical and abstract aspects of domestic daily life at several simultaneous spatio-temporal scales, normally activitated by the connection to a person or community, such as a nuclear family. It is thus the autonomous interpretation of domestic life, and that which is interpreted (Benjamin Forthcoming).

Perhaps the *home* should not be defined once and for all. Its role as a concept that encourages scholarly study and creativity across the boundaries of many disciplines may be more important than what might be gained by holding down the meaning to one set of words.

Other homes

Finally, I present a short comparison of western and non-western descriptions of the meaning content of *home*. It is evident in the following that not only are non-western conceptions similiar to the home at present, but they also recall what we know of past conceptions of the western home. Because these societies live in different physical and cultural conditions, many of them in a more intimate and interdependent relationship to the natural ecology of the nearby environment, their conception of home may be instructive as to how such interpretations as the home, when made throughout society, can lead to a more harmonious relationship with the natural environment.

A worrying trend in the opposite direction is the use of simplistic definitions of the western home (i.e., such as home = house), to help in studying and designing domestic space for a non-western clientele. An example of this is Mills' (1993) use of Hillier and Hanson's space syntax theory to mathematically describe indigenous South African "homes," to assume that certain of the described spaces are "social" or "good," and then to reproduce some of these desirable elements in new towns that meet modern building standards.

It seems rash to impose on other cultures one's own conception of the home without ever having attempted to investigate their own native conceptions of space, or home$_2$, let alone considering whether they even have conceptions that have to do with affection for the living space.

The western home. This describes a physical and/or psychic area and place where one lives, and where one has an emotional, often profound and affectionate relationship to this place throughout the lifespan (Brink in this volume).

The Dogon home. Morgenthaler (1969) has recorded the words of Dommo, a native of the village Andiumbolo, concerning the Dogon conceptions of the living space. First, it is the objective of return, as after a party in a neighboring village, Dommo comments, "...and then it is time to go home again" (ibid., 195). But this home itself has a surprisingly complex structure. Dommo must show Morgenthaler more than his own houses to indicate his home. He must take him around to the variety of important places, physical structures, situations, people, and show him human relationships in order to reveal his home. Thus, when Dommo (ibid., 203) says, "I don't live where we just were – when my wife is working in the fields or is sick and can't cook, I eat in the big house. I'm home here," he confirms that his conception of home is relative to the situation of his personal relationships, as well as space and time. Home is apparently the entire village, but each part of the village plays on different aspects of being home. The home is thus not a single house, but the order and complexity of life of his Dogon village, and even though understood community-wide, it is "emotionally differentiated from person to person" (Van Eyck 1969, 209).

The Kurdish home. Hoshiar Nooraddin, from Erbil and a doctoral student in Architecture at the Norwegian Institute of Technology, describes the Kurdish sense of the home thus: It is the place where the individual can breathe freely, where he owns all that is around him, where his memories, his love, and his relatives are, and where the voice of *adan* (the town crier) is heard. Perhaps unique to this cultural group, the home is a literal physical feeling in the breath, being perhaps a symbol for life itself.

The Ghanian home. Jennifer Na Dei Nunoo, from Accra and also a doctoral student in Architecture at the Norwegian Institute of Technology, describes the Ghanian home. She claims that it has meaning at several scales simultaneously. In the Ga dialect of Ghana, the meaning of the *shiä* (home) is relative to the context within which the term is used. Thus, for each scale, different aspects of the place determine what it is that conditions the meaning:

1. The entire country: a juridical/political entity one belongs to.

2. The house (in modern towns): the private residence where one can be oneself, not bound by customs, to do what one likes.

3. The village: the place of ethnic origin, personal ancestry, containing relations, and the structures and physical environments housing these

relations, in addition to being the place where the individual returns to from the modern world for homecoming and other rituals.

This ancestral home existed even before the Europeans came. Even westernized Ghanians point to the ancestral home as theirs, because it is a specific place where they belong. Na Dei Nunoo has also studied other homes in her research on the domestic architecture of Islamic societies in Nigeria. She found it necessary to learn about their concept of home to help one as a researcher define the space they used. She concludes by claiming that cultures all over the world have some sort of home since belonging is universal.

Issues from the plenary session

In the scholarly context, there are generally problems with definitions of important terms. What fields of study are different definitions valid for? What should be the criteria of these definitions? Should the term be derived from empirical studies or synthesized through scientific contemplation? If there is a gender to the home, should the opposite gender define the term?

The basic criteria for a definition could be:

1. Are the ideas in the meaning of the term applicable to cultures or descriptions used today? (In other words, can the meaning be tested empirically, or must it be studied relative to extinct phenomena?)

2. Is the definition logical?

3. Does the definition have internal coherence?

4. Does the term describe a real phenomenon, or is it a metaphor for some other phenomenon?

Other questions brought up as inspiration to debate and research were the following:

1. What are the modern mythologies concerning houses/homes qualifying and distorting inhabitant's and scholar's use and understanding of the concept?

2. Can changes in the definition of the term or use of the term be linked or correlated to other major processes in society, such as economic changes, political turnovers, historical changes, or natural/climatic

changes? If such a correlation can be found, then it may be possible to develop a form of prediction concerning the use of the term, and in general a way of studying the use of symbols as they change in societies, atleast for limited cultural groups.

3. What is happening to homes at present? The old home is being slowly destroyed with the historical progression of culture, and a new one is taking shape in the process. What does this new home look like? This is apparently an example of the larger study of contemporary cultural phenomena from an historical-integrative perspective (see Lawrence this volume).

4. What is the cosmology of the home? What would this be like (certainly different relative to the cultural membership of the study group)?

5. How does the home work as a medium or expression of social stratification or egalitarianism?

6. Is it possible to see a coordinated interplay among the different viewpoints on the home, from the eco-functionalistic, the symbolic, to the structural?

7. Why does the home exist at all?

Because users associate the home with the dwelling environment, it may help in studying subjects in the scholar's own society that are otherwise difficult to conceive of since the scholar him/herself lives within the same society. Thus, it may help researchers to look at certain issues from a perspective, even though it is flawed and subjective, it is still a perspective that can be tested. This is another reason why the ancient/historical home is so pregnant with possibilities for research; we can study the long term *development* of the concept to enlighten ourselves about the significance of such environmental terms still in use today. Other areas of study are the following:

1. The implications for public policy with identifiable changes in the home.

2. The study of community-household links.

3. The cosmology and world view qualified by the home.

4. The gender of home$_{x...n}$.

5. The home as an artistic expression (see for example *chowk* from India, or floor painting used on the home, Brown 1994).

6. The home as a category of place as defined by informants, *also* outside the Euro-American cultural sphere.

7. The home can be seen as a metaphor or focus for how to represent diverse perspectives on the nature of phenomena, such as human built space, and as such, it can be an interdisciplinary concept for studying many phenomena.

8. The home could be used as a sort of filter to become aquainted with the spatial culture of any society under study (see Na Dei Nunoo above).

9. The home can be seen as a possible way of linking 'idea' and 'form.'

10. The home can be the focus for attempts to join the different explanations of a term, so that one integrates them into a whole as an inclusive conceptualization.

Perhaps the real contribution of the home concept is that it gathers together the physical and mental aspects of our environment and domestic family life into a conceptual space that we know, but that is problematic to explicitly define and manipulate. Further, it links the environment and the rituals of daily life, showing that they are consequential for one another. Thus, it is a concept badly needed in today's world where very few acknowledge or manifest any sense that one's own construction of settlement and striving for comfort in the home has any bearing on the degradation or destruction of the natural premises for a healthy life.

This is basically a question of what are our societal norms and their meanings, and how they are proposed and enforced. From the viewpoint of the social sciences and humanities, there is thus a need for some overarching framework concerning the definition of the home that can influence policy, otherwise any research will have a limited effect.

The present spatial and conceptual isolation between our domestic life, and the prevalent economy and culture of society, is in contrast to the agrarian life of the earliest known users of the term *home*.

The "wandering villages" of Iron Age Denmark are a case in point (Becker 1987). Here, the economy, architecture, site planning, and likely social life and the cultural interpretation of the above, all seem to have been integrated into a *dwelling tradition*. This involved the use of highly flammable and bio-degradable materials for all building construction so entire villages were burned down and plowed under at specific intervals. These massive conflagrations enriched the mineral poor earth of the west coast of Jutland, providing new grain fields for future generations, while the village moved to a location nearby, close to other resources and the site of earlier conflagrations. This cycle of build, cultivate, burn down, plow under, build, etc., or the cycling between creation and destruction, lasted in some cases for up to 300 years.

Each generation in this tradition repeated the rituals of their ancestors, and knew that their own offspring would do the same. thus, these dwelling cycles served to recreate the *past* and the *future* in the present. Further, since the fertility of the earth from these conflagrations and the plowing was vital to their livelihood, they very likely *interpreted* the landscape filled with the remnants of past villages for what it said about where their own village and grain fields should be, both for their own prosperity, but also for where their own offspring would beneficially be able to cultivate from their own present efforts.

In this sense, the Iron Age Jutland coastal inhabitants may have not only developed a very sophisticated *archaeology* (cf. Herschend this volume), but also, by perhaps planning for their offspring's future, they may have had a sense of wholistic *site planning*. Here, we see in the past, the contours of a sort of dwelling as *process,* or a *continuous home,* moveable, transformable, and re-cyclable.

Other new issues: What the symposium did not mention

With the increase in homelessness in the world, the continued growth of huge megalopolises, and the general transformation of settlements into marketable commodities for the maximization of corporate profit, the contention over the definition of both the term *home,* and its physical manifestation and cultural interpretation are becoming more and more important. Thus, Philip Langdon (1994, 49), not an architect, writes about the present-day scene in America: "Modern suburbs are not known as satisfying hometowns" (see also Kunstler 1993, for a similiar view).

Architects such as Nigel Gilbert (1993, 69–70) have started to identify, in a half ironic – half sorrowful – tone, the contours of this coming home, based on the latest trends. In his vision, home becomes a disjointed phenomenon, the outside responding to the necessity of showing wealth, status, and good aesthetic neighborliness, while the interior becomes a hyper-electronic enclave for the complete indulgence of sensual narcissism. Such a vision would only really be damaging for a few rich, addictive personalities, were it not for the fact that such images are marketed worldwide as the home of the future, without even making a nod at any sort of integration with local tradition or the ecological premises of the site.

AFTERWORD

The investigation of spatio-temporal demarcations of settlement space from outside the Euro-American culture group will assist in validating other conceptions. Thus, geographers will find it harder to justify the destruction of non-literate people's settlements in order to make way for the "highest and best use of the land" if the destruction they are justifying concerns someone's *home*.

In this way, the term *home* is a kind of *provaceteur* in research, goading scholars and other interested parties to think again concerning how people interpret the living environment, and how these interpretations should be manifested. Amos Rapoport's role at the 1992 symposium can be seen in a similiar way: By his criticism and rejection of the term, he demands that we think again and think deeper about a concept that researchers have for too long taken as a given.

References

Barnstone, Willis, trans. 1967. *Greek Lyric Poetry*. Bloomington, Ind.: Indiana University Press.

Becker, C. J. 1987. Farms and Villages in Denmark from the Late Bronze Age to the Viking Period. *Proceedings of the British Academy* 63.

Benjamin, David N. Home. In *Encyclopedia of Vernacular Architecture of the World*. Forthcoming.

Birkeli, Emil. 1932. *Høgsætet*. Stavanger, Norway: Dreyers Grafisk Forlag.

Black, H. 1979. *Black's Law Dictionary*. 5th. edition. St. Paul, Minn.: West Publishing Company.

Bradshaw, John. 1990. *Homecoming. Reclaiming and Championing Your Inner Child*. N.Y.: Bantam Books.

Brink, Stefan. 1988. Folkvandringstida Namn? In *Folkevandringstid i Norden*, ed. Ulf Näsman et al. Århus: Aarhus Universitetsforlag.

Brown, Patricia L. 1994. Immigrants Bring Traditions to New Homes. *The Plain Dealer* (March 27).

Caplow, Theodore, Howard Bahr, and David Sternberg. 1968. Homelessness. In *International Encyclopedia of the Social Sciences*, ed. David Sills. N.Y.: The Macmillan Co. and the Free Press.

Carlsson, Lizzie. 1935. Högsätet och Hemfriden. *Rig* 18.

Collins English Dictionary. 3rd. edition. 1991. Glasgow: HarperCollins Publishers.

Douglas, Mary. 1991. The Idea of a Home: A Kind of Space. *Social Research* 58(1).

Erik den Rødes Saga (Eiríks Saga Rauda). 1961. Copenhagen: Foreningen "Fremtiden."

Gilbert, Nigel. 1994. Information Plus Vernacular Equals the Future. *World Architecture* 29.

Goodal, Brian. 1987. *Dictionary of Human Geography*. N.Y.: Facts on File Publications.

Gullestad, Marianne. 1984. *Kitchen Table Society*. Oslo: Universitetsforlaget.

———. 1993. Home Decoration as Popular Culture. Constructing Homes, Genders and Classes in Norway. In *Gendered Anthropology*, ed. Teresa del Valle. London: Routledge.

Halle, David. 1993. *Inside Culture. Art and Class in the American Home*. Chicago: The University of Chicago Press.

Hartfiel, Günter, ed. 1972. *Wörterbuch der Soziologie*. Stuttgart: Alfred Kröner Verlag.

Hight, G.A., ed. 1914. *Gretti's Saga*. London: Everyman's Library.

Hodder, Ian. 1990. *The Domestication of Europe*. Oxford: Basil Blackwell.

Hultkrantz, Åke, ed. 1960. *International Dictionary of Regional European Ethnology and Folklore*. Vol. 1. Copenhagen: Rosenkilde & Bagger.

Jobes, Gertrude, ed. 1961. *Dictionary of Mythology, Folklore and Symbols*. N.Y.: The Scarecrow Press.

Koefoed, Aa., et al., eds. 1989. *Old var årle. Nordens gamle religioner*. Copenhagen: Gjellerup and Gad.

KLNM Kulturhistorisk leksikon for nordisk middelalder, ed. Finn Hødnebo. 1956. Oslo: Gyldendal.

Kunstler, James Howard. 1993. *The Geography of Nowhere*. N.Y.: Simon and Schuster.

Langdon, Philip. 1994. *A Better Place to Live. Reshaping the American Suburb*. Amherst, Mass.: The University of Massachussets Press.

Levi-Strauss, Claude. 1972. Structuralism and Ecology. *Social Science Information* 12 (1).

Madge, John. 1968. Housing. In *International Encyclopedia of the Social Sciences*, ed. David Sills. N.Y.: The Macmillan Co. and the Free Press.

McCann, Willis. 1941. Nostalgia: A Review of the Literature. *Psychological Bulletin* 38.

Mejborg, R. 1888. *Gamle Danske Hjem i det 16., 17., og 18. Aarhundrede*. Copenhagen.

Mills, Glenn, and Sue Armstrong. 1993. Africa Tames the Town Planners. *New Scientist* 138 (1871).

Morgenthaler, Fritz. 1969. The Dogon People: 2. In *Meaning in Architecture*, ed. Charles Jencks. London: Barrie & Rockliff: Cresset Press.

Nouwen, Henri J.M. 1992. *The Return of the Prodigal Son. A Story of Homecoming.* N.Y.: Doubleday.

Page, Jr., Hugh R. 1992. Burusho. In *Encyclopedia of World Cultures.* Vol. 3, ed. Paul Hockings. Boston: G.K. Hall & Co.

Porteous, J. D. 1982. *Environment and Behavior.* Reading, Penn.: Addison-Wesley.

Rapoport, Amos. 1990a. *History and Precedent in Environmental Design.* N.Y.: Plenum Press.

———. 1990b. Systems of Activities and Systems of Settings. In *Domestic Architecture and the Use of Space,* ed. Susan Kent. Cambridge: Cambridge University Press.

———. 1980. Vernacular Architecture and the Cultural Determinants of Form. In *Buildings and Society,* ed. Anthony D. King. London: Routledge & Kegan Paul.

———. 1977. *Human Aspects of Urban Form.* Oxford: Pergamon Press.

———. 1970. The Study of Spatial Quality. *The Journal of Aesthetic Education* 4(4).

Reinhold, Gerd, ed. 1991. *Soziologie Lexikon.* Munich: R. Oldenburg Verlag.

Sack, Robert D. 1986. *Human Territoriality.* Cambridge: Cambridge University Press.

Saile, David. 1985. The Ritual Establishment of Home. In *Home Environments.* Vol. 8 of *Human Behavior and Environments. Advances in Theory and Research,* ed. Irwin Altman and Carol Werner N.Y.: Plenum Press.

Sills, David, ed. 1968. *International Encyclopedia of the Social Sciences.* N.Y.: The Macmillan Co. and the Free Press.

Spradley, James, and D. McCurdy. 1975. *Anthropology: The Cultural Perspective.* N.Y.: John Wiley & Sons, Inc.

Van Eyck, Aldo. 1969. The Interior of Time. In *Meaning in Architecture,* ed. Charles Jencks. London: Barrie & Rockliff: Cresset Press.

Winick, Charles. 1956. *Dictionary of Anthropology.* N.Y.: Philosophical Library.

Wrenn, C.L., ed. 1954. *Beowulf and the Finnsburg Fragment.* Transl. by J.R.C. Hall. London: Geo. Allen & Unwin.

Contributors

Eje Arén has produced several archaeological reconstructions in Sweden, and has his own consulting firm in Slimminge, Sweden.

David N. Benjamin recieved his Ph.D. in Architecture from the Norwegian Institute of Technology in Trondheim, Norway with a study on the ancient Scandinavian home, and is presently a consultant to architects and research organizations in the U.S. and Europe.

Stefan Brink is a professor at the Institute for Nordic Name Research of Uppsala University, Uppsala, Sweden.

Marjorie Bulos is an Assoc. Professor in the School of Land Management and Urban Policy at Southbank University, London, England.

Waheed Chaker is a political scientist and an Assoc. Professor at the School of Land Management and Urban Policy at Southbank University, London, England.

Frands Herschend is a long-term visiting researcher in Archaeology at the Institute for Archaeology of Uppsala University, Uppsala, Sweden.

Susan Kent is an assoc. professor in Anthropology at Old Dominion University, Norfolk, Virginia, U.S.A.

Roderick J. Lawrence is a professor at the Institute for Human Ecology of the University of Geneva, in Geneva, Switzerland.

Juhani Pallasmaa has his own architectural practice in Helsinki, Finland, and is a professor of Architecture at the University of Helsinki.

J. Douglas Porteous is professor of Geography at the University of Victoria, British Columbia, Canada.

Neil Price did his doctoral work on colonial Scandinavian Architecture, and is now a consultant in archaeology for Arkeologi Konsult in Uppsala, Sweden.

Amos Rapoport is distinguished professor of Architecture at the University of Wisconsin– Milwaukee, in Milwaukee, Wisconsin, U.S.A.

David Saile is Professor of Architecture and director of the Center for the Study of the Practice of Architecture at the University of Cincinnati, in Cincinnati, Ohio, U.S.A.

David Stea is a visiting lecturer at several American universities, and is director of the International Center for Culture and Environment in Mexico City, Mexico.

Ruth Tringham is professor of Anthropology at the University of California–Berkeley, in Berkeley, California.

Bror Westman has lectured for many years at the Royal Danish Academy of Arts School of Architecture, and is presently an independent Danish ethnologist.

Jørn Ørum-Nielsen has written widely on architectural subjects in Danish, and is presently an independent consultant in Architecture.

For Product Safety Concerns and Information please contact our EU
representative GPSR@taylorandfrancis.com
Taylor & Francis Verlag GmbH, Kaufingerstraße 24, 80331 München, Germany

www.ingramcontent.com/pod-product-compliance
Lightning Source LLC
Chambersburg PA
CBHW071153300426
44113CB00009B/1197